A Celtic Primer

Brendan O'Malley is Dean of Chapel and Part Time Lecturer at the University of Wales, Lampeter. He is a Canon of St David's Cathedral and his interests lie particularly in Practical Theology and Spirituality. His previous publications include the award winning *The Animals of St Gregory* (Paulinus Press, 1981); *A Pilgrim's Manual*, St David's (Paulinus Press, 1985); *A Welsh Pilgrim's Manual* (Gomer Press, 1989); *God at Every Gate* (Canterbury Press and Morehouse Publishing, 1997); *Celtic Blessings* (Canterbury Press and Twenty-Third Publications, 1998); *A Celtic Eucharist* (Canterbury Press and Morehouse Publishing, 2001).

A Celtic Primer

*The Complete Celtic Worship Resource
and Collection*

Edited and Compiled by
Brendan O'Malley

CANTERBURY
PRESS
Norwich

© in this compilation Brendan O'Malley 2002

The text of A Celtic Eucharist (pp. 205–254) is published
separately under the title *A Celtic Eucharist* by the Canterbury
Press in the UK and by Morehouse Publishing in North America.

First published in 2002 by the Canterbury Press Norwich
(a publishing imprint of Hymns Ancient & Modern Limited, a
registered charity)
St Mary's Works, St Mary's Plain,
Norwich, Norfolk, NR3 3BH

www.scm-canterburypress.co.uk

British Library Cataloguing in Publication data

A catalogue record for this book is available
from the British Library

ISBN 1-85311-490-1

Typeset in Britain by Regent Typesetting
and printed by
Biddles Ltd, Guildford and King's Lynn

To

The Right Reverend D. Huw Jones, MA

Bishop of St David's

1996–2001

with gratitude

BEFORE, BEHIND, BENEATH,
CREATION, CONCEPTION, BIRTH,
REDEMPTION
THIS PRAYER, THIS MOMENT:
CREATOR'S SPIRIT.

HOLY SPIRIT,
INFINITUDE
ETERNALLY POURING FORTH,
ENERGY OF LOVE
SUSTAINING THE UNIVERSE.

COME
CREATOR SPIRIT
CONCEIVING SPIRIT
INITIATING SPIRIT
LIFE - GIVING
BIRTH - GIVING
SPIRIT
LIFE-BREATH OF LOVE.

HOLY SPIRIT
YOUR BLESSED UNCTION FROM ABOVE
IS FIRE OF LOVE.

adapted from 'Veni Creator Spiritus'
(A Welsh Pilgrim's Manual,
Brendan O'Malley)

CONTENTS

INTRODUCTION

The traditional concept of a Primer is that it is an aid to teach people their prayers for use in private devotion, as well as to teach children how to read.

The origin of the Primer as a manual of devotion lies in the Prayer of the Hours chanted in early medieval monasteries. Eventually the monastic liturgical prayer was adapted for lay use and known as the 'Primer' (first prayers), becoming a veritable little office book. By the early fourteenth century the Primer contained the Little Office of the Blessed Virgin Mary, the Penitential Psalms, Gradual Psalms, the Litany of the Saints and the Office of the Dead. Eventually, by the sixteenth century, in England, the Primer was superseded by the *Book of Common Prayer* which was in itself a distillation of the original monastic office of public prayer.

This *Celtic Primer* is an attempt to reflect the above tradition albeit in the Celtic idiom, and is intended to be a resource of prayer inspired by that tradition. It is to be used as a companion to the Bible, encouraging the use of the Bible itself as the ideal Book of Prayer.

The Celtic Eucharist, too, is offered for modern use. Its words, its art and its shape are designed to serve the ongoing Celtic Tradition, reflecting a people who lived and died liturgically, and it is authentic by virtue of its being both traditional and radically new.

This collected text is very much a working liturgy. In common with the *Stowe Missal*, little in it is unique. The Eucharistic Prayers used are the Gelasian (from the Stowe), as well as the Gallican and the earliest known Eucharistic text, the text of Hippolytus, from the early church circa AD 215. This latter prayer may not be an invariable form although it may have been a model for all later Eucharistic Prayers. I have employed these prayers because of their beauty of form and because they are the spiritual font from which the Church of the Celts drew their inspiration.

I would like to express my gratitude to my friend Jane Main for her patience and good humour in typing the manuscript.

Brendan O'Malley
Lampeter, 2002

HOW TO USE THE PRIMER

The Elements which make up the order of the daily prayer or office are these:

1. **A Sentence** to focus mind and heart and prepare our thoughts for the worship of God.
2. A short **Litany** seeking God's forgiveness.
3. An **Invocation** asking for Divine help and continual presence.
4. **Antiphon** and **Psalmody**. A selection of appropriate psalms are presented for ease of use. As an alternative the perpetual psalter may be said in the continuous manner, i.e. begin at the first psalm and then pray as many psalms as wished in consecutive order. At each new office carry on from the last psalm recited. This is the ancient monastic method of keeping the psalter going in a continuous cycle of prayer. After the 'Glory be to the Father' at the end of the psalmody, a pause for silent recollection is to be recommended. The silent repetition of a sentence chosen from the psalms as a mantra enables 'psalm-prayer' to become 'prayer of the heart'.
5. **Canticle**. At each office a canticle is said after the recitation of the psalms. Note the canticle from the list provided and place a marker at the correct page in the Bible before saying the office. After the office has been said move the marker to the appropriate page for the next canticle in the order.
6. **Reading: Lectio Continua**. Read a chapter or portion from a particular book of the Bible so that whole sections or books may be read over a period of time. Obviously, a wise choice of suitable readings needs to be made. There are many calendars and lectionaries, almanacs, ordos (orders) and reading-plans available, should the method recommended not suffice.
7. **Silence** is to be recommended at this point, simply for being in God's presence or for reflecting on the word through the practice of **Lectio Divina**.

Lectio Divina

It is important to be incessant in attention to God's Word as a means of self-purification, and so a love of the scriptures illuminates life as a whole.

The practice of meditating on the Word enables us to understand better the psalms and the reading. It is better to 'surrender' to what is read in a spirit of humility rather than to try to 'interpret' or 'master' the Word. An experience of a real encounter with Christ at the level of sacramental communion through listening to the written sounded Word enables reading and prayer to become 'one'. Through the meditative reading of Scripture we are drawn into a personal encounter with the Divine.

The practice of 'muttering' or gently and slowly reading aloud (lectio), by constant repetition of the words (meditatio), and then repeating and ruminatively savouring (ruminatio), and lingering over them for nourishment; praying over them in a dialogue (oratio) with God, and then resting silently in his presence in a state of contemplative (contemplatio) awareness and focused attention, is to discover the art of Lectio Divina. To practise this method for its own sake, through the experience of slow meditative reading, is to achieve a personal experience of God rather than the acquisition of intellectual knowledge.

The method of Lectio Divina applied to the praying of the office encourages a communion of prayer and listening to God, resulting in an increased attention to God and purity of heart which consists in charity.

8. **Gospel Canticle**. The **Benedictus** at Morning Prayer and the **Magnificat** at Evening Prayer celebrate Christ as the fulfilment of God's promise to Israel, and the sign of the new covenant. The world of the Old Testament, expressed in the Psalms, is thus united with the proclamation of Jesus Christ in the New Testament.

9. **Intercessions** may be made for the needs of others or personal needs, as well as contemporary concerns of the Church and world, ending with the **Lord's Prayer**.

10. The **Collect** of the day gathers together all that has gone before, encapsulating the theme of the psalms and readings.

11. The **Conclusion** of the order is marked by **verses** and **responses**.

My KING OF MYSTERIES,
OF FAIR FAME,
WHEREVER IN HIS CREATION
HE DWELLS ABOVE THE WORLD,
MIGHTY AND GLORIOUS
··· IN MY LIFE
I CAN DO NOTHING
BUT WORSHIP HIM

SALTAIR NA RANN

MORNING PRAYER

(Matins/Lauds)

Sentence

Litany

Invocation

Antiphon and Psalmody

Canticle

Reading

Benedictus

Intercession

Lord's Prayer

Collect

Conclusion

Sentences

1. Lord, hear my voice when I call to you. My heart has prompted me to seek your face; I seek it Lord; do not hide from me, alleluia.

2. Guide me in your truth and teach me, Lord, for you are the God who saves me.

adapted from Psalm 25

3. The maker of all things,
   The Lord God worship we;
   Heaven white with angels' wings,
   Earth and the white-waved sea.

Early Irish (1)

4. O King of Kings!
   O sheltering wings, O guardian tree!
   All, all of me,
   Thou Virgin's nurseling, rest in thee.

Early Irish (1)

5. The heavenly sky
   Where Christ the son of Mary is,
   There if he die a man lives still
   And whatso'er he will 'tis his.

Early Irish (1)

6. The path I walk, Christ walks it,
   May the land in which I am be without sorrow.

Celtic Spirituality (7)

7. May the Trinity protect me wherever I stay, Father, Son and Holy Spirit.

(7)

8. Bright angels walk with me – dear presence – in every dealing.

(7)

9. May I arrive at every place, may I return home; may the way in which I spend be a way without loss.

(7)

10. May every path before me be smooth, man, woman, and child welcome me.

(7)

11. A truly good journey! Well does the fair Lord show us a course, a path.

(7)

12. May Jesus and the Father, may the Holy Spirit sanctify us! May the mysterious God not hidden in darkness, may the bright King save us!

(7)

13. May the cross of Christ's body and Mary guard us on the road. May it not be unlucky for us, may it be successful and easy!

(7)

14. Fair Lord, I pray to you
    Concerning my excesses and deficiencies:
    Grant me forgiveness here
    For my misdeeds, my ignorance.

    Saltair na Rann (18)

15. My Christ ever faithful,
    With glory of angels
    And stars in thy raiment,
    Child of the whitefooted
    Deathless inviolate
    Brightbodied maïden!

    Early Irish (1)

16. The praise of Christ is illustrious speech,
    The worship of God's Son is an art full of virtue.
    May everyone who has sung it or heard it
    Belong to God's kingdom without rejection.

    from Broccain's Hymn to Saint Brigit (17)

17. The world's strength is a deception
    To whoever dwells therein;
    There is no strength
    Save great love for the Son of Mary.

    from Feilire Oengusso (18)

18. You have nothing more precious
    Than the love of God, if you perform it:
    You will not regret
    Adoring the King of clouds.

    from Feilire Oengusso (18)

19. May our purpose be strong:
     To strive for what is fittest.
     Let us all love Jesus,
     For this is the highest thing.

from Feilire Oengusso (18)

20. Lord, O Lord, hear me
     Fill my soul, Lord, with Thy love's ray,
     Fill my soul, Lord, with Thy love's ray,
     Lord, O lord, hear me.

Early Irish
(trans. George Sigerson) (4)

21. Have mercy on me,
     Royal abundant Lord,
     Jesus whom I love,
     Great God to whom I pray.

from Feilire Oengusso (18)

22. Christ, Christ, hear me!
     Christ, Christ of thy meekness!
     Christ, Christ love me!
     Sever me not from thy sweetness!

Suibhne Geilt, eighth-century Irish

23. Praise and gratitude to you, Holy Father,
     Who created the skies and heaven first
     And after that created the big wet sea
     And the heaps of fish in it swimming closely.

Peig Sayers

24. God, give me a well of tears
     my sins to hide,
     or I am left like arid earth
     unsanctified.

Medieval Irish

25. It's evil
     to shun the King of righteousness
     and make compact with demons.

Medieval Irish

Litany

1.

Have mercy on us O God, Father almighty,
God of hosts,
noble God,
Lord of the world,
unutterable God,
Creator of the elements,
invisible God.
Heavenly Father, you who abide in heaven,
Have mercy on us.

The Celtic Monk (6)

2.

Have mercy on us O God, Father almighty.
immeasurable God.
patient God.
incorruptible God.
immortal God.
eternal God.
perfect God.
merciful God.
wonderful God.
heavenly Father, who abides in heaven,
Have mercy on us.

(6)

3.

Have mercy on us O God, Father almighty,
God of earth.
God of fire,
God of the waters of wonder.
God of the gusting and blustering air.
God of the many languages found
Throughout the world.
heavenly Father, you who abide in heaven,
Have mercy on us.

(6)

A Celtic Primer

4.

Have mercy on us O God, Father almighty,
God of the waves from the depths of the ocean.
God of the planets and the many bright stars.
God, creator of the universe and inaugurator of the night and day.
God, Lord of Hell and its infernal host.
God, ruler through the archangels.
Golden Good.
Heavenly Father, you who abide in heaven,
Have mercy on us.

(6)

5.

Have mercy on us, O God the Almighty,
Jesus Christ Son of the Living God.
O Son twice born,
O sole-begotten of the Father.
O First-born of the Virgin Mary,
O Son of David,
O Son of Abraham.
O Beginning of all things.
O Fulfilment of the world.
O Word of God.
– O Christ crucified.
O eternal Judge, have mercy on us.

(6)

6.

Have mercy on us, O God the Almighty
Jesus Christ Son of the Living God.
O Path to the heavenly realms.
O Life of all things.
O eternal Truth.
O Image, O Likeness, O Model of God the Father (Heb. 1.3).
O Hand of God.
O Arm of God.
O Power of God
O Right-Hand of God.
– O Christ crucified.
O eternal Judge, have mercy on us.

(6)

7.

Have mercy on us, O God the Almighty,
Jesus Christ Son of the living God,
O true Knowledge.
O true Light of love, who enlightens all darkness,
O guiding Light.
O Sun of truth.
O Morning Star.
O Brightness of the divinity.
O Radiance of eternal brightness.
– O Christ crucified.
O eternal judge, have mercy on us.

(6)

8.

Have mercy on us, O God the Almighty,
Jesus Christ Son of the living God.
O Fountain of eternal life.
O Intelligence of mystic life.
O Mediator of God and humanity.
O Promised One of the Church.
O loyal Shepherd of the flock.
O Hope of believers.
– O Christ crucified,
O eternal judge, have mercy on us.

(6)

9.

Have mercy on us, O God the Almighty,
Jesus Christ Son of the living God.
O Angel of great counsel.
O true Prophet.
O true Apostle.
O true Teacher.
O High Priest
O Nazarene.
O Christ crucified.
O eternal judge, have mercy on us.

(6)

10.

>Have mercy on us, O God the Almighty.
>Jesus Christ Son of the living God.
>O true Vine.
>O Rod of the root of Jesse.
>O King of Israel.
>O Saviour.
>O Door of life.
>O Choice Flower of the field.
>O Lily of the valleys.
>– O Christ crucified,
>O eternal judge, have mercy on us.

(6)

11.

>Have mercy on us, O God the Almighty.
>Jesus Christ Son of the Living God.
>O Rock of strength.
>O Cornerstone.
>O heavenly Sion.
>O Foundation of the faith.
>O Innocent Lamb.
>O Crown.
>– O Christ crucified.
>O eternal judge, have mercy on us.

(6)

12.

>Have mercy on us, O God the Almighty.
>Jesus Christ Son of the living God.
>O gentle Sheep (Isa. 53.7).
>O Redeemer of the human race.
>O Tree of God.
>O true Man.
>O Lion.
>O Calf.
>O Eagle.
>O Christ crucified.
>O eternal judge, have mercy on us.

(6)

13.

Have mercy on us Almighty God,
O Holy Spirit.
O Spirit, greatest of all spirits.
O Finger of God.*
O Protector of Christians.
O Comforter of the sorrowful,
O Lenient One.
O Merciful Mediator.
– O Holy Spirit, who rules all creation, visible and invisible,
Have mercy on me.

(6)

14.

Have mercy on us Almighty God,
O Holy Spirit.
O Teacher of true wisdom,
O Spirit of understanding.
O Spirit of Counsel.
O Spirit of strength.
O Spirit of knowledge.
O Spirit of tenderness
– O Holy Spirit, who rules all creation, visible and invisible,
Have mercy on me.

(6)

15.

Have mercy on us Almighty God,
O Holy Spirit.
O Spirit of love.
O Spirit of grace.
O Spirit, from whom all good comes.
O Spirit, who annuls all guilt.
O Spirit, who wipes out sin.
– O Spirit, who rules all creation, visible and invisible,
Have mercy on me.

(6)

* Isa. 53.7.

16.

Have mercy on me, Father, Son and Holy Spirit.
Have mercy on me, one only God.
O God of heaven, have mercy on me.
Have mercy on me, O God,
From whom and through whom
Is the direction of all created things for you, O God.
To you be glory and honour
For ever and ever. Amen.

(6)

17.

Great God to Whom I pray,
Hear my sad groan!
May I, after this struggle,
Be with the angels and saints forever.

Hail, choir of heaven!
May one of you give heed to me.
It troubles me greatly
That I am not in your company,

You can help me,
For your compassion is great
Heal my heart
For the sake of Mary's Son.

from Feilire Oengusso (18)

Invocation

Either

Lord, be with us this day,
Within us to purify us;
Above us to draw us up;
Beneath us to sustain us;
Before us to lead us;
Behind us to restrain us;
Around us to protect us.

St Patrick

Or

We must get up before the sun to bless you, O God,
And adore you at the break of day.

Wisdom 16.28

Antiphon and Psalmody

O Lord, open my/our lips:
And my/our mouth shall proclaim your praise.
Glory to the Father and to the Son,
And to the Holy Spirit;
As it was in the beginning, is now,
And shall be for ever.
Amen.

Either

Venite
Psalm 95.1–8

Come, let us sing to the Lord;*
let us shout for joy to the rock of our salvation.

Let us come before his presence with thanksgiving*
and raise a loud shout to him with psalms.
For the Lord is a great God,*
and a great king above all gods.

In his hands are the depths of the earth,*
and the heights of the hills are his also.

The sea is his, for he made it,*
and his hands moulded the dry land.

Come, let us bow down and bend the knee,*
and kneel before the Lord our Maker.

For he is our God,
and we are the people of his pasture
and the sheep of his hand.*
O that today you would hearken to his voice!

'Harden not your hearts,
as your forebears did in the wilderness,*
at Meribah, and on that day at Massah, when they tempted me.'

Glory to the Father and to the Son:*
And to the Holy Spirit;
As it was in the beginning, is now:
And shall be for ever.
Amen.

Or

Psalm 63.1–9

O God, you are my God; eagerly I seek you;*
my soul thirsts for you, my flesh faints for you,
as in a barren and dry land where there is no water.

Therefore I have gazed upon you in your holy place,*
that I might behold your power and your glory.

For your loving-kindness is better than life itself;*
my lips shall give you praise.

So will I bless you as long as I live*
and lift up my hands in your name.

My soul is content, as with marrow and fatness,*
and my mouth praises you with joyful lips,

When I remember you upon my bed,*
and meditate on you in the night watches.

For you have been my helper,*
and under the shadow of your wings will I rejoice.

My soul clings to you;*
your right hand holds me fast.

May those who seek my life to destroy it*
go down into the depths of the earth;

Glory to the Father and to the Son:
And to the Holy Spirit;
As it was in the beginning, is now:
And shall be for ever.
Amen.

Or

Psalm 90.1–4

Lord, you have been our refuge*
from one generation to another.

Before the mountains were brought forth,
or the land and the earth were born,*
from age to age you are God.

You turn us back to the dust and say,*
'Go back, O child of earth.'

For a thousand years in your sight
are like yesterday when it is past*
and like a watch in the night.

Glory be to the Father and to the Son:
And to the Holy Spirit;
As it was in the beginning, is now:
And shall be for ever.
Amen.

Or

Jubilate
Psalm 100

Be joyful in the Lord in triumph all you lands;*
serve the Lord with gladness
and come before his presence with a song.

Know this: The Lord himself is God;*
he himself has made us and we are his;
we are his people and the sheep of his pasture.

Enter his gates with thanksgiving;
go into his courts with praise;*
give thanks to him and call upon his name.

For the Lord is good; his mercy is everlasting;*
and his faithfulness endures from age to age.

A Celtic Primer

Glory to the Father and to the Son:
And to the Holy Spirit;
As it was in the beginning, is now:
And shall be for ever.
Amen.

Or

Easter Anthems
1 Corinthians 5.7; Romans 6.9; 1 Corinthians 15.20

Christ our Passover
Has been sacrificed for us:
So let us celebrate the feast,

Not with the old leaven
of corruption and wickedness:
but with the unleavened bread of
sincerity and truth.

Christ once raised from the dead dies no more:
Death has no more dominion over him.

In dying he died to sin once for all:
In living he lives to God.

See yourselves therefore as dead to sin:
And alive to God in Jesus Christ our Lord.
Christ has been raised from the dead:
The first fruits of those who sleep.

For as by man came death:
By man has come also
The resurrection of the dead;

For as in Adam all die:
Even so in Christ shall all be made alive.

Glory to the Father and to the Son:
And to the Holy Spirit;
As it was in the beginning, is now:
And shall be for ever.
Amen.

Antiphon

Ordinary

O God, you are my God;
Eagerly I seek you, my soul is athirst for you.

Advent/Christmas

All you that thirst come to the waters;
Seek the Lord while he may be found.

Lent

'As I live,' says the Lord,
'I do not desire the death of a sinner,
But rather that he/she may turn from his/her way and live.'

Easter

'I am the resurrection and the life.'

WE BEHOLD
    SOMETHING NEAR AT HAND:
    A BLESSED PSALM
CONCERNING THE MIGHT OF GOD;
    A VIGOROUS DISCOURSE
    TODAY AND AT THE
    END OF THE WORLD

FROM FEILIRE OENGUSSO

FOUR WEEK PSALTER

Week One

Morning Prayer   **Evening Prayer**

Day	Matins	Lauds	Midday	Vespers
Monday	95, 6, 9	5, 29	19, 7	11, 15
Tuesday	95, 10, 12	24, 33	119 (1–8), 13, 14	20, 21
Wednesday	95, 18 (1–30)	36, 47	119 (9–16), 17	27, 23
Thursday	95, 18 (31–51)	57, 48	119 (17–24), 25	30, 32
Friday	95, 35	51, 100	119 (25–32), 26, 28	41, 46
Saturday	95, 105	119 (145–52), 117	119 (33–40), 34	119 (105–112), 16
Sunday	95, 104	118, 150	23, 76	110, 115

Week Two

Morning Prayer   **Evening Prayer**

Day	Matins	Lauds	Midday	Vespers
Monday	95, 31	42, 19	119 (41–48), 40	45
Tuesday	95, 37	43, 55	119 (49–56), 53, 54	49
Wednesday	95, 39, 52	77, 97	119 (57–64), 55	62, 67
Thursday	95, 44	80, 81	119 (65–72), 56, 57	72
Friday	95, 38	51, 147	119 (73–80), 59, 60	116 (1–9), 121
Saturday	95, 106	92, 8	119 (81–88), 61, 64	113, 116 (10–19)
Sunday	95, 145	93, 148	118	110, 111

WEEK THREE

	Morning Prayer			Evening Prayer
Day	Matins	Lauds	Midday	Vespers
Monday	95, 50	84, 96	119 (89–96), 71	123, 124
Tuesday	95, 68	85, 67	119 (97–104), 74	125, 131
Wednesday	95, 89 (1–38)	86, 98	119 (105–112), 70	126, 127
Thursday	95, 89 (39–52)	87, 99	119 (113–120), 79, 80	132, 75
Friday	95, 69	51, 100	22	135, 65
Saturday	95, 107	119 (145–152), 117	119 (121–128), 34	122, 130
Sunday	95, 24, 66	118, 150	23, 76	110, 112

WEEK FOUR

	Morning Prayer			Evening Prayer
Day	Matins	Lauds	Midday	Vespers
Monday	95, 73	90, 135	119 (129–136), 82, 120	136
Tuesday	95, 102	101, 144	119 (137–144), 88	137, 138
Wednesday	95, 103	108, 146	119 (145–152), 94	139
Thursday	95, 44	143, 147	119 (153–160), 128, 129	144
Friday	95, 78 (1–39)	51, 147	119 (161–168), 133, 140	145
Saturday	95, 78 (40–72)	92, 8	119 (169–176), 45	141, 142
Sunday	95, 1, 2, 3	63, 149	118	110, 114

THE CANTICLES

(The following canticles may be found in the Scriptures)

Exodus 15.1–18
The Canticle of Moses and Miriam

Deuteronomy 32.1–12
The Canticle of Moses

1 Samuel 2.1–10
The Canticle of Hannah

1 Chronicles 29.10–13
The Canticle of David

Tobit 13.1–7
13.8–11, 13–15

Judith 16.2–3a, 13–15

Proverbs 9.1–6, 10–12

Wisdom 3.1–9
9.1–6, 9–11
10.17–21
16.20–21, 26; 171a

Sirach 14.20; 15.3a, 6b
31.1–7, 13, 16–22
29.13–16a

Isaiah 2.2–5
9.1–6
12.1–4, 7–9
33.2–10
33.13–16
38.10–14, 17–20
40.10–17
42.10–16

A Celtic Primer

45.15–25
49.7–13
61.10–62.7
63.1–5
66.10–14a

Jeremiah 7.2–7
14.17–21
17.7–8
31.10–14

Lamentations 5.1–7, 15–17, 19–21

Ezekiel 36.24–28

Daniel 3.26, 27, 29, 34–41
The Canticle of Azariah
3.52–57
3.56–88
The Canticle of Shadrach, Meshach and Abednego

Hosea 6.1–6

Habakkuk 3.2–4, 13a, 15–19

Zephaniah 3.8–13

Luke 1.46–55
The Canticle of Mary
1.68–79
The Canticle of Zechariah
2.29–32
The Canticle of Simeon

Ephesians 1.3–10

Philippians 2.6–11

Colossians 1.12–20

1 Timothy 3.16

1 Peter 2.21–24

Revelation 4.11, 5.9, 10, 12
11.17–18; 12.10b–12a
15.3–4
19.1–7

SCRIPTURE READING CHART

Four Week Cycle

Week One

	Morning	Midday	Evening
Monday	Isaiah 26.1–8	Galatians 6.7–10	Ephesians 2.1–10
Tuesday	Tobit 13.1–8	Proverbs 3.13–15	1 Cor. 15.12–28
Wednesday	Jud. 16.2–3, 13–15	Joel 2.11–13	Colossians 2.9–15
Thursday	Jeremiah 31.10–14	1 Kings 8.56–60	Romans 8.31–39
Friday	Isaiah 11.1–9	Jeremiah 32.36–40	Revelation 15.2–4
Saturday	Isaiah 30.15–16, 18	Deut. 1.16b–17a	Hebrews 4.12–16
Sunday	1 Chron. 29.10–13	Jeremiah 4.3–4	1 Peter 2.19–25

Week Two

	Morning	Midday	Evening
Monday	Jeremiah 7.3–11	Romans 13.8–10	Luke 9.22–27a
Tuesday	Isaiah 38.10–20	Job 5.17–23	John 3.16–21
Wednesday	Deut. 32.1–12	Hosea 12.6	John 6.44–51
Thursday	Isaiah 12.1–6	Romans 5.1–5	1 John 4.7–12
Friday	Isaiah 2.2–6	Ezekiel 34.31	Gal. 5.13–15, 22–24
Saturday	Hosea 6.1–6	Isaiah 55.6–9	1 Timothy 6.6–10
Sunday	Micah 6.6–8	Baruch 4.27–30	Revelation 21.1–5a

A Celtic Primer

WEEK THREE

	Morning	Midday	Evening
Monday	Exodus 20.1–7	1 Peter 1.17–19	Luke 6.20–23
Tuesday	Exodus 20.8–17	1 Peter 1.13–16	Matthew 5.13–16
Wednesday	Deut. 6.4–7	2 Cor. 13.4	Luke 17.5–10
Thursday	Deut. 7.6–9	2 Cor. 1.19–28	Luke 18.9–14
Friday	Jeremiah 6.16	Romans 8.14–17	Luke 9.57–62
Saturday	Job 1.21	1 Samuel 16.76	Mark 10.35–40
Sunday	Job 38.1–7	Wisdom 1.13–15	1 John 3.1–3

WEEK FOUR

	Morning	Midday	Evening
Monday	Ecclesiastes 3.1–8	Jeremiah 17.5–8	Luke 10.38–42
Tuesday	Sirach 1.1–20	1 Peter 3.8–9	Matthew 1.13–14
Wednesday	Sirach 18.1–7	Colossians 3.12–15	Matthew 11.28–30
Thursday	Sirach 39.13–21	Jeremiah 31.33	Luke 17.20–21
Friday	Sirach 42.15–25	1 Cor. 12.12–13	Luke 14.25–27
Saturday	Sirach 50.22–24	Galatians 5.16–18	Ephesians 4.22–32
Sunday	Jeremiah 16.19–21	Deut. 8.5–18	Philippians 2.14–18

Te Deum Laudamus

(Optional – may be said on Sundays)

[Bracketed verses may be omitted]

You are God and we praise you:
You are the Lord and we acclaim you;

You are the eternal Father:
All creation worships you.

To you all angels, all the powers of heaven:
Cherubim and seraphim sing in endless praise,

Holy, holy, holy Lord, God of power and might:
Heaven and earth are full of your glory.

The glorious company of apostles praise you:
The noble fellowship of prophets praise you,
The white-robed army of martyrs praise you.

Throughout the world the holy Church acclaims you:
Father of majesty unbounded;

Your true and only Son, worthy of all worship:
And the Holy Spirit advocate and guide.

You Christ are the King of glory:
The eternal Son of the Father.

When you became man to set us free:
You did not abhor the Virgin's womb.

You overcame the sting of death:
And opened the kingdom of heaven to all believers.

You are seated at God's right hand in glory:
We believe that you will come and be our judge.

Come then Lord and help your people:
Bought with the price of your own blood;

And bring us with your saints:
To glory everlasting.

[Save your people Lord and bless your inheritance:
govern and uphold them now and always.

Day by day we bless you:
We praise your name for ever.

Keep us today Lord from all sin:
Have mercy on us, Lord have mercy.

Lord show us your love and mercy:
For we put our trust in you.

In you Lord is our hope:
Let us not be confounded at the last.]

Glory to the Father and to the Son:
And to the Holy Spirit;
As it was in the beginning, is now:
And shall be for ever.
Amen.

The Song of Zechariah
Benedictus Luke 1.68–79

Blessed be the Lord the God of Israel:
For he has come to his people and set them free.

He has raised up for us a mighty Saviour:
Born of the house of his servant David.

Through his holy prophets he promised of old that he would save us from our enemies:
From the hands of all that hate us.

He promised to show mercy to our forebears:
And to remember his holy covenant.

This was the oath he swore to our father Abraham:
To set us free from the hands of our enemies,

Free to worship him without fear:
Holy and righteous in his sight all the days of our life.

You my child shall be called the prophet of the Most High:
For you will go before the Lord to prepare his way.

To give his people knowledge of salvation:
By the forgiveness of all their sins.

In the tender compassion of our God:
The dawn from on high shall break upon us,

To shine on those who dwell in darkness and the shadow of death:
And to guide our feet into the way of peace.

Glory to the Father and to the Son:
And to the Holy Spirit;
As it was in the beginning, is now:
And shall be for ever.
Amen.

The Lord's Prayer

Intercessions (optional, see page 55)

Office Collect (see page 58)

Or

Celtic Prayers (see page 83)

Or prayers from the Old Testament or New Testament may be used.

Conclusion

Let us bless the Lord.
Thanks be to God.
May the souls of the faithful departed through the mercy of God, rest in peace,
And rise in glory.
May the Divine assistance remain with us always,
And with our absent brothers and sisters.
Amen.

MIDDAY PRAYER

Sentence
Invocation
Antiphon
Psalmody
Reading
Collect
Conclusion

———

The Angelus
(optional)

Sentence (see page 5)

Invocation

O God come to my aid
O Lord make haste to help me.

Glory be to the Father, and to the Son:
And to the Holy Spirit;
As it was in the beginning, is now:
And shall be for ever.
Amen.

Let us worship the Lord.
All praise to his name.

(A hymn may be sung or said if prayed in private)

Antiphon

Help me keep my flesh chaste for love of the Lord,
Flesh which He has prepared as a temple for the Holy Spirit.

Psalmody

Either use the Perpetual Psalter mode or choose from the following chart.

Psalms for Midday Prayer

Sunday	Terce: 119.1–32	Sext: 1, 8, 12	None: 112, 113, 115
Monday	Terce: 119.33–56	Sext: 20, 23, 24	None: 120, 121, 122
Tuesday	Terce: 119.57–80	Sext: 43, 46, 47	None: 123, 124, 125
Wednesday	Terce: 119.81–104	Sext: 48, 67, 70	None: 126, 127, 128
Thursday	Terce: 119.105–128	Sext: 72, 84	None: 129, 130, 131
Friday	Terce: 119.129–152	Sext: 96, 97, 98	None: 133, 138, 146
Saturday	Terce: 119.153–176	Sext: 100, 101, 111	None: 147, 148, 150

Reading

The continual reading mode may be used, a short reading may be chosen from the 'Readings' section on page 24 or the following alternative reading may be used:

Seek good, and not evil,
That you may live,
That the Lord, the God of Hosts,
May be with you, as you claim He is.
Hate evil and love good;
Establish justice in the courts;
It may be that the Lord, the God of Hosts,
Will show favour to the survivors of Joseph.

Amos 5.14ff.

Collect

Dear, chaste Christ,
Who can see into every heart and read every mind,
Take hold of my thoughts.
Bring my thoughts back to me
And clasp me to yourself.

Irish, eighth century

Let us bless the Lord
Thanks be to God.

THE ANGELUS

(May be recited after Midday Prayer
other than during Eastertide)

The Angel of the Lord declared unto Mary,
And she conceived of the Holy Spirit.

Hail Mary, full of grace, the Lord is with thee:
blessed art thou among women, and blessed is the fruit of thy womb, Jesus.
Holy Mary, Mother of God, pray for us sinners,
now and at the hour of our death.
Amen.

Behold the handmaid of the Lord,
Be it done unto me according to your word.

Hail Mary.

And the Word was made flesh,
And dwelt among us.

Hail Mary.

Pray for us, O holy Mother of God,
That we may be worthy of the promises of Christ.

Let us pray.

Pour forth, we beg you, O Lord, your grace into our hearts: that we, to whom
the Incarnation of Christ your Son was made known by the message of an
angel, may by his passion and cross be brought to the glory of his Resurrection.
Through the same Christ our Lord.
Amen.

During the Easter Season: *Regina Coeli*

Queen of Heaven, rejoice, alleluia:
For he whom you merited to bear, alleluia,
Has risen, as he said, alleluia.

Rejoice and be glad, O Virgin Mary, alleluia.
Because the Lord is truly risen, alleluia.

Let us pray.

O God, who by the resurrection of your Son, our Lord Jesus Christ, granted joy
to the whole world: grant, we beg you, that through the intercession of the
Virgin Mary, his mother, we may lay hold of the joys of eternal life. Through
the same Christ our Lord.
Amen.

EVENING PRAYER

(Vespers)

Sentence
Invocation
Antiphon
Psalmody
Reading
Silence
Hymn
Gospel Canticle
Intercessions
Lord's Prayer
Collect
Conclusion

Evening Prayer

Let us adore the Lord,
Maker of marvellous works,
Bright heaven with its angels,
And on earth the white-waved sea.

Old Irish

Sentence (see page 5)

Invocation

O God, come to my aid
O Lord, make haste to help me.

Antiphon

Ordinary

Consecrate my prayer, O Christ, Lord of the heavens!

Advent/Christmas

God's greatness shall reach to the ends of the earth.
God shall be peace.

Lent

Create in me a clean heart, O God, and renew a right spirit within me.

Easter

Although Jesus was crucified, O Lord, our champion,
He has now arisen as the pure King of all that he created.

Psalmody

Reading: Old Testament

Hymn/Meditation (see page 113)

Reading: New Testament

Gospel Canticle
Magnificat

My soul proclaims the greatness of the Lord:
my spirit rejoices in God my Saviour;

for he has looked with favour on his lowly servant:
from this day all generations will call me blessed;

the Almighty has done great things for me:
and holy is his name.

He has mercy on those who fear him:
in every generation.

He has shown the strength of his arm:
he has scattered the proud in their conceit.

He has cast down the mighty from their thrones:
and has lifted up the lowly.

He has filled the hungry with good things:
and the rich he has sent away empty.

He has come to the help of his servant Israel:
for he has remembered his promise of mercy,

the promise he made to our forebears:
to Abraham and his children for ever.

Glory to the Father and to the Son:
and to the Holy Spirit;
as it was in the beginning, is now:
and shall be for ever.
Amen.

Intercessions (see page 55)

The Lord's Prayer

Collect (see page 58)

Conclusion

May Almighty God bless us,
deliver us from all evil,
and bring us to everlasting life.
May the souls of the faithful departed
through the mercy of God, rest in peace.
And rise in glory.
May the divine assistance remain with us always.
And with our absent brothers and sisters.

MONASTIC COMPLINE

May the almighty Lord grant me/us
A peaceful night and a perfect end.
Amen.

Be sober and watch, because your adversary the devil prowls around like a roaring lion, seeking someone to devour. Resist him, strong in faith. But you, O Lord,
have mercy on me/us. Thanks be to God.

Our/my help is in the name of the Lord
Who made heaven and earth.

O God, make speed to save me/us
O Lord, make haste to help me/us.

Glory to the Father, and to the Son:
And to the Holy Spirit;
As it was in the beginning, is now:
And shall be for ever.
Amen.

Psalm 4

Answer me when I call, O God, defender of my cause*
you set me free when I am hard-pressed;
have mercy on me and hear my prayer.

'You mortals, how long will you dishonour my glory*
how long will you worship dumb idols
and run after false gods?'

Know that the Lord does wonders for the faithful;*
when I call upon the Lord, he will hear me.

Tremble, then, and do not sin;*
speak to your heart in silence upon your bed.

Offer the appointed sacrifices*
and put your trust in the Lord.

A Celtic Primer

Many are saying, 'O that we might see better times!'*
lift up the light of your countenance upon us, O Lord.

You have put gladness in my heart,*
more than when grain and wine and oil increase.

I lie down in peace; at once I fall asleep;*
for only you, Lord, make me dwell in safety.

Glory to the Father, and to the Son:
And to the Holy Spirit;
As it was in the beginning, is now:
And shall be for ever.
Amen.

Psalm 91

He who dwells in the shelter of the Most High,*
abides under the shadow of the Almighty.

He shall say to the Lord,
'You are my refuge and my stronghold,*
my God in whom I put my trust.'

He shall deliver you from the snare of the hunter*
and from the deadly pestilence.

He shall cover you with his pinions,
and you shall find refuge under his wings;*
his faithfulness shall be a shield and buckler.

You shall not be afraid of any terror by night,*
nor of the arrow that flies by day;

Of the plague that stalks in the darkness,*
nor of the sickness that lays waste at midday.

A thousand shall fall at your side
and ten thousand at your right hand,*
but it shall not come near you.

Your eyes have only to behold*
to see the reward of the wicked.

Because you have made the Lord your refuge,*
and the Most High your habitation.

There shall no evil happen to you,*
neither shall any plague come near your dwelling.

For he shall give his angels charge over you,*
to keep you in all your ways.

They shall bear you in their hands,*
lest you dash your foot against a stone.

You shall tread upon the lion and the adder;*
you shall trample the young lion and the serpent under your feet.

Because he is bound to me in love,
therefore will I deliver him;*
I will protect him, because he knows my name.

He shall call upon me and I will answer him;*
I am with him in trouble,
I will rescue him, and bring him to honour.

With long life will I satisfy him,*
and show him my salvation.

Glory to the Father and to the Son:
And to the Holy Spirit;
As it was in the beginning, is now:
And shall be for ever.
Amen.

Psalm 134

Behold now, bless the Lord,
all you servants of the Lord,*
you that stand in the house of the Lord.

Lift up your hands in the holy place
and bless the Lord;*
the Lord who made heaven and earth
bless you out of Zion.

Glory to the Father and to the Son:
And to the Holy Spirit;
As it was in the beginning, is now:
And shall be for ever.
Amen.

Hymn

Te Lucis

To you before the end of day,
Creator of the world, we pray:
In love unfailing hear our prayer
And keep us in your watchful care.

Bid anxious dreams and fears depart,
Enfold in peace each mind and heart.
Restore our flagging strength with rest
No wiles of evil can molest.

O Father, that we ask be done
Through Jesus Christ, your only Son,
Who, with the Spirit and with you,
Shall live and reign all ages through.
Amen.

Chapter Jeremiah 14.9

You, O Lord, are among us, and your holy name is called upon by us; do not forsake us.
Thanks be to God.
Keep me/us, O Lord, as the apple of your eye.
Protect me/us under the shadow of your wings.
Lord, have mercy;
Christ, have mercy;
Lord, have mercy.

The Lord's Prayer

Collect (see page 72)

Or

Visit this house, O Lord, and drive from it all the snares of the enemy. May your holy angels dwell herein to preserve us in peace, and may your blessing be always upon us. Through Jesus Christ our Lord, who with you and the Holy Spirit, lives and reigns one God, now and for ever.
Amen.

Let us bless the Lord;
Thanks be to God.
May the almighty and merciful Lord,
Father, Son and Holy Spirit,
Bless and keep us.
Amen.

The 'Salve Regina'

Hail! Holy Queen, Mother of mercy,
Our life, our sweetness, and our hope.
To thee do we cry, poor banished children of Eve.
To thee do we send up our sighs, mourning and weeping in this vale of tears.
Turn then, most gracious advocate, thine eyes of mercy towards us
And after this our exile, show unto us the blessed fruit of thy womb, Jesus!
O clement, O loving, O sweet Virgin Mary.

Prayer

Almighty and everlasting God, Who by the cooperation of the Holy Spirit made ready the body and soul of the glorious Virgin and Mother Mary to be a fit dwelling for Your Son, grant that we, who rejoice in her memory, may be freed from present ills and from eternal death by her prayers. Through the same Christ our Lord.
Amen.

May the divine assistance remain always with us.
And with our absent brothers and sisters.
May the souls of the faithful departed through the mercy of God rest in peace.
Amen.

CELTIC COMPLINE

May your Holy Angels, O Christ, son of the living God,
tend our sleep, our rest, our bright bed.
Let them reveal true visions to us in our sleep, O High Prince of the universe,
O great and mysterious King.
May no demons, no evil, no injury or terrifying dreams disturb our rest,
our prompt and swift repose.
May our waking, our work, and our living be holy;
our sleep, our rest, without hindrance or harm.

Celtic Spirituality (6)

Antiphon

Keep us safe, O Lord, in the darkness of this night,
for the eternal kingdom, where there is flaming radiance forever.

Early Irish Lyrics (19)

Psalmody

Psalm 139.1–11, 16, 17

Lord, you have searched me out and known me;*
you know my sitting down and my rising up;
you discern my thoughts from afar.

You trace my journeys and my resting-places*
and are acquainted with all my ways.

Indeed, there is not a word on my lips,*
but you, O Lord, know it altogether.

You press upon me behind and before*
and lay your hand upon me.

Such knowledge is too wonderful for me;*
it is so high that I cannot attain to it.

Where can I go then from your Spirit?*
where can I flee from your presence?

If I climb up to heaven, you are there;*
if I make the grave my bed, you are there also.

If I take the wings of the morning*
and dwell in the uttermost parts of the sea,

Even there your hand will lead me*
and your right hand hold me fast.

If I say, 'Surely the darkness will cover me,*
and the light around me turn to night',

Darkness is not dark to you;
the night is as bright as the day;*
darkness and light to you are both alike.

How deep I find your thoughts, O God!*
how great is the sum of them!

If I were to count them,
they would be more in number than the sand;*
to count them all, my life span would need to be like yours.

Glory to the Father, and to the Son:
And to the Holy Spirit;
as it was in the beginning, is now:
and shall be for ever.
Amen.

Psalm 16

Protect me, O God, for I take refuge in you;*
I have said to the Lord, 'You are my Lord,
my good above all other.'

All my delight is upon the godly that are in the land,*
upon those who are noble among the people.

But those who run after other gods*
shall have their troubles multiplied.

Their libations of blood I will not offer,*
nor take the names of their gods upon my lips.

A Celtic Primer

O Lord, you are my portion and my cup;*
it is you who uphold my lot.

My boundaries enclose a pleasant land;*
indeed, I have a goodly heritage.

I will bless the Lord who gives me counsel;*
my heart teaches me, night after night.

I have set the Lord always before me;*
because he is at my right hand I shall not fall.

My heart, therefore, is glad and my spirit rejoices;*
my body also shall rest in hope.

For you will not abandon me to the grave,*
nor let your holy one see the Pit.

You will show me the path of life;*
in your presence there is fullness of joy,
and in your right hand are pleasures for evermore.

Glory to the Father and to the Son:
And to the Holy Spirit;
As it was in the beginning, is now:
And shall be for ever.
Amen.

Psalm 17.1–8

Hear my plea of innocence, O Lord; give heed to my cry;*
listen to my prayer, which does not come from lying lips.

Let my vindication come forth from your presence;*
let your eyes be fixed on justice.

Weigh my heart, summon me by night,*
melt me down; you will find no impurity in me.

I give no offence with my mouth as others do;*
I have heeded the words of your lips.

My footsteps hold fast to the ways of your law;*
in your paths my feet shall not stumble.

I call upon you, O God, for you will answer me;*
incline your ear to me and hear my words.

Show me your marvellous loving-kindness,*
O Saviour of those who take refuge at your right hand
from those who rise up against them.

Keep me as the apple of your eye;*
hide me under the shadow of your wings.

Glory to the Father and to the Son:
And to the Holy Spirit;
As it was in the beginning, is now:
And shall be for ever.
Amen.

Repeat Antiphon

Keep us safe, O Lord, in the darkness of this night,
for the eternal kingdom, where there is flaming radiance for ever.

Reading

Either

They shall see God's face, and his name shall be on their foreheads. And night
shall be no more; they shall not need the light of the lamp nor the light of the sun,
because the Lord God shall enlighten them, and they shall reign for ever and ever.

Revelation 22.4–5

Or

I lie down this night with God,
And God will lie down with me;
I lie down this night with Christ,
And Christ will lie down with me;
I lie down this night with the Spirit,
And the Spirit will lie down with me;

God and Christ and the Spirit
Be lying down with me.

Gaelic (13)

Or

O God, Lord of Creation, I invoke you.
You are my gracious counsellor.
Do not turn your face toward me,
for you are my judgment without betrayal.

You are my king. You are my law.
Yours is my flesh, my body, I love you, blessed Christ,
for my soul is yours tonight.

Let me not conceal it, O King.
May I be in your royal dwelling all my days.
May I eat the feast from your table.
Do not leave me behind, O God.

Early Irish

Thanks be to God.
Into your hands, Lord, I commend my spirit.
For you have redeemed us, Lord God of truth.

Antiphon

Guide us waking, O Lord, and guard us sleeping; that awake we may watch with
Christ, and asleep we may rest in peace.

Nunc Dimittis

Lord, now you let your servant go in peace: your word has been fulfilled.
My own eyes have seen the salvation: which you have prepared in the sight of
every nation.
A light to reveal you to the nations: and the glory of your people Israel.

Glory to the Father, to the Son:
And to the Holy Spirit;
As it was in the beginning, is now:
And shall be for ever.
Amen.

Repeat Antiphon

Guide us waking, O Lord, and guard us sleeping; that awake we may watch with
Christ, and asleep we may rest in peace.

Lord have mercy.
Christ, have mercy.
Lord, have mercy.

The Lord's Prayer

May we do the will of God, sharing in the death of Christ,
and rise in the light of heaven.
May we rest safely this night, sleep in perfect peace,
and rise with the morning light.
May the Father watch over our beds, Christ fill our dreams,
and the angels guard our souls.

May the peace of the Spirit be mine this night,
the peace of the Son be mine this night,
and the peace of the Father be mine this night,
Each morning and evening of my life.
Amen.

Gaelic (13)

A Celtic Primer

Hymn

Tota pulchra es

Thou are all-lovely O
Mary, and the stain of sin
is not found in thee.
You are the glory of Jerusalem.
You are the joy of Israel,
You are the greatest honour of our people.
You are the advocate of sinners.
O Mary, O Mary,
Virgin most prudent,
Mother most merciful,
Pray for us,
Intercede for us with our Lord Jesus Christ.

Ancient Hymn to the Blessed Virgin Mary

Prayer

Let me have from you my three petitions beautiful Mary, little bright-necked one; get them, sun of women, from your son who has them in his power.

That I be in the world till old with the Lord who rules starry heaven, and that thereafter there be a welcome for me into the eternal, ever-enduring kingdom.

Blathmac, seventh century (10)

Or

Gentle Mary, noble maiden, give us help!
Shrine of our Lord's body, casket of the mysteries!
Queen of queens, pure holy maiden,
Pray for us that our wretched transgressions
be forgiven for Thy sake.

Irish, tenth century

May the Divine Assistance remain always with us.
And with our absent loved ones.
Amen.

LOVE
the people,
LOVE them well.
LOVE the Word,
LOVE the Eucharist.
LOVE your work
and try to
be good.

BRENDANUS

INTERCESSIONS

FOR THE CHURCH

Introduction

'On this rock I will build my Church, and the powers of death shall never conquer it.'

Matthew 16.18

Intentions

We pray for all who work through the power of Christ in the Church today, serving the needs of the poor and healing the wounds of injustice, division and materialism in our society.
(Silence)
We pray for the elderly, the sick and the lonely among us: that they may receive comfort, companionship and care from those around them.
(Silence)
We pray that those who have been persecuted or seriously wronged by others may experience warmth and love with Christ, and be able to forgive those who have hurt them.
(Silence)
We pray for the members of the Church, that we may humbly admit our failure to meet the needs of others.
(Silence)
We pray that the Christian churches may grow together towards unity of faith, and witness to the values of the gospel.
(Silence)

Concluding Prayer

O God of unchangeable power and eternal light, look favourably on your Church, that wonderful and sacred mystery; and by the tranquil operation of perpetual providence, carry out the work of the salvation of humankind; and let the whole world feel and see that things which were cast down are being made new, and that all things are returning to perfection through Him from whom they took their origin, through our Lord Jesus Christ.
Amen.

Gelasian

For Others

Introduction

With expectant faith we pray to the Father, confident in his love and infinite wisdom.

Intentions

Let us pray for all Christians: that they may seek the kingdom of God before all else.

Let us pray for those who are distressed, whether in body, mind or spirit.

Let us pray for ourselves: that we may seek more energetically to work with the Lord in establishing justice and peace on earth.

Let us pray for all married couples: that they remain loving and faithful to each other in good times and in bad.

Let us pray for all those who have asked for our prayer, especially those whose names are written on our hearts at this moment.

A Celtic Primer

Concluding Prayer

Almighty Father, we ask you to grant our petitions. Help us to seek and to love you more every day of our lives. Teach us to reach out to our neighbour, that we may follow the example of Jesus, the Christ, your Son our Lord.
Amen.

For Ourselves

Introduction

The Lord our God listens to the needs of his children. Let us make them known to him now in quiet confidence and hope.

Intentions

We pray that when we are discouraged, we may find strength in the signs of a loving and faithful God in those around us.

We pray for the trust and openness to give our hearts and lives to God as Jesus did.

We pray for those who have lost hope: that they may find the joy of the Holy Spirit within their hearts.

We pray that we may be a sign of the love of God to all whom we meet today.

We pray for the souls of all those whom we have loved but now no longer see; those who have gone beyond the veil of this mortal life. May their souls and the souls of all the faithful departed rest in peace.
And rise in glory.

Concluding Prayer

We thank you Father for all that you have given us. In your love grant us what your word has prompted us to ask for in the name of Jesus Christ our Lord.
Amen.

OFFICE COLLECTS

Morning Prayer

Sunday (1)

Father of mercy,
your love embraces everyone
and through the Resurrection of your Son
you call us all into your wonderful light.
Dispel our darkness
and make us a people with one heart and one voice,
forever singing your praise,
in Jesus, the Christ, our Lord.

Unity
Rom. 2.11; 1 Tim. 2.4; 1 Peter 2.9; Eph. 2.14, 1.14

Sunday (2)

God of the universe,
when you raised your servant Jesus,
you made him the light of the nations.
May the salvation he brings us
shine out to the ends of the earth,
and may your name be blessed for ever and ever.

The light of Christ. Universality of salvation
1 Cor. 6.14; Acts 4.27–30; Isa. 49.6; Acts 13.47

A Celtic Primer

Monday (1)

Lord God,
you have created us in your own Image,
to find freedom in a love that knows no bounds.
Lead us further today along this path of freedom
to which you call us,
through Jesus, your beloved Son, our Lord.

Our image of God. Love and liberty
Gen. 1.27; Eph. 5.1–2; Gal. 5.1, 18

Monday (2)

Lord Jesus, eternal splendour,
on this day which is given us by the Father's love,
do not let us lose sight of you
but always bring us back to the light of your face,
for you reign for ever and ever.

Jesus and the love of the Father. The face of Christ
Heb. 1.3; Isa. 17.7; 2 Cor. 4.6

Tuesday (1)

Lord Jesus,
you know each of us by name
and have called us to follow you;
teach us how to respond anew
in every opportunity this day will bring.
We ask you this, you who love us
with the Father and the Spirit,
for ever and ever.

To follow Christ. The meaning of daily life
John 1.3–4

Tuesday (2)

Father of Jesus Christ,
open our hearts to your Word
and to the power of the Spirit.
Give us love to discover your will
and strength to carry it out today;
for you are our light,
for ever and ever.

To do the will of the Father
Acts 16.14; Eph. 3.16; Rom. 12.2; Eph. 5.10; 2 Cor. 8.11; Col. 1.9–10; Phil. 2.13; Heb. 13.21

Wednesday (1)

God our Creator,
today you bring us to a new stage of our journey to you;
May the presence of your
Son guide us,
the love of your Spirit enlighten us,
until we come at last to you,
God blessed for ever and ever.

The meaning of time
Eph. 2.10; Deut. 1.31; Heb. 2.10; Col. 1:11

Wednesday (2)

Father almighty,
you revealed to us that you are light.
Help us to live our lives in your radiance
and we will be in fellowship with one another
in the Christ, our Lord.

To live in the light. Communion with one another
1 John 1.5, 7

Thursday (1)

God our Father,
your light came into the world.
May we welcome him in our lives,
and thus be a light for our brothers and sisters.
We ask you this
through Jesus, the Christ, our Lord.

To welcome Christ. To live in the light
John 3.16; Isa. 58.8; Matt. 5.16; Eph. 5.8

Thursday (2)

Lord our Father,
each morning you welcome us as we are;
give us a heart that is pure and free,
to receive your Word,
and discover in our brothers and sisters
the message of life that you bring us,
through Jesus, the Christ, our Lord.

Spiritual poverty. Welcoming the Word. Welcoming the brothers and sisters
Luke 8.15; 1 Thess. 1.6, 2.13; James 1.21; 1 John 1.5

Friday (1)

Lord Jesus,
your food was to do the will of your Father.
Make us attentive this day to the call of the Spirit,
and give us the strength to respond to him in humility,
for you are our help
for ever and ever.

Attentiveness to the Spirit
John 4.34; Rev. 2.7; Rom. 12.2

Friday (2)

Lord God,
you know we long to give ourselves to you;
come and help our weakness;
then we shall emerge victorious
from the struggle of this day,
thanks to him who has loved us so much,
Jesus Christ, your Son, our Lord.

The spiritual combat
1 Cor. 12.9; Rom. 8.37; 1 John 5.5

Saturday (1)

Father, source of all holiness,
help us to live in mutual love throughout this day,
for according to your Word, we must shine in the world
like beacons of light.
This we ask through Jesus, the Christ, our Lord.

Eternal love
Phil. 2.1–2; Col. 3.13–14; 1 Peter 1.22; 2 John 6; Matt. 5.16

Saturday (2)

Lord Jesus, true light,
we believe in you;
increase our faith,
so that today we shall become more fully
children of the light.
We ask you this,
who are resplendent in the glory of the Father,
for ever and ever.

Faith. To live in the light
John 1.9; Luke 17.5; John 12.36

A Celtic Primer

Midday Prayer

Sunday (1)

Father, at noontime on this day
hallowed by the Resurrection of your Son,
we give you thanks for your presence among us.
Yours is the earth and its fullness.
May the hearts and desires of all peoples
be turned to you, through Jesus, the Christ, our Lord.

The presence of God. The desire for God
Ps. 23.1, 88.12; Isa. 45.22; 1 Kgs 8.58

Sunday (2)

God our Father,
on this, the day of the Risen Lord,
we have received the gift of his life,
and have given thanks to you.
Keep alive in us the memory of your covenant,
and the desire to praise you,
today and for ever.

The life of Christ in us. Recalling the Covenant
Rom. 6.23; 1 Chron. 16.15; Luke 22.20; 1 Cor. 11.25

Monday (1)

God of mercy,
we thank you for this morning
which has brought us closer to you.
Accept all human labour,
make it fruitful,
and bless every creature in your love for us,
which endures for ever and ever.

God welcomes our work
Deut. 33.11, 28.1; Ps. 89.16–17; Gen. 1.28

Office Collects

Monday (2)

God our Father
revive our strength
and renew our vision
at noontime on this day.
Teach us to discern your presence
in ourselves,
and in our brothers and sisters,
through Jesus, the Christ, our Lord.

Spiritual discernment. The presence of God
Isa. 4.29; Ps. 18.9b; Luke 24.31

Tuesday (1)

Lord our God,
midway through the work of this day
draw our minds and hearts to you.
Renew us in love,
that we may serve you in joy until evening,
through Jesus, the Christ, our Lord.

Recollection. The service of God
Ps. 88.11; Zeph. 3.17; Ps. 99.2

Tuesday (2)

Lord Jesus, our Shepherd,
at this hour when you draw us together,
and give us a time of rest;
teach us to leave everything aside
so that we may gaze on you,
know you,
and love you with all our hearts,
who live with the Father,
in the unity of the Holy Spirit,
for ever and ever.

Contemplating Christ. To love Christ
Ps. 22.2–3; Acts 2.46; Phil. 2.1–2; 2 Cor. 13.13

Wednesday (1)

Lord Jesus, Saviour of the word,
this is the hour when you were lifted up from the earth.
By looking on your Cross
and seeing the depth of your love for us,
may we never again stray from you,
who reign with the Father for ever and ever.

The love of Christ. Contemplating the Cross
John 3.14, 19.37; Gal. 3.1; Heb. 12.2; John 13.1, 15.13; Gal. 2.20; Ps. 79.19

Wednesday (2)

You are always at work within us,
Lord our God,
drawing us into the unity of the Spirit;
guide our hearts
so that we may be open in love,
to our brothers and sisters
while always remaining closely united to you,
through Jesus, the Christ, our Lord.

The unity of the Church. Attentiveness to God. Attentiveness to others
1 Thess. 2.13; 1 Cor. 6.17; Eph. 4.3–4; Ps. 85.11c

Thursday (1)

Gathered together again at noontime,
God our Father,
we make our prayer to you;
keep your children united in the one Spirit,
that we may be witnesses
to the peace which you give us,
in Jesus, the Christ, our Lord.

Unity. To give witness to peace
Eph. 4.3; Col. 3.13–14; John 14.27

Thursday (2)

Lord God,
you give us the grace
to stand in your presence and serve you.
Keep us vigilant in prayer,
and in love of our neighbour,
so that our work may not be in vain,
but may always give glory to you,
through the Christ, our Lord.

Vigilance. Prayer and love of one another
Luke 1.74–75; Rom. 12.10–13; Col. 4.2; Heb. 13.1; 1 Cor. 10.31; Col. 3.17

Friday (1)

Lord Jesus,
when you were crucified for the salvation of the world;
you promised the kingdom to the repentant thief.
With him we implore you:
pardon our sins,
and grant that we may be with you always,
where now you live and reign,
with the Father and the Spirit,
for ever and ever.

Pardon for sins
John 11.51–52; Gal. 3.13; 2 Cor. 5.14–15; Col. 1.22; Luke 23.43

Friday (2)

Lord, at this midday hour
we call to mind in your presence
the agony of your Son on the Cross;
and we entrust to you
all the suffering and weariness
that weigh on so many of our brothers and sisters;
let them know in their lives
the power of your love,
in Jesus Christ, our Lord.

Human suffering. The love of God
Isa. 53; 2 Cor. 12; Heb. 12.2

Saturday (1)

Father, at midday you give us a time of rest;
may we accept it gratefully
and be strengthened by it,
to serve you and our neighbour
through Jesus, the Christ, our Lord.

The meaning of a time of rest. The service of God and of each other
Wisd. 1.7; Eph. 5.16; Philemon 6

Saturday (2)

Lord our God,
amid the uncertainties of our human life,
may we pause and draw strength from you,
trusting in your faithful love.
We ask this through Jesus, your Son, our Lord.

Confidence in God
Sir. 2.4; 2 Chron. 14.10

EVENING PRAYER

Sunday (1)

Ever faithful God,
you love us and bless us
in Jesus Christ your Son.
By him alone
you are perfectly glorified.
At this evening hour,
may your Spirit in us
sing the marvels of your salvation;
God most high,
who lives for ever and ever.

The action of the Spirit. Praise
Eph. 1.3–13; 2 Cor. 1.20; Eph. 3.21; Isa. 12.5; Luke 10.21; Acts 2.11; Eph. 5.19

Sunday (2)

We give you thanks, Lord our God,
for this day, now drawing to a close.
May our prayer, rising before you like incense,
be pleasing to you;
and may our outstretched hands
be filled with your mercy,
through Jesus, your Son, our Lord.

The evening offering. To welcome mercy
Ps. 140.2; Jude 21

Monday (1)

Lord Jesus, as once you looked with pity
on the weary crowds,
look again this evening on us,
your people.
Good Shepherd, who gave your life for your flock,
guide us to the peace of your kingdom,
where we shall know you
in the glory of the Father,
and the unity of the Spirit,
for ever and ever.

Human distress. The peace of God
Matt. 9.36; John 10.11; Matt. 16.27; John 17.5–25

Monday (2)

In the peace of evening,
we come to you, Lord God.
May your Word free our hearts
from the cares of this day.
As we experience your forgiveness in Jesus,
may we too forgive in him
our brothers and sisters who have injured us.
We ask this in his name,
Jesus, the Christ, our Lord.

The mercy of God. Pardon
Luke 8.11, 6.26; Col. 3.13

A Celtic Primer

Tuesday (1)

Father, we thank you
for showing us your mercy today;
may that mercy extend to all those
whom you entrust to our prayer;
and may it bring your peace to all people,
through Jesus Christ, our Lord.

Intercession. The mercy of God
1 Peter 1.3; Ex. 33.19, 34.6; Sir. 50.22–23; Isa. 57.19; Eph. 2.17

Tuesday (2)

As once you walked in the garden, Lord,
in the calm of evening,
so this evening you come seeking us.
If we are tempted to flee from your presence,
change our fear to confidence.
Confessing our sin,
without blaming others;
we place our hope
in your mercy and forgiveness,
through Jesus, your Son, our Lord.

Confidence. Trust. Recognizing oneself as a sinner
Gen. 3.8–10, 3.12; 1 John 1.9

Wednesday (1)

It is for you that we live,
Lord our God,
and to you we have consecrated this day;
perfect and purify our offering,
so that our prayer of thanksgiving
may rise to you,
in Jesus, your Son, our Lord.

The evening offering. Thanksgiving
Rom. 12.1; Zeph. 3.9–10; Matt. 1.11; Heb. 9.14, 12.28

Wednesday (2)

We have worked this day, Lord,
at the tasks you gave us.
Now the night is coming,
when no one can work.
May your light remain with us always,
so that during the night of our earthly life
we may accomplish the one work
which endures to eternal life –
to believe in him
whom you have sent,
Jesus Christ, your Son, our Lord.

The night of the world. Faith
John 9.4, 6.28–29

Thursday (1)

Lord God, ever faithful,
see us gathered before you
as the day draws to a close;
confirm our hearts in your love,
and keep alive in us
the memory of your goodness and kindness,
which have appeared in Jesus Christ, our Lord.

The faithfulness of God. To remember God and his goodness to us
2 Tim. 2.13; 2 Thess. 3.3–5; James 5.8; Ps. 102.2

Thursday (2)

We come to you, Lord Jesus,
tired from the burdens of this day.
Teach us your gentleness and humility,
and our heart will find rest and peace,
because you are faithful to your promises,
now and for ever.

The mildness and humility of Christ. His faithfulness
Matt. 11.28–29, 20.12; Ps. 61.6, 130.2

Friday (1)

Lord Jesus, Mediator of the new Covenant,
sustain our confidence,
and despite our falls,
confirm us in the hope in which we glory.
So that, purified by your Blood,
we may come to the City of the Living God,
where you reign,
with the Father and the Holy Spirit, for ever and ever.

The City of God
Heb. 8.6, 9.15, 3.6, 12.24, 12.22

Friday (2)

As each day passes, Lord,
and the knowledge of our weakness
lies heavily upon us,
grant that we may so love you
as never to despair of your mercy;
for it endures for ever
in Jesus, the Christ, our Lord.

Trust. The mercy of God
Rule of St Benedict 4.74

Saturday (1)

Lord our God,
this day is drawing to a close.
At the hour of evening sacrifice
you gather us in praise.
Keep us from all anxiety,
and stir up in our hearts
a longing for your day.
Hear us in the love you bear us,
through Christ and the Holy Spirit,
for ever and ever.

Praise. The day of God
Luke 24.29; Ex. 30.8; Num. 28.4; Ps. 140.2; Sir. 44.15; Acts 2.47; Eph. 5.19;
Col. 3.16; Phil. 4.6; 1 Peter 5.7; 2 Tim. 4.8

Saturday (2)

Lord our God,
you called us to begin this day.
Now at its ending
our tasks lie incomplete,
our hopes are not achieved.
Grant that we may be with you
where our weakness will be overcome,
and all our longing be fulfilled,
in Jesus, your Son, our Lord.

The desire for heaven
Rom. 7.18; Eph. 4.1; Gal. 5.7; 2 Cor. 8.11; 1 Cor. 15.43; 1 Peter 5.10

Night Prayer: Compline

Sunday (1)

Jesus, our risen Lord,
you deliver us from darkness
and from the spirit of slavery;
give us the freedom of the children of God,
through the certainty that we are loved by your Father,
who is also our Father, blessed for ever and ever.

Children of God. Liberty
Isa. 42.7; John 8.12; Rom. 8.15, 8.39

Sunday (2)

As the day ends and darkness falls, O Lord our God,
may the darkness be for us
a reminder of your mercy which blots out all our sins.
Strengthen our hearts,
so that beyond all darkness
they may remain ever fixed in your light,
in Jesus, the Christ, our Lord.

The mercy of God. To live in the light
Ps. 64.4, 84.3; Sir. 2.11, 18; Micah 7.18–19; Isa. 49.10

Monday (1)

Have pity on your children, Father,
when their hearts condemn them;
for you are greater than our hearts.
We take shelter in you
for you will be our refuge
at the hour of our death;
give us also your protection this night
through Jesus, the Christ, our Lord.

Trust
1 John 3.20; Ps. 10.1, 31.7, 90.2, 140.8–10; Matt. 3.16

Monday (2)

To those who love you,
God our Father,
grant your peace;
may it so fill our hearts and our spirits
that not even the powers of darkness
may separate us from you.
Hear our prayer,
in Jesus, your Son, our Lord.

Darkness. The peace of God
Ps. 118.165; Phil. 4.7; 2 Thess. 3.16; Ps. 22.4; Rom. 8.38–39

Tuesday (1)

Jesus. Light and Salvation of the World,
reveal yourself to those
who search for you in darkness.
Light up their lives in hope;
may they see your power at work,
and recognize that you are God-with-us,
for ever and ever.

The light of Christ. The activity of Christ
Ps. 26.1; Luke 2.33–34; Acts 17.27; Isa. 9.1; Matt. 1.23, 28.20

Tuesday (2)

Bless our sleep, Lord God,
and make it a continuation of our trustful prayer;
so that even while we rest,
our hearts may remain watchful,
through Jesus, the Christ, our Lord.

Trust. Prayer
Wisd. 5.2

Wednesday (1)

God our Father,
you have been our guide and our help
throughout this day;
stay with us now throughout the night.
May your light
enlighten and purify our hearts,
and keep them vigilant in faith,
through Jesus, the Christ, our Lord.

The light of God. Vigilance
Ps. 22.3; Deut. 1.32–33; 1 Cor. 16.13; 2 Cor. 1.24; Heb. 3.14

Wednesday (2)

We have sought your ways this day,
Lord God,
but we have also followed our own.
Forgive us for straying
and lead us back to you.
Strengthened by your help
we shall be able to support one another,
in Jesus, the Christ, our Lord.

Our Sin. Love of one another
Ps. 24.5, 85.11, 142.8, 80.13; Jer. 18.12, 23.27; Bar. 1.22; Eph. 2.3; Ps. 68.8,
24.8; Isa. 35.3–4, 41.14; 2 Cor. 1.4; 1 Thess. 4.18, 5.11

Thursday (1)

Lord Jesus,
as you look upon us this evening,
may the light of your countenance
pass beyond our sins,
even to the depths of our hearts;
and bring to birth there
a deep and trustful love.
Hear us, Lord, who reign for ever and ever.

The light of Christ. Purity of heart
Hab. 1.13; Luke 22.61; Rule of St Benedict 72.10

Thursday (2)

Lord Jesus,
support the sick, the dying,
and all for whom this coming night will be a trial.
Lead us with all our brothers and sisters,
from darkness into your own wonderful light,
which shines for ever and ever.

The sick. The action of Christ
1 Peter 2.9

Friday (1)

Unseen God,
you reveal your presence in the hearts
of those who love you and keep your Word.
Forgive the sins we have committed this day,
and come make your home with us,
together with your Son,
and the Holy Spirit,
one God, blessed for ever and ever.

The presence of God. Pardon for sins
John 1.18, 14.21–23

Friday (2)

You seek us tirelessly,
God our Father.
Forgive us our resistance,
and grant that the recognition
of your infinite goodness
may draw us closer to one another in forgiveness.
We ask this through Jesus, your Son, our Lord.

The goodness of God. Mutual forgiveness
Isa. 65.1–2; Jer. 7.25, 25.4–6; Ezek. 34.15; Rom. 2.4; Eph. 4.32

Saturday (1)

May the noise and turmoil of our world
rise to you, Lord God,
to be taken up into your silence;
and may your peace come down upon us,
Jesus, the Christ, our Lord.

The silence of God. The peace of God
Phil. 4.7; 2 Thess. 3.16

Saturday (2)

Lord our God,
there is no limit to your forgiveness;
at the evening of this day,
trusting in your mercy,
we ask you not to hold our sins against us,
but to open our hearts
to the peace which was promised us
by Jesus, the Christ, our Lord.

The mercy of God. Trust
Neh. 9.17; Ps. 129.3–4, 7; Sir. 2.7–11; John 14.27

COLLECTS OF THE SEASONS

ADVENT

Morning Prayer

Ever faithful God,
your prophets foretold the coming of the light.
In your name they promised
that the eyes of the blind would be opened.
We confidently await the coming of your Son,
and the day when he will gather all people
to live in your light, for ever and ever.

Evening Prayer

God our Father,
you overcame the stubbornness of human hearts,
and their resistance to your call,
as you prepared the coming of the Messiah.
Grant that we too may be faithful
and persevere to the end in the ways that you have called us,
and in waiting for him who is to come,
Jesus, our Lord.

CHRISTMAS

Morning Prayer

God our Father,
by his coming on earth,

your Son revealed your glory to us.
May your Spirit awaken us to this radiance,
so that we may live in your presence through love,
straining forward to the day of eternity.
Hear us, through Jesus, your Son, our Lord.

Evening Prayer

Loving Father,
your final word to us is your Word incarnate;
Grant that we may welcome him with all our hearts,
respond in love to your unending love,
and gain eternal life,
through Christ, our Lord.

LENT

Morning Prayer

Lord Jesus,
you fulfilled the Father's will to the very end.
Speak to our hearts
and we will follow the path of your commands.
May the way of the Cross
lead us to the joy of Easter,
for ever and ever.

Evening Prayer

God our Father,
your will is that everyone be saved and no one be lost.
You draw us to yourself by prayer and penance.
Grant that we may so follow Christ in love
that our lives may help others and our weakness never hinder them.
We make this prayer in his name,
Jesus, the Christ, our Lord.

EASTER

Morning Prayer

God of truth,
in the Resurrection of your Son,
you reveal to us the meaning of all things.
Increase our faith
so that we may see your presence
in all that comes to us this day.
Hear us, through Jesus, the Christ, our Lord.

Evening Prayer

God, most holy Father,
in the Resurrection of Jesus
you have given us the blessed hope
of a never-ending day.
Lead us now, through the darkness and the night,
to the vision of your glory,
in the kingdom of your son,
for ever and ever.

PENTECOST

Morning Prayer

Father, you are the God of life,
who created all things
by the power of your Spirit.
We pray you, on this day,
when your blessing was poured out on the Apostles:
renew your Church,
so that all may find in her
the seeds of the new creation,
through Jesus, the Christ, our Lord.

Evening Prayer

God of power and holiness,
we rejoice in your enduring love for the Church,
the beloved Bride of your Son.
Today your Spirit comes upon her;
may he be light in her darkness,
strength in her trials,
and joy in her hope.
Hear us, God, living for ever and ever.

Collects for the Office are from Proclaiming all Your Wonders (31)

A Celtic Primer

IF you
want
to understand
the CREATOR
seek to
understand
CREATED
things

ST COLUMBANUS

CELTIC PRAYERS

Dear, chaste Christ,
Who can see into every heart and read every mind,
Take hold of my thoughts,
Bring my thoughts back to me
And clasp me to yourself.

Prayer of a Celtic monk, eighth century

O Son of God, change my heart,
Your spirit composes the songs of the birds and buzz of the bees.
I ask of you only one more miracle:
Beautify my soul.

Traditional

He is pure gold, he is sky around the sun,
He is a vessel of silver with wine,
He is an angel, he is holy wisdom,
Whoso doth the will of the King.

Ancient Irish (9)

Rule this heart of mine,
O dread God of the elements,
That Thou mayest be my love,
That I may do Thy will.

(9)

Whoso doth the will of God's Son from Heaven
Is a brilliant summer-sun,
Is a dais of God of Heaven,
Is a pure crystalline vessel.

(9)

O God I pray to you for help in every trouble,
in every way of which my lips are capable!
deeper than seas, greater than reckoning,
Three, One, more wondrous than can be told.

from Broccain's Hymn to Saint Brigid

Morning Poem

O Holy Spirit of Love
In us, round us, above;
Holy Spirit we pray
Send, sweet Jesus, this day.

Holy Spirit, to win
Body and Soul within
To guide us that we be
From ills and illness free.

From sin and demons' snare,
From hell and evils there,
O Holy Spirit, come!
Hallow our heart, thy home.

Máel Iśu ó Brolcháin (3)

O holy Jesus,
Gentle friend,
Morning Star,
Midday sun adorned
Brilliant flame of righteousness, life everlasting and eternity,
Fountain ever-new, ever-living, everlasting,
Heart's desire of Patriarchs
Longing of prophets,
Master of Apostles and disciples,
Giver of the Law,
Prince of the New Testament,
Judge of doom,
Son of the merciful Father without mother in heaven,
Son of the true Virgin Mary, without father on earth,
True and loving brother.

from The Broom of Devotion (2)

A Celtic Primer

Daily Offering

Thanks to Thee, God,
Who brought'st me from yesterday
To the beginning of today,
Everlasting joy
To earn for my soul
With good intent.
And for every gift of peace
Thou bestowest on me,
My thoughts, my words,
My deeds, my desires
I dedicate to Thee.
I supplicate Thee,
I beseech Thee,
To keep me from offence,
And to shield me tonight,
For the sake of Thy wounds
With Thine offering of grace.

Gaelic

O God, listen to my prayer,
Let my earnest petition come to you
For I know that you hear me
As surely as I see you with my own eyes.

Gaelic

Almighty God,
Father, Son, and Holy Spirit
to me the least of saints,
to me allow that I may keep even the smallest door,
the farthest, darkest, coldest door,
the door that is least used, the stiffest door.
If only it be in Your house, O God,
that I can see Your glory even afar,
and hear Your voice,
and know that I am with You, O God.

St Columba

Let us praise God
at the beginning
and the end of time.
Who ever seeks Him out
He will not deny
not refuse.

Black Book of Carmarthen,
tenth to eleventh century (22)

Prayer of St Columba

Have mercy, Christ, have mercy
on all that trust in Thee,
for Thou are God in glory
to all eternity.

O God, make speed to save us
in life's abounding throes:
O God, make haste to help us
in all our weary woes.

O God, Thou art the Father
of all that have believed:
from whom all hosts of angels
have life and power received.

O God, Thou art the Maker
of all created things,
the righteous Judge of judges,
the Almighty King of kings.

High in the heavenly Zion
Thou reignest God adored;
and in the coming glory
Thou shalt be sovereign Lord.

Beyond our ken Thou shinest,
The everlasting Light;
ineffable in loving,
unthinkable in might.

Thou to the meek and lowly
Thy secrets dost unfold;
O God, Thou doest all things,
all things both new and old.

I walk secure and blessed
in every clime or coast,
in the Name of God the Father,
and Son, and Holy Ghost.

attributed to St Columba

O Lord our Father, almighty everlasting God, we ask you to send your holy Angel
from heaven to guard, cherish, protect, visit, and defend all who dwell in this
house; through Jesus Christ our Lord.
Amen.

Gelasian

Stretch forth, O Lord, the right hand of your mercy upon your servants, that,
seeking you with their whole heart, they may have all their needs supplied;
through Jesus Christ our Lord.
Amen.

Gelasian

Christ the lowly and meek,
Christ the all powerful,
Be in the heart of each to whom I speak,
In the mouth of each who speaks to me,
In all who draw near me,
Or see me, or hear me!

St Patrick

Prayer to the Trinity

Teach me O Trinity,
All men sing praise to Thee;
Let me not backward be,
Teach me O Trinity.

Come Thou and dwell within me,
Lord of the holy race;
Make here Thy resting-place,
Hear me O Trinity.

That I Thy love may prove,
Teach Thou my heart and hand,
Even at Thy command
Swiftly to move.

Like a rotting tree,
Is the vile heart of me;
Let me Thy healing see,
Help me O Trinity.

Welsh (26)

God, kindle Thou in my heart within
A flame of love to my neighbour,
To my foe, to my friend, to my kindred all,
To the brave, to the knave, to the thrall,
O Son of the loveliest Mary,
From the lowliest thing that liveth
To the name that is highest of all.

Gaelic

For Family and Friends

Almighty and everlasting God, you are Lord both of the living and the dead, and you love all those whom you know to be yours by faith and good works; we humbly entreat you that all those for whom we pray, both living and dead, whom the world to come has received, may by your goodness and mercy be counted worthy to obtain pardon of their sins and everlasting happiness; through Jesus Christ our Lord.
Amen.

Sarum Primer

Have mercy, O Lord, upon my family and friends, and grant us to be subject to you with our whole heart, that being filled with the sprit of your love, we may be cleansed from earthly desires and made worthy by your grace of heavenly blessedness; through Jesus Christ our Lord.
Amen.

Gallican

A Celtic Primer

For a Departed Friend

O God, whose mercies are without number, accept my prayer for the soul of your servant (N) and grant him/her the fellowship of all your saints in the land of light and joy; through your Son, our Lord Jesus Christ, the Saviour and Guardian of our souls and bodies.
Amen.   *Sarum Primer*

Prayer for a Bishop

O God, the Pastor and Ruler of your faithful servants, look down in your mercy upon your servant (N) our bishop, to whom you have given charge over this diocese; evermore guide, defend, comfort, sanctify and save him; and grant that he, with the flock committed to his charge, may attain to everlasting life, through Jesus Christ our Lord.
Amen.   *Ambrosian*

Patrick's Evensong

Christ, Thou Son of God most High,
May Thy Holy Angels keep
Watch around us as we lie
In our shining beds asleep.

Time's hid veil with truth to pierce
Let them teach our dreaming eyes,
Arch-King of the Universe,
High-Priest of the Mysteries.

May no demon of the air,
May no malice of our foes,
Evil dream or haunting care
Mar our willing prompt repose!

May our vigils hallowed be
By the tasks we undertake!
May our sleep be fresh and free,
Without let and without break.

(21)

Celtic Prayers   89

Evening Prayer

Spirit, give me of Thine abundance,
Father, give me of Thy wisdom,
Son, give me in my need,
Jesus beneath the shelter of Thy shield.

I lie down tonight,
With the Triune of my strength,
With the Father, with Jesus,
With the Spirit of might.

(13)

The Bible

O Lord, you have given us your word for a light to shine upon our path; grant us so to meditate on that word, and to follow its teaching, that we may find in it the light that shines more and more until the perfect day; through Jesus Christ our Lord.

Saint Jerome

PRAYER READINGS FROM THE OLD TESTAMENT AND APOCRYPHA

Genesis 12.1–3	God's call to Abraham
Genesis 28.11–18, 20–22	Jacob's dream
Exodus 15.1–13, 17–18	The Canticle of Moses
Exodus 20.1–17	The Ten Commandments
Deuteronomy 1.29–31	The Lord your God will lead you
1 Chronicles 16.8–18, 23–36	David's Song of Praise
Nehemiah 9.6–21, 26–28, 31–33	The Prayer of Confession
2 Maccabees 1.2–6	A Blessing to the Jews in Egypt
Proverbs 8.11–31, 34–35	In Praise of Wisdom
Ecclesiastes 3.1–8	There is a Season for Everything
Sirach 1.1–20	In Praise of Wisdom
Sirach 18.1–7	The Greatness of God
Sirach 39.14–21, 33–35	Hymn in Praise of God
Sirach 42.15–25	The Glory of God in Nature
Sirach 43.27–33	The Lord is Everything
Sirach 51.1–3, 6–12	A Song of Thanksgiving
Isaiah 15.1–5	A Canticle of Praise
Isaiah 40.1–11	The Lord is coming. Prepare in the wilderness a road for the Lord.
Isaiah 40.12–14, 18–22, 25–31	Hymn to the Incomparable God
Isaiah 44.1–8	The Lord is the only God
Isaiah 45.9–19	Canticle of Isaiah
Isaiah 55.1–3, 5–13	Song of God's mercy
Isaiah 57.14–15, 18–19	'Let my people return to me. Remove every obstacle from their path! Build the road and make it ready!'
Jeremiah 10.12–13, 16	Hymn of Praise to God
Lamentations 3.22–33	God's unfailing love
Daniel 3.52–90	Song of the Three Young Men – Praise of the Lord of Creation
Amos 4.13	God is the One who made the mountains

Amos 9.11–15	Words of hope from the Lord, 'The mountains will drip with sweet wine, and the hills will flow with it!'
Micah 4.1–4	A song of universal peace
Micah 6.6–8	What the Lord wants of you – 'to walk humbly with your God'.

PRAYER READINGS FROM THE NEW TESTAMENT

Matthew 5.3–10	The Beatitudes
Matthew 5.43–48	Love your enemies
Luke 6.27–31	Love your enemies
Luke 22.14–20	Prayer of Thanksgiving
Luke 12.22–31	You cannot serve both God and Money
Luke 11.9–13	Ask and you will receive
Matthew 11.25–37	Jesus prays to the Father
Luke 10.21–22	Jesus prays to the Father
Matthew 11.28–30	Come to me and rest
Matthew 18.19–20	Anything you pray for, it will be done
Matthew 21.18–22	When you pray . . . Believe
Mark 12.28–31	The two great commandments
Luke 1.46–55	Canticle of Mary
Luke 1.67–79	Canticle of Zechariah
Luke 3.21–22	While Jesus was praying
Luke 24.13–35	The Emmaus walk
John 1.1–15	Canticle of the Word
John 3.16–17	God so loved the World
John 10.10–18	Song of the Good Shepherd
John 13.34–35	A new commandment
John 14.1–4, 6–7, 9, 12–14	Jesus is the Way to the Father
John 14.15–18, 23, 25–26	The Promise of the Holy Spirit
John 14.27–31	My own peace I give you
John 15.1–5, 7, 10–17	Jesus is the True Vine
John 16.4–5, 7–8, 13–15	The work of the Holy Spirit
John 16.20–24	Whatever you ask in my name
John 17.1–26	The priestly prayer of Christ
Romans 5.6–11	Christ made us his Friends
Romans 8.31–35, 37–39	Hymn to God's Love
Romans 10.9–13	Everyone who calls on the Lord will be saved

Romans 11.33–36	A Hymn to God's Wisdom
Romans 12.12	Pray at all times
Romans 16.25–27	Prayer of Praise
1 Corinthians 1.3–9	Blessings in Christ
1 Corinthians 13.1–13	Canticle to love
1 Corinthians 15.51–55	Hymn of triumph over death
2 Corinthians 1.2–5	Let us give thanks to God
Galatians 4.6–7	Abba, Abba
Ephesians 1.3–14	Spiritual Blessings in Christ
Ephesians 1.15–23	Prayer of the Light, love and power of Christ
Ephesians 3.14–21	The root and foundation of Christ's love
Ephesians 4.4–6	There is one Lord
Ephesians 5.19–20	With Psalms and Hymns
Ephesians 6.10–20	The Armour of God
Philippians 1.2–11	Paul's Prayer for his readers
Philippians 2.5–11	Christ's humility and greatness
Philippians 4.4–9	Ask for what you need with a thankful heart
Colossians 1.15–20	Hymn to Christ
Colossians 3.1–4	Set your hearts on things that are in Heaven
Colossians 3.23–24	Christ is the Real Master you serve
Colossians 4.2–4	Be persistent in prayer
1 Thessalonians 4.13–14	The Truth about those who have died
1 Thessalonians 5.16–26	Pray at all times
Hebrews 1.1–13	A Hymn to God's Word
Hebrews 1.4–14	Hymn to the greatness of God's Son
Hebrews 4.12–13	The Word of God is alive and active
Hebrews 12.2–3	Let us keep our eyes fixed on Jesus
1 Peter 2.20–25	Christ carried our sins
1 John 1.1–4	The Word of Life
1 John 1.5–7	God is Light
1 John 3.1–3	We are God's children
1 John 4.7–21	God is Love
Revelation 1.4–8	Hymn of Thanksgiving to Christ
Revelation 5.7–14	A New Song
Revelation 7.9–17	The saints proclaim God's glory
Revelation 21.1–7	The New Heaven and the New Earth

A Celtic Primer

PRAYERS OF REPENTANCE

Repentance

God's will would I do,
My own will bridle.

God's due would I give,
My own due yield.

God's path would I ponder,
My own death remember;

Christ's agony would I meditate,
My love to God make warmer;

Christ's cross would I carry,
My own cross forget;

Repentance of sin would I make,
Early repentance choose;

A bridle to my tongue would I put,
A bridle on my thoughts I would keep;

God's judgement would I judge,
My own judgement guard;

Christ's redemption would I seize,
my own ransom work;

The love of Christ would I feel,
My own love know.

Jesus, forgive my sins.
Forgive the sins that I can remember, and also the sins I have forgotten.
Forgive the wrong actions I have committed, and the right actions I have omitted.
Forgive the times I have been weak in the face of temptation, and those when I have been stubborn in the face of correction.
Forgive the times I have been proud of my own achievements, and those when I have failed to boast of your works.
Forgive the harsh judgements I have made of others, and the leniency I have shown to myself.

Forgive the lies I have told to others, and the truths I have avoided.
Forgive me the pain I have caused others, and the indulgence I have shown to
myself.
Jesus have pity on me, and make me whole.

Early Irish

To others I am always honest;
myself I sometimes deceive.
To others I say what I believe to be true;
myself I can make believe a lie.

To others my smile is intended to be sincere;
myself I can fool into hiding my anger.
To others I always wish to do good;
myself I can blind to my evil motives.

Lord, let me be as honest with myself
as I am with others.

Early Irish

I read and write and teach, philosophy peruse.
I eat and freely drink, with rhymes invoke the muse,
I call on heaven's throne both night and day,
Snoring I sleep, or stay awake and pray.
And sin and fault inform each act I plan.
Ah! Christ and Mary, pity this miserable man.

Sedulius Scottus
(trans. J. Carney)

Forgiveness, God, for all my sins
I seek at last,
the sin in word, the deed in heart,
foul sin compared.

In heedless youth I broke the rule,
made grievous slips,
offered fair women of gleaming teeth
lascivious lips.
Now I am an old, old man
and after sinful years
I seek no feast but that my cheeks
be wet with tears.

Máel Iśu ó Brolcháin
(trans. J. Carney)

A Celtic Primer

The will of God be done by us;
The law of God be kept by us;
Our evil will controlled by us;
Our sharp tongue checked by us;
Quick forgiveness offered by us;
Speedy repentance made by us;
Temptation sternly shunned by us;
Blessed death welcomed by us;
Angels' music heard by us;
God's highest praises sung by us.

Anon.

O helper of workers,
ruler of all good,
guard on the ramparts
and defender of the faithful,
who lift up the lowly
and crush the proud,
ruler of the faithful,
enemy of the impenitent,
judge of all judges,
who punish those who err,
pure life of the living,
light and Father of lights
shining with great light,
denying to none of the hopeful
your strength and help,
I beg that me, a little man
trembling and most wretched,
rowing through the infinite storm of this age,
Christ may draw after Him to the lofty
most beautiful haven of life
. . . an unending
holy hymn for ever.
From the envy of enemies you lead me
into the joy of paradise.
Through you, Christ Jesus,
who live and reign . . .

attributed to St Columba (14)

Prayers of Repentance

Fair Lord, I pray to you
concerning my excesses and deficiencies:
grant me forgiveness here
for my misdeeds, my ignorance.

Saltair na Rann (18)

Gentle Mary, Branch of Jesse's tree in the beauteous hazel-wood,
Pray for me until I obtain forgiveness of my sins.

Mary, splendid diadem, You have saved our race,
Glorious noble torch, orchard of Kings!

Brilliant one, transplendent one, with the deed of pure chastity
Fair golden illumined ark, holy daughter from Heaven!

Mother of righteousness, You who excel all else,
Pray for me with Your first-born to save me on the day of Doom.

from 'A Prayer to the Virgin', tenth century

God above us,
God before us,
God rules.
May the King of Heaven
give now the portion of mercy.

Black Book of Carmarthen,
tenth to eleventh century (22)

Re-Dedication

How great the tale, that there should be,
In God's Son's heart, a place for me!
That on a sinner's lips like mine,
The cross of Jesus Christ should shine!

Christ Jesus, bend me to Thy will,
My feet to urge, my griefs to still;
That even my flesh and blood may be
A temple sanctified to Thee.

A Celtic Primer

No rest, no calm, my soul may win,
Because my body craves to sin
Till Thou, dear Lord, Thyself impart
Peace to my head, light to my heart.

May consecration come from far
Soft shining like the evening star!
My toilsome path make plain to me,
Until I come to rest in Thee.

Muredach Albanach, twelfth century (26)

GOD is Breath,
for the breath of the wind is shared by all,
goes EVERYWHERE; nothing shuts it in,
NOTHING holds it prisoner

Maximus the Confessor

BODY PRAYER

'What I do is pray, how I pray is breathe.'

Thomas Merton

To relax properly before practising Lectio Divina or Contemplative Prayer it is recommended that you release mental and physical tension.

The function of this exercise is to bring the body into tune with mind and spirit so that the whole person may experience the living Word made flesh. The prayer of the Word cannot happen without the body, through the praying of the scriptures the Spirit takes possession of the body, which is the temple of the Holy Spirit.

Inhale through your nose and imagine your abdomen is like a balloon filling with air. Hold, then exhale slowly, imagining the balloon deflating. Your chest should remain motionless. Repeat three times and then commence reading or silent prayer.

'The Word of God is something alive and active; it cuts like any double-edged sword but more finely; it can skip through the place where the soul is divided from the spirit, or joints from marrow; it can judge the secret emotions and thoughts.' (Heb. 4.12)

The next short exercise is also an exercise or 'ascesis' of the breath. It not only relaxes the body through breathing away the tensions, it also prepares the whole person for Lectio Divina, the praying of the Word.

BASIC RELAXATION TECHNIQUE

When you sit, keep your body as erect as possible (like a puppet on a string): and become aware of your breathing.

As you breathe out, relax the muscles, beginning with the head: breathing away the tensions . . .

Relaxing the scalp and the sides of the face . . . and the jaw line where so much tension gathers.

Breathe away the tensions of the shoulders . . . dropping the shoulders and the arms . . . and the hands . . . and the fingers . . . letting them completely relax.

Relax the chest muscles . . . the waist . . . and the thighs . . . and the legs, breathing away the tensions.

Now, as you breathe out . . . breathe out as though you are breathing through all the pores of your body . . .

Completely alert and in control . . . at the same time, as much as possible, relaxed.

For a few moments breathe out through all the pores of the body.

Silence.

DAILY MEDITATION TEXTS

These short readings are for reflection and meditation on the Word of God. They are primarily for those who cannot spend much time over the Office but look for a sentence of Scripture to nourish heart conversation with the Lord during a busy day.

These readings may also be used at Morning, Midday or Evening Prayer.

LECTIO DIVINA JOURNAL

The daily Scripture Meditation Texts printed below are for reflection, meditation and Lectio Divina (see also page xi). They may be used for study of the Word, as well as an experience of God sought through the practice of praying the Word in his presence.

As the Scripture sentence or phrase is read in a murmured manner, it is echoed in the heart. An interior expansion is experienced and an inner-space is realized to accommodate the Word. This is a deeply experiential method of prayer, which effectively allows the reader to deepen his or her received knowledge of the inspired Word of God.

A suggested method of practising Lectio and combining it with study is to keep a Lectio Divina Journal. If possible, use an Annotated or Study Bible with cross-references and footnotes.

Read the text taken from the daily reading list and write a chosen sentence on to the top of the left-hand page of the open journal. Underneath the sentence, write any of the cross-reference texts which relate to it and are suitable for the developing theme.

When you have completed your thematic journey into the Word through marrying the texts, write 'Meditatio' on the right-hand page. Under this heading, write the sentence which sums up the Lectio or study of the previous page. It may be the original words which strike your attention, or an additional biblical sentence which has emerged from the experience. Keep praying over the word, muttering it, chewing, ruminating and digesting this inner word of life. Then, when you are ready, write 'Oratio' underneath the meditatio section, for prayer written as a response to the meditated word which has preceded it.

Finally, under the heading 'Contemplatio', write down a single word or mantra phrase which sums up the whole exercise. This phrase will remain in the heart to be remembered and repeated frequently throughout the day.

Date and Bible reference	
Text Lectio: Using comparable texts from a study Bible build up a theme for prayer.	Meditatio: Read the passage over and over again and write down the sentences and phrases which strike the attention. Oratio: A written prayer summing up the whole experience. Contemplatio: A prayer phrase for the day.

If wished, another page may be used for personal spiritual journal.

DAILY BIBLE MEDITATION TEXTS

January			February	
1	Luke 2.16–21		1	Deut. 15.7–11
2	Acts 10.34–43		2	2 Cor. 1.18–22
3	John 1.1–18		3	Eph. 6.18–20
4	Wisd. 11.21–26		4	1 John 3.13–16; Mark 3.7–12
5	Matt. 6.6–8		5	1 Cor. 15.54–58
6	Matt. 2.1–12		6	Acts 17.22–28
7	Isa. 12.2–6		7	Ps. 40.7–12
8	Isa. 12.5–6; John 1.14–18		8	Amos 8.8–11
9	Luke 3.15–22		9	John 6.27–29
10	Matt. 3.13–17		10	1 John 4.15–18; Mark 4.13–20
11	Ps. 96		11	Matt. 5.17–37
12	Zech. 2.15; Luke 6.20–23		12	1 John 5.1–4; Luke 11.9–13
13	Isa. 43.1–4a		13	Heb. 11.8–16
14	2 Tim. 1.9–10; John 2.1–12		14	Mark 4.30–34
15	Isa. 46.3–5, 9		15	Mark 5.35–43; Deut. 8.2–16
16	Rom. 8.5–11		16	Matt. 6.1–6, 16–18
17	Jer. 31.31–34		17	Ps. 143
18	Phil. 4.4–7		18	John 5.24–27
19	1 John 3.17–20; John 5.1–9		19	John 6.41–51
20	Rev. 3.20–22		20	1 Cor. 3.18–23
21	John 5.1–9; Acts 10.37–38		21	Matt. 25.34–40
22	Isa. 50.7–9		22	Isa. 61.10–11
23	Eph. 4.29–32		23	John 12.20–33
24	Mark 1.14–20		24	Isa. 49.14–15
25	1 John 1.1–4; Luke 4.1–14		25	Mark 8.34–35
26	Isa. 49.13–15		26	Ps. 51
27	Eph. 3.7–12		27	Isa. 65.17–18
28	Luke 4.14–30		28	Deut. 4.29–31; Matt. 5.43–48
29	Jer. 2.1–13			
30	Matt. 6.7–15			
31	Eph. 1.15–23			

March

1	Rom. 12.1–13
2	Wisd. 11.23–24; Matt. 20.20–28
3	Matt. 7.7–12
4	Ps. 147
5	Jer. 17.7–8
6	Rom. 12.3–13
7	Rev. 3.7–8
8	Matt. 6.19–21
9	1 Thess. 5.12–22
10	Matt. 7.18–20
11	Job 19.23–27
12	Hos. 6.3–6; Luke 18.9–14
13	Phil. 2.1–11
14	Matt. 18.1–4
15	Ps. 42
16	James 5.7–12
17	John 9.35–39; Ezek. 37.12–14
18	Luke 11.9–13
19	Matt. 1.16–21
20	Rom. 11.29, 33–36
21	John 4.14–26
22	Micah 7.14–16
23	John 11.1–45; Isa. 49.1–6
24	Ex. 14.5–31
25	John 16.32–33
26	1 Tim. 4.12–16
27	Matt. 19.27–29
28	Matt. 26.36–46
29	Matt. 27.45–46
30	Ps. 118
31	Luke 23.33–46

April

1	John 8.1–11
2	Mark 9.17–29
3	Micah 6.1–8
4	Acts 1.6–11
5	Gal. 5.16–18, 22–23
6	Acts 5.17–33
7	Acts 26.1–23
8	John 20.19–23; Acts 3.11–21
9	Rom. 8.1–11
10	Bar. 5.1–9
11	John 20.24–29
12	Zech. 8.16–19
13	Acts 5.34–42; John 3.16–17
14	Phil. 4.4–7
15	Acts 15.5–12
16	Acts 4.1–12
17	Luke 4.14–30
18	Gal. 2.15–21
19	Matt. 14.44–46
20	Hos. 14.2–9
21	Hos. 6.3–6
22	Eph. 1.3–10
23	Matt. 28.1–10
24	Isa. 42.10–17
25	Mark 16.15–20
26	2 Cor. 5.16–21
27	1 Peter 1.6–9; John 10.22–30
28	John 12.44–50
29	John 13.31–35
30	2 Cor. 3.16–18

A Celtic Primer

May

1	Matt. 9.17–29
2	Acts 15.7–12
3	Luke 1.39–56
4	1 Cor. 15.20–28
5	John 20.11–18
6	Acts 2.14, 36–41
7	1 Cor. 15.54–58
8	Ps. 55.17–19
9	2 Tim. 2.1–7
10	1 Peter 1.1–5
11	1 Peter 1.6–9
12	Luke 24.1–12
13	1 John 3.14–20
14	Isa. 45.1–7
15	Ps. 105.1–5
16	Isa. 43.18–21
17	Col. 3.12–17
18	Matt. 10.38–39
19	Hab. 2.1–4
20	Rom. 12.9–13
21	Micah 7.7–8
22	John 14.15–21
23	Matt. 28.16–20
24	Ps. 37
25	1 John 2.24–28
26	Ps. 62
27	1 Peter 4.7–11
28	Ezek. 36.24–27
29	1 Cor. 12.3–13
30	Dan. 9.18–19
31	Zeph. 3.14–18a

June

1	Rom. 13.8–10
2	Mark 10:17–22
3	1 Peter 5.6–11
4	Gen. 12.1–4
5	Luke 19.1–10
6	John 6.47–51
7	Deut. 30.11–14
8	Matt. 5.13–16
9	Mark 3.20–35
10	Gen. 28.12–17
11	Luke 12.22–31
12	Mark 4.26–34
13	1 John 1.1–7
14	Isa. 55.6–11
15	2 Peter 1.12–18
16	Mark 12.28–34
17	Ps. 119.1–16
18	Ps. 36
19	Luke 17.20–21
20	2 Cor. 4.7–10
21	Luke 19.1–10; 2 Cor. 3.16–18
22	John 7.37–39
23	Matt. 7.7–11
24	1 Kgs 17.17–24
25	Matt. 5.1–12
26	Isa. 63.7, 10–14
27	Hos. 11.1–4
28	Col. 2.12–14
29	Matt. 16.13–19
30	Matt. 9.1–8

July

1	Hos. 6.2–6
2	Hos. 11.7–9
3	John 20.24–29
4	Isa. 2.2–5
5	1 Thess. 3.12–13
6	John 3.16–17
7	Deut. 30.11–14
8	Rev. 2.8–11
9	Luke 6.36–38
10	Col. 3.12–17
11	Isa. 40.25–28
12	Matt. 11.28–30
13	Matt. 12.1–8
14	Isa. 43.1–4
15	Isa. 40.29–31
16	Deut. 7.7–8
17	2 Cor. 12.1–10
18	Gal. 6.1–10
19	Matt. 6.25–34
20	1 Cor. 4.10–13
21	James 1.17–27
22	John 20.1, 11–18
23	Isa. 42.10, 16
24	Isa. 44.21–23
25	Matt. 20.20–28
26	Luke 11.1–13
27	Rom. 15.7–13
28	Jer. 17.7–8
29	Heb. 11.8–16
30	Isa. 48.20–21
31	Isa. 46.3–4, 8–9

August

1	Jude 20–21
2	Matt. 12.1–8
3	John 6.24–35
4	Gal. 5.16–18, 22–23
5	Matt. 13.18–23
6	Luke 9.28b–36
7	Isa. 54.8, 10–14
8	Prov. 4.18–27
9	2 Cor. 5.1–5
10	Matt. 18.12–14
11	Isa. 56.1–7
12	John 3.16–17
13	Sir. 2.1–9
14	Phil. 1.3–11
15	Luke 1.39–56
16	2 Cor. 4.7–12
17	Matt. 16.24–28
18	John 6.47–51
19	Isa. 30.15
20	Eph. 4.1–7
21	Isa. 58.7–10
22	1 Kgs 8.22–40
23	1 John 4.16–21
24	2 Thess. 1.11–12
25	Ps. 138
26	Heb. 10.22–25
27	Rom. 11.29, 33–36
28	Neh. 8.8–12
29	2 Cor. 13.11–13
30	Matt. 10.1–10
31	John 12.47–50

A Celtic Primer

September

1	Eph. 1.15–23
2	Isa. 45.1–7
3	James 1.17–27
4	Matt. 18.21–22
5	Isa. 49.1–6
6	Luke 18.18–23
7	John 11.1–45
8	John 10.1–10
9	Matt. 1.18–23
10	1 Cor. 7.29–31
11	Eph. 2.14–18
12	Isa. 32.15–20
13	2 Cor. 1.3–7
14	John 3.16–18
15	1 Sam. 16.1–13
16	Rom. 14.13–19
17	Luke 22.24–27
18	Mark 9.30–37
19	Luke 5.1–11; Sir. 4.9
20	Eph. 2.11–13
21	Matt. 9.9–13
22	2 Cor. 1.3–7
23	John 11.1–45
24	Eph. 5.8–14
25	Col. 1.15–20
26	Luke 8.4–8
27	Luke 7.18–23
28	Ezek. 36.25–28
29	Luke 8.43–48
30	Luke 12.22–31

October

1	Rom. 5.1–5
2	Lam. 3.54–57
3	Luke 7.1–10
4	Matt. 11.25–30
5	Luke 5.1–11
6	Rom. 6.12–14, 22–23
7	Matt. 21.33–43
8	John 15.14–17
9	Sir. 30.21–25
10	Rom. 12.9–13
11	1 Peter 5.5–7
12	Micah 7.7–8
13	Zeph. 3.14–18a
14	Gal. 2.15–21
15	Isa. 2.2–5
16	Matt. 6.7–15
17	Isa. 40.1–5
18	Luke 6.27–35
19	Phil. 1.3–11
20	Sir. 2.1–11
21	2 Cor. 5.1–7
22	Heb. 10.19–25
23	1 Peter 5.1–4
24	Ps. 23
25	Isa. 12.2–6
26	John 14.22–26
27	Sir. 14.1–6, 14–16
28	Heb. 10.19–25
29	Ezek. 3.10–11
30	Acts 20.17–38
31	Luke 10.1–9

November

1	Matt. 5.1–12
2	1 Tim. 4.7–16
3	Hos. 6.3–6
4	1 Cor. 12.3–13
5	Micah 4.1–3
6	Luke 14.27–33
7	1 Chron. 29.10–15
8	Neh. 9.17–19
9	Gen. 12.1–5
10	Eph. 3.14–21
11	Matt. 4.12–17
12	2 Thess. 2.3, 5–16
13	Luke 11.9–13
14	Ps. 130
15	Ps. 5
16	Isa. 25.6–9
17	Matt. 25.31–32
18	1 John 2.7–10
19	Wisd. 6.12–19
20	Matt. 12.46–50
21	Rev. 2.8–10
22	Luke 18.35–42
23	Luke 19.1–10
24	Phil. 1.27–30
25	Rom. 12.1–2
26	Luke 15.8–10
27	Rev. 21.5–7
28	Luke 21.1–4
29	Luke 21.8, 12–19
30	Matt. 4.18–22

December

1	Ps. 94.14–22
2	Jer. 1.4–8
3	John 14.19–23
4	Isa. 8.11–18
5	Matt. 7.21–27
6	Isa. 11.5–9
7	Eph. 1.11–12
8	Isa. 25.1–5
9	Wisd. 1.11–15
10	Matt. 18.12–14
11	Matt. 11.28–30
12	Isa. 35.1–10
13	Isa. 28.16–17
14	1 Thess. 5.12–22
15	2 Cor. 5.18–21
16	2 Peter 1.19–21
17	James 5.7–11
18	Rev. 21.5–7
19	Sir. 2.1–11
20	John 15.15–17
21	Luke 1.26–38
22	Ps. 103
23	Luke 1.67–79
24	Eph. 1.15–23
25	John 1.1–18
26	Matt. 25.31–40
27	1 John 1.1–4
28	Isa. 40.29–31
29	Col. 3.12–17
30	1 John 4.7–11
31	John 3.16–17

HYMNS

PRIODAS CALON A DUW YW EMYN

A HYMN IS THE MARRIAGE OF THE HEART OF HUMANKIND WITH THE HEART OF GOD

BEN BOWEN

Hymn of Praise

I praise Thee:

My King, the king of noble heaven,
without pride, without boasting,
made the world with its true nature –
my King ever living, ever triumphant;

King over the creation, on which the sun looks down,
King over the depths of the ocean,
King south, north, west, and east,
against whom no struggle can be maintained;

King of the mysteries, who has been, who is,
before the creation, before the ages,
King living forever still, fair his semblance,
King without beginning, without end.

from Saltair na Rann (18)

Lord, be it thine,
Unfaltering praise of mine!
To thee my whole heart's love be given,
Of earth and Heaven thou King Divine!

Lord, be it thine,
Unfaltering praise of mine!
And, O pure prince! Make clear my way
To serve and pray at thy sole shrine!

Lord, be it thine,
Unfaltering praise of mine!
O Father of all souls that long,
Take this my song and make it thine!

Irish (1)

Be Thou my Vision, O Lord of my heart:
Naught is all else to me, save that Thou art,
Thou my best thought, by day and by night,
Waking or sleeping, Thy presence my light.

Be Thou my Wisdom, Thou my true Word;
I ever with Thee, Thou with me Lord.
Thou my great Father, I Thy dear son,
Thou in me dwelling, I with Thee one.

Be Thou my breastplate, my sword for the fight;
Be Thou my whole armour, be Thou my true might;
Be Thou my soul's shelter, be Thou my strong tower:
O raise Thou me heavenward, great Power of my power.

Riches I heed not, nor man's empty praise:
Be Thou mine inheritance now and always;
Be Thou and Thou only the first in my heart;
O Sovereign of heaven, my treasure Thou art.

High King of heaven, Thou heaven's bright Sun,
O grant me its joys after vict'ry is won;
Great Heart of mine own heart, whatever befall,
Still be Thou my vision, O Ruler of all.

Early Irish

In Eden – I shall always remember this –
I lost blessings numberless as the dew;
Down fell my bright crown:
But the victory of Calvary
Won them back for me again;
I shall sing as long as I live.

Faith! Yonder is the place, and yonder the tree,
On which the Prince of heaven was nailed,
Innocent, in my place;
The dragon has been crushed by the One;
As two were wounded, One has conquered,
And that one was Jesus.

William Williams, Pantycelyn

A Celtic Primer

His left hand, in heat of noonday,
Lovingly my head upholds,
And his right hand, filled with blessings,
Tenderly my soul enfolds.
I adjure you, nature's darlings,
Beautiful in field and grove,
Stir not up, till he be willing,
Him who is my glorious Love.

Ann Griffiths
(trans. H. A. Hodges) (24)

Wondrous sight for men and angels!
Wonders, wonders without end!
He who made, preserves, sustains us,
He our Ruler and our Friend,
Here lies cradled in the manger,
Finds no resting-place on earth,
Ye the shining hosts of glory
Throng to worship at his birth.

When thick cloud lies over Sinai,
And the trumpet's note rings high,
In Christ the Word I'll pass the barrier,
Climb, and feast, nor fear to die;
For in him all fullness dwelleth,
Fullness to restore our loss;
He stood forth and made atonement
Through his offering on the cross.

He between a pair of robbers
Hung, our Making-good to be;
He gave power to nerve and muscle
When they nailed him to the tree;
He, his Father's law exalting,
Paid our debt and quenched our flame;
Righteousness, in fiery splendour,
Freely pardons in his name.

See, my soul, where our Peace-maker,
King of kings, was lowly laid,
He, creation's life and movement,
Of the grave a tenant made,
Yet on souls fresh life bestowing;
Angels view it with amaze;
God in flesh with us adoring;
Heaven's full chorus shouts his praise.

Thanks for ever, thanks ten thousand,
While I've breath, all thanks and praise
To the God who all his wonders
For my worship here displays,
In my nature tried and tempted
Like the meanest of our race,
Man – a weak and helpless infant,
God – of matchless power and grace.

Gone this body of corruption,
Mid the fiery hosts on high,
Gazing deep into the wonders
Wrought of old on Calvary,
God, the Invisible, beholding,
Him who lives, yet once was slain,
Clasped in close eternal union
And communion I'll remain.

There, new-fashioned in his likeness,
Veils and fancies done away,
To the Name by God exalted
Highest homage I shall pay.
There, communing in the secret
Seen in those deep wounds he bore,
I shall kiss the Son for ever,
Turning from him nevermore.

(24)

A Celtic Primer

I'll walk on softly day by day,
The cross o'ershadowing all my way,
And as I walk, my course I'll run,
And as I run I'll stand and see
The full salvation that shall be
When I'm no more beneath the sun.

(24)

Lo, to us is born a brother,
Born for hard and troublous days,
Faithful, full of consolation,
Worthy of yet higher praise,
Freedom sealing, sickness healing.
Way to Zion straight and free,
Fount clear-flowing, life bestowing,
God our saving ark is he.

(24)

Not the great wide-rolling oceans
E'er can hide man's sin away;
Not the mighty Flood could drown it,
It is living still today;
But the precious blood and merits
Of the Lamb that once was slain –
There's the ocean that can hide it;
It will ne'er be seen again.

(24)

There is not on earth an object
That can bring content to me;
My sole pleasure, my sole comfort
Is thy glorious face to see;
This can break the bonds that bind me
to all creatures here below;
Friends and kinsfolk shrink to nothing
If but thy great name I know.

(24)

Lord God, from whose deep counsels
Salvation had its birth,
Thou only art the ruler
Of all in heaven and earth;
In face of tribulation,
Whatever may betide,
Let thy strong grace assist me
Beneath thy hand to hide.

(24)

Diolch am yr Efengyl

Diolch I Ti, Hollalluog Dduw,
Am yr Efengyl, am yr Efengyl,
Am yr Efengyl Sanctaidd.
Haleliwia, haleliwia, haleliwia, Amen.

We thank thee and praise thee for the holy Gospel
For the good news; for the good news;
For the Holy Gospel.
Halleluya, halleluya, halleluya, Amen.

Cariad at Grist
(Ton: Blaen Cefn)

Beth sydd imi mwy a wnelwyf
ag eilunod gwael y llawr?
Tystio'r wyf nad yw eu cwmni
I'w gystadlu a'm Jesu mawr:
O! am aros,
Yn Ei gariad ddyddiau f'oes.

What have I to do henceforward
With base idols of the earth?
One and all I here proclaim them
Matched with Jesus, nothing worth.
O! May I abide
All my lifetime in His love!

Ann Griffiths
(trans. Sir I. Bell)

A Celtic Primer

Cariad Crist
(Ton: Y Botel)

Dyma gariad fel y moroedd,
Tosturiarthau fel y lli:
Twysog Bywyd pur yn marw –
Marw I brynu'n bywyd ni.
Pwy all beidio a chofio amdano?
Pwy all beidio a thraethu'i glod?
Dyma gariad nad a'n angof
Tra fo nefoedd wen yn blod.

Here is love, wide as the ocean,
Mercies, boundless like the sea!
Prince of life in anguish dying –
Dying thus to set us free.
Who His love can but remember?
Who His Name can but adore?
Ne'er such love can be forgotten
While heaven lasts for evermore.

Gwilym Hiraethog
(trans. V. Lewis)

Arweiniad Dwyfol
(Ton: Bryn Calfaria)

Ymddiriedaf yn Dy allu,
Mawr yw'r gwaith a wnest erioed;
Ti gest Angau; Ti gest uffern,
Ti gest Satan dan dy droed:
Pen Calfaria,
Nac aed hwnnw byth o'm cof.

I do trust in Your power,
Great the deed you have performed;
Death you conquered; hell was conquered;
Crushed was Satan, once for all:
Hill of Calvary,
May I not forget that place.

William Williams

Guide me, O thou great Redeemer
Pilgrim through this barren land;
I am weak but thou art mighty;
Hold me with thy powerful hand:
Bread of heaven, bread of heaven,
Feed me now and evermore.

Open now the crystal fountain
Whence the healing stream doth flow;
Let the fiery cloudy pillar
Lead me all my journey through:
Strong deliverer, strong deliverer,
Be thou still my strength and shield.

When I tread the verge of Jordan,
Bid my anxious fears subside;
Death of death, and hell's destruction,
Land me safe on Canaan's side:
Songs and praises, songs and praises
I will ever give to thee.

W. Williams
(Tune: Cwm Rhondda)

St David and the Welsh Saints
(Tune: 'Hyfrydol')

Lord, who in Thy perfect wisdom
Times and seasons dost arrange, –
Working out Thy changeless purpose
In a world of ceaseless change:
Thou didst form our ancient nation
In remote barbaric days,
To unfold in it a purpose
To Thy glory and Thy praise.

To our shores remote, benighted,
Washed by distant western waves,
Tidings in Thy love Thou sentest,
Tidings of the Cross that saves.

A Celtic Primer

Men of courage strove and suffered
Here Thy holy Church to plant:
Glorious in the roll of heroes
Shines the name of Dewi Sant.

Lord, we hold in veneration
All the saints our land has known,
Bishops, priests, confessors, martyrs
standing now around Thy throne; –
Dewi, Dyfrig, Deiniol, Teilo, –
All the gallant saintly band,
Who of old by prayer and labour
Hallowed all our fatherland.

Still Thy ancient purpose standeth
Every change and chance above;
Still Thy ancient Church remaineth –
Witness to Thy changeless love.
Vision grant us, Lord, and courage
To fulfil the work begun;
In the Church and in the nation
Lord of Lord, Thy will be done. Amen.

Bishop Timothy Rees

PLYGAIN

A Plygain is a Welsh Christmas Carol Service traditionally held very early in the morning between 3 a.m. and 6 a.m. on Christmas Day, although it may be held up to the end of January. In many parts of Wales the service has been abandoned in favour of Midnight Mass. The Plygain was a shortened form of Morning Prayer interspersed with and accompanied by carols sung by soloists and choirs. There is evidence of Holy Communion being administered during The Plygain.

Today the service of Plygain is making a come-back as a distinctive Welsh liturgy thanks to the pioneering effort of the one time Rector of Mallwyd, Canon Geraint Vaughan Jones and The Reverend Enid Morgan of the Church in Wales.

The following few Plygain Carols are offered as a sample.

Carol Eliseus – Gwyr Llanymawddwy
(Beth yw'r melys seiniau glywaf?)

Beth yw'r melys seiniau glywaf?
Clychau aur Caersalem fry.
Beth yw tinc y dôn hoffusaf?
Diolch gân y nefol lu.
Yn yr uchelderau cenwch
felys odlau cerdd yn rhydd,
Nos wylofain, nos wylofain,
O cydfloeddiwch,
Nos wylofain, O cydfloeddiwch,
Arwain wnaeth i olau dydd.

Pwy sy'n gorwedd yn y Preseb?
Anfeidroldeb rhyfedd iawn.
Pwy all ddirnad ei diriondeb?
Gabriel, na, er maint ei ddawn.
Ei amgyffred Ef nis gellir,
Goruwch nef a daear yw –
Y mynyddoedd, y mynyddoedd
Oll a dreulir,
Y mynyddoedd, oll a dreulir
Erys ein Meseia gwiw.

A Celtic Primer

Pwy mewn gwael gadachau rwymwyd
Tragwyddoldeb dim yn llai.
I ba beth y'i darostyngwyd?
Er mwyn codi euog rai.
Cyfrin bydoedd a olrheinir;
Daw'r dirgelion oll heb len,
Erys un nas, erys un nas
Llwyr ddatguddir
Erys un nas llwyr ddatguddir
Wedi elo'r byd i ben.

Pwysa, enaid beunydd arno,
Person dwyfol ddynol ryw,
Cadw, cynnal, cydymdeimlo,
yw melusaf waith Mab Duw;
Rhoi ei hunan dros yr aflan,
Dyna wnaeth er garw loes,
Mentraf innau, mentraf innau
Iddo f'hunan
Mentraf innau iddo f'hunan
Fel yr wyf wrth droed y groes.

Cilwern Davies, Llanymawddwy
(o Cyff Mawddwy)

Elisha's Carol

What are these sweet sounds I hear?
The golden bells of Jerusalem on high.
What is the key of the favourite melody?
The thanksgiving song of the host of heaven.
In the highest sing
Sweet rhymes of music freely,
The night of wailing, the night of wailing,
O shout together
The night of wailing, O shout together
Has led to light of day.

Who is it who lies in the Manger?
A very strange immortality.
Who can discern his gentleness?

Not Gabriel despite his skill.
It is not possible to imagine Him,
He is above heaven and earth –
The mountains, the mountains
May all be worn out,
The mountains may all be worn out,
Our wonderful Messiah remains.

Who was wrapped in poor napkins?
None less than eternity.
To what purpose was he subjected?
In order to raise up the guilty.
Secret worlds shall be described;
All secrets shall be without a curtain before them.
One remains, one remains
Who will never be completely revealed.
One remains who will never be completely revealed
When the world comes to an end.

Lean, my soul, daily upon him,
The Divine and human person.
Saving, sustaining, sympathising,
Is the sweetest work of the Son of God.
He gave himself for the unclean,
That's what he did despite harsh pain,
I shall venture, I shall venture
To him myself
I shall venture to him myself
Just as I am to the foot of the cross.

Ar Gyfer Heddiw'r Bore
Triawd Ty Cerrig, Llangadfan
(Ar gyfer heddiw'r bore)

Ar gyfer heddiw'r bore'n
Faban bach, yn faban bach,
Y ganwyd gwreiddyn Jesse'n
Faban bach.
Y Cadarn ddaeth o Bosra
Y Deddfwr gynt ar Seina

       A Celtic Primer

Yr Iawn gaed ar Galfaria'n
Faban bach, yn faban bach,
Yn sugno bron Maria'n
Faban bach.

Caed bywiol ddwr Eseciel
Ar lin Mair, ar lin Mair
A gwir Feseia Daniel
Ar lin Mair;
Caed bachgen doeth Eseia,
'Raddewid roed i Adda,
Yr Alffa a'r Omega
Ar lin Mair, ar lin Mair;
Mewn côr ym Methlem Jiwda, ar lin Mair.

Am hyn, bechadur, brysia,
Fel yr wyt, fel yr wyt,
Ymofyn am y Noddfa,
Fel yr wyt.
I ti'r agorwyd ffynnon
A ylch dy glwyfau duon
Fel eira gwyn yn Salmon
Fel yr wyt, fel yr wyt,
Am hynny, tyrd yn brydlon
Fel yr wyt.

O Carolau Hen a newydd

For This Morning

For this morning, today
A little baby, a little baby
Was born of the root of Jesse
A little baby.
The strong One who came from Bosra
The law giver formerly on Sinai
The Atonement on Calvary
A little baby, a little baby
Sucking Mary's breast,
A little baby.

The living water if Ezekiel was found
At Mary's knee, at Mary's knee
And the true Messiah of Daniel
At Mary's knee;
The wise boy of Isaiah was found,
The promise given to Adam
The Alpha and the Omega
At Mary's knee, at Mary's knee
In a stall in Bethlehem of Judea,
At Mary's knee.

For this reason then, sinner, make haste
Just as you are, just as you are,
Seek out the Sanctuary,
Just as you are.
A spring of water has been opened for you
That will wash your black wounds,
Like the white snow of Salmon,
Just as you are, just as you are,
Therefore, come promptly,
Just as you are.

Emyn

Wele cawsom y Meseia,
Cyfaill gwerthfawroca' 'rioed;
Darfu i Moses a'r proffwydi
Ddweud amdano cyn ei ddod:
Iesu yw, Gwir Fab Duw,
Ffrind a Phrynwr dunol-ryw.

Dyma gyfaill haedda'i garu,
A'i glodfori'n fwy nag un;
Prynu'n bywyd, talu'n dyled,
A'n glanhau â'i waed ei hun;
Frodyr dewch, llawenhewch,
Diolchwch iddo, byth na thewch.

Dyma'r Cyfaill mwyn a'n cofiodd
Ac a'n carodd eyn bod byd;
Dyma'r Oen a ddaeth o'r nefoedd,
Ac a'n prynodd ni mor ddrud:
Tra bôm fyw, dyled yw
Cofio cariad pur Mab Duw. Amen

Dafydd Jones (Caeo)

Hymn

Behold we have the Messiah,
The most precious friend ever;
Moses and the prophets
Told about him before he came:
He is Jesus, True Son of God
Friend and Redeemer of humanity.

Here is a friend who deserves to be loved
And praised more than any one;
He redeemed our lives, paid our debt
And cleansed us with his own blood:
Brothers come, rejoice,
Thank him, never be silent.

This is the gentle friend who remembered us
And loved us before the world existed;
This is the Lamb who came from heaven,
And bought us in such a costly way:
As long as we live, it is our duty
To remember the pure love of the Son of God.

Y Trwsgwl Mawr
Parti Tŷ Cerrig, Llangadfan
(Deffrown, deffrown, a rhown fawrhad)

Deffrown, deffrown, a rhown fawrhad
    Cyn toriad dydd,
I ddwyfol Aer y nefol wlad,
    Croesawiad sydd;

Fe ganodd sêr er bore'r byd,
Sef holl angylion Duw ynghyd,
Fe ganodd y Proffwydi i gyd,
  Heb fod yn gau;
A pham na chanwn ninnau'n un
Am gael Jehofa mawr ei hun
Mewn dull fel dyn ac ar ein llun
  i'n gwir wellhau.

Ond er ei waelder ar y llawr
  Mae'n fawr un fodd.
Mae pob trysorau dan ei sêl
  Goruchel rodd;
Mae'n Hollgyfoethog enwog un,
Yn gadarn Dwr i gadw dyn,
Mae pob cyflawnder ynddo'i hun
  i Adda a'i hâd;
Mae'n fywyd meirwon i ail fyw
Mae'n Feddyg llon il'r fron sy'n friw,
Gwisg lawn i'r noeth, a chyfan yw
  A chyfiawnhad.

Robert Davies, Bardd Natglyn
(O Cyff Eos Llechid)

The Great Clumsy Carol

Let us awake, awake and give praise
  Before daybreak,
To the divine heir of the heavenly land
  There is a welcome.
The stars sang from the morning of the world,
All God's angels together.
All the prophets sang
  Without being false;
And why should we not sing as one
For having great Jehofa himself
In the manner of a man, and in our image
  To truly heal us.

But despite his poverty on earth
    He is still great.
All treasure under his seal
    A gift of the most High;
He is the All-rich, famous One,
A strong tower to save humanity
He has every fullness in Himself
    For Adam and his seed;
He is life for the dead to live again
He is a joyful physician to the broken heart,
A garment for the naked, complete and just
    And justification.

Carol Y Swper – Parti Llanrwst, Parti
Penrhyncoch, Gwŷr Llanymawddwy
(Cydganed dynoliaeth ar ddydd gwaredigaeth)

Cydganed dynoliaeth are ddydd gwaredigaeth,
Daeth trefn y Rhagluniaeth i'r goleuni,
A chân Haleliwia o fawl i'r Gorucha
Meseia Jiwdea, heb dewi.
Moliannwn o lawenydd, gwir ydyw fod Gwaredydd
Fe anwyd Geidwad inni, sef Crist y Brenin Iesu,
Cyn dydd, cyn dydd, ym Methlem yn ddigudd,
Y mae Gwaredydd ar ddydd, o wele ddedwydd ddydd!

Ein Meichiau a'n Meddyg, dan fflangell Iddewig,
Ar agwedd un diddig, yn dioddef,
A'i farnu gan Peilat, a'i wisgo mewn sgarlat
Gan ddynion dideimlad, rhaid addef;
A phlethu draenen bigog, yn goron anrhygarog,
A'i gosod mewn modd creulon, ar ben Iachawdwr dynion:
Fel hyn, fel hyn, y gwisgwyd Iesu gwyn,
O dan arteithiau, ein mawrion feiau, i boenau pen y bryn.

Defnyddiwn ein breintiau, mae perygl o'u holau,
Cyn del dydd angau, dihangwn;
Mae heddiw'n ddydd cymod, a'r swper yn barod,
A'r bwrdd wedi ei osod, o brysiwn.
Mae'r dwylaw fu dan hoelion, yn derbyn plant afradlon

I wlad y Ganaan nefol, i wledda yn dragwyddol.
Amen, Amen, boed moliant byth, Amen.
Haleliwia i'r Meseia sy'n maddau byth. Amen

The Supper Carol

Let humanity sing together on the day of salvation.
The plan of Providence has come to light,
A song of Halelujah of praise to the most High
The Messiah of Judah, without ceasing.
Let us praise from joy, the truth is that there is a Redeemer
A Saviour is born to us, that is Christ, King Jesus,
Before day, before day, in Bethlem without being hidden,
There is a Redeemer at the dawning of the day, O Happy Day!

Our redeemer, and our healer, beneath the Jewish scourge
In appearance as content, yet suffering,
And judged by Pilate, and dreamed in Scarlet,
By men without feeling, it must be confessed.
And weaving of spiky thorn into a merciless crown,
And set in a cruel manner, on the head of the Saviour of men;
Thus, thus was holy Jesus dressed
Beneath tortures, our great failures, to pains on the hilltop.

Let us make use of our privileges, there is a danger behind them,
Before the day of death, let us escape;
Today is a day of reconciliation, and supper is ready
The table is set, O let us hurry.
The hands that bore nails, receives prodigal children
To the land of heavenly Canaan, to feast eternally,
Amen, Amen, Let there be praise for ever, Amen
Hallelujah to the Messiah who forgives for ever. Amen

San-cti ve-ni - te, Chri-sti cor-pus su-mi-te;

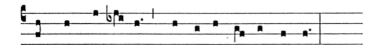

San-ctum bi - ben-tes, Quo re-dem-pti san-gui-nem

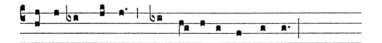

Sal-va - ti Chri-sti   Cor-po - re et san-gui-ne,

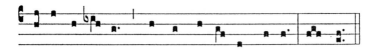

A quo re - fe - cti,   Lau-des di - ca-mus De - o.   A - men

Sancte, venite

The verses in italics are sung by all.

1.   *Come, Christ's beloved, feed on his body true,*
     Drink your salvation in his precious blood.

2.   Saved by his body, hallowed by his blood,
     Here in God's banquet, let us thank our Lord.

3.   *Christ, in this myst'ry gives us his flesh and blood,*
     Guiding us safely through death's shade to light.

4.   Son of the Father, King of all the world,
     Christ is our Saviour, by his cross and blood.

5.   *Christ, priest and victim, offers himself for all,*
     At once the giver, and the gift divine.

6.   Priests of the old law, offering blood outpoured,
     Did but foreshadow Christ, the victim-priest.

7.   *Christ our redeemer, Christ now the light of men,*
     Does thus enrich us by his grace sublime.

8.   Bring to this banquet faithful hearts sincere;
     Take hence the promise of eternal life.

9.   *Come, Christ's beloved, feed on his body true,*
     Drink your salvation in his precious blood.

Latin, freely adapted from the
seventh-century Antiphonary of Bennchar

A Celtic Primer

Sancti venite,	Approach, you who are holy,
Christi corpus sumite;	Receive the body of Christ,
Sanctum bibentes,	Drinking the sacred blood
Quo redempti sanguinem.	By which you were redeemed.
Salvati Christi	Saved by the body
Corpore et sanguine,	and blood of Christ,
A quo refecti,	Now nourished by it
Laudes dicamus Deo.	Let us sing praises unto God.
Hoc sacramento,	By this sacrament
Corporis et sanguinis,	Of the body and blood,
Omnes exuti	All are rescued
Ab inferni fauchibus.	From the power of hell.
Dator salutis,	The giver of salvation,
Christus filius Dei,	Christ, the Son of God,
Mundum salvavit,	Redeemed the world
Per crucem et sanguinem.	By his cross and blood.
Pro universes	For the whole world
Immolatus Dominus	The Lord is offered up;
Ipse sacerdos	He is at the same time
Existit et hostia.	High-priest and victim.
Lege praeceptum	In the law it is commanded
Immolari hostias:	To immolate victims:
Qua adumbratur	By it were foreshadowed
Divina mysteria.	These sacred mysteries.
Lucis indultor	The giver of all light,
Et salvator omnium,	And the saviour of all,
Praeclaram sanctis	Now bestows upon the holy
Largitus est gratiam.	An exceeding great grace.
Accedant omnes,	Let all approach,
Pura mente creduli;	In the pure simplicity of faith;
Sumant aeternam	Let them receive the eternal
Salutis custodiam:	Preserver of their souls.
Sanctorum custos,	The guardian of the saints,
Rector quoque Dominus,	The supreme ruler and Lord,
Vitae perennis	The bestower of eternal life,
Largitor credentibus.	On those who believe in him.

Coelestem panem	To the hungry he gives to eat
Dat esurientibus;	Of the heavenly food;
De fonte vivo	To the thirsty he gives to drink
Praebet sitientibus.	From the living fountain.
Alpha et omega	The alpha and omega
Ipse Christus Dominus	Our Lord Christ himself
Venit venturus	Now comes he who shall one day come
Judicare homines.	To judge all mankind.

A CELTIC READER

A hedge
of trees
surrounds me,
a blackbird's lay sings to me,
praise I shall not conceal,
above my lined book the trilling
of the birds sings to me.
A clear-voiced cuckoo sings
to me in a grey cloak
from the tops of the bushes,
May the Lord save me from judgement;
well do I write under
the greenwood.

OLD IRISH

The Pilgrim's Rune

King of Elements – Love-Father of Bliss,
In my pilgrimage from airt to airt,
From airt to airt,
May each evil be a good to me,
May each sorrow be a gladness to me,
And may Thy Son be my foster-brother,
Oh may Thy Son be my foster-brother.

Holy Spirit – Spirit of Light,
A pilgrim I throughout the night,
Throughout the night,
Lave my heart pure as the stars,
Lave my heart pure as the stars,
Nor fear I then the spells of evil,
The spells of evil.

Jesu – Son of the Virgin pure,
Be thou my pilgrim-staff throughout the lands,
Throughout the lands,
Thy love in all my thoughts, Thy likeness in my face,
May I heart-warm to others, and they heart-warm to me,
For love of the love of Thee,
For love of the love of Thee.

Gaelic (13)

St Columba on Iona

Delightful it would be
From a rock pinnacle to trace
Continually
The Ocean's face:
That I might watch the heaving waves
Of noble force
To God the Father chant their staves
Of the earth's course.
That I might mark its level strand,
To me no lone distress,
That I might hark the seas-bird's wondrous band –

Sweet source of happiness.
That I might hear the clamorous billows thunder
On the rude beach.
That by my blessed church side might I ponder
Their mighty speech.
Or watch surf-flying gulls the dark shoal follow
With joyous scream,
Or mighty ocean monsters spout and wallow,
Wonder supreme!
That I might well observe of ebb and flood
All cycles therein;
And that my mystic name might be for good
But 'Cul-ri. Erin'.
That gazing toward her on my heart might fall
A full contrition,
That I might bewail my evils all,
Though hard the addition;
That I might bless the Lord who all things orders
For their good.
The countless hierarchies through heaven's bright borders –
Land, strand and flood
That I might search all books and from their chart
Find my soul's calm.
Now kneel before the Heaven of my heart,
Now chant a psalm;
Now meditate upon the king of heaven,
Chief of the Holy Three;
Now ply my work by no compulsion driven
What greater joy could be?
Now plucking dulse from rocky shore,
Now fishing eager on,
Now furnishing food unto famished poor;
In hermitage anon:
The guidance of the king of kings
Has been vouchsafed to me;
If I keep watch beneath His wings,
No evil shall undo me.

(19)

A Celtic Primer

Columba's Affirmation

Alone with none but Thee, my God,
I journey on my way;
What need I fear, when Thou art near,
O king of night and day?
More safe I am within Thy hand,
than if a host did round me stand.

My destined time is fixed by Thee,
and death doth know his hour.
Did warriors strong around me throng,
they could not stay his power;
no walls of stone can man defend
when Thou Thy messenger dost send

My life I yield to Thy decree,
and bow to Thy control
in peaceful calm, for from Thine arm
no power can wrest my soul.
Could earthly omens e'er appal
A man that heeds the heavenly call!

The child of God can fear no ill,
His chosen dread no foe;
we leave our fate with Thee and wait
Thy bidding when we go.
Tis not from chance our comfort springs,
Thou art our trust, O king of kings.

St Columba
(trans. unknown)

Columba's Farewell to Ireland

Delightful to be on the hill of Howth
Before going over the white-haired sea:
The dashing of the waves against its face,
The bareness of its shores and of its border.

Delightful to be on the hill of Howth
After coming over the white-bosomed sea;
To be rowing one's little coracle,
Alas! on the wild-waved shore.

Great is the speed of my coracle,
And its stern turned upon Derry:
Grievous is my errand over the main,
Travelling to Alba of the beetling brows.

My foot in my tuneful coracle,
My sad heart tearful:
A man without guidance is weak,
Blind are all the ignorant.

There is a grey eye
That will not look back upon Ireland:
It shall never see again
The men of Ireland nor her women.

I stretch my glance across the brine
From the firm oaken planks:
Many are the tears of my bright soft grey eye
As I look back upon Erin.

(trans. Kuno Meyer) (20)

I adore not the voice of birds,
Nor sneezing, nor lots in this world,
Nor a boy, nor lots, nor women:
My Druid is Christ, the Son of God,
Christ, Son of Mary, the Great Abbot,
The Father, the Son, and the Holy Spirit.

attributed to Columba

Behold Iona!
A blessing on each eye that seeth it!
He who does a good for others there,
will find his own redoubled
Many-fold!

attributed to Columba

A Celtic Primer

God of All

Our God is the God of all,
The God of heaven and earth,
Of the sea and of the rivers;
The God of the sun and of the moon and of all the stars;
The God of the lofty mountains
and of the lowly valleys.
He has His dwelling around heaven and earth,
and sea, and all that in them is.
He inspires all,
He gives life to all,
He dominates all,
He supports all.
He lights the light of the sun.
He furnishes the light of the night.
He has made springs in dry land . . .
He is the God of heaven and earth,
of sea and rivers,
of sun, moon and stars,
of the lofty mountain and the lowly valley,
the God above heaven,
and in heaven,
and under heaven.

St Patrick

Holy Patrick, Full of Grace

When holy Patrick, full of grace,
Suffered on Cruach, that blest place,
In grief and gloom enduring then
For Eire's women, Eire's men.

God for his comfort sent a flight
Of birds angelically bright
That sang above the darkling lake
A song unceasing for his sake.

'Twas thus they chanted, all and some:
'Come hither, Patrick, hither come!
Shield of the Gael, thou light of story,
Appointed star of golden glory!'

Thus singing, all those fair birds smite
The waters with soft wings in flight
Till the dark lake its gloom surrenders
And rolls a tide of silvery splendours.

(1)

Rune of St Patrick

At Tara today in this fateful hour
I place all Heaven with its power,
And the Sun with its brightness,
And the snow with its whiteness,
And Fire with all the strength it hath,
And lightning with its rapid wrath,
And the winds with their swiftness along the path,
And the sea with its deepness,
And the rocks with their steepness,
And the Earth with its starkness:
All these I place
By God's almighty help and grace,
Between myself and the powers of Darkness.

Gaelic

Alexander's Breastplate

On the face of the world
There was not born
His equal.
Three-person God,
Trinity's only Son,
Gentle and strong.
Son of the Godhead,
Son of humanity,
Only Son of wonder.

A Celtic Primer

The Son of God is a refuge,
Mary's Son a blessed sanctuary,
A noble child was seen.
Great his splendour,
Great Lord and God,
In the place of glory.
From the line of Adam
And Abraham
We were born.
From David's line,
The fulfilment of prophecy,
The host was born again.
By his word he saved the blind and deaf,
From all suffering,
The ragged
Foolish sinners,
And those of impure mind.
Let us rise up
To meet the Trinity,
Following our salvation.
Christ's cross is bright,
A shining breastplate
Against all harm,
Against all our enemies may it be strong:
The place of protection.

Welsh, twelfth century

Invocation to Bride

The genealogy of the holy maiden Bride,
Radiant flame of gold, noble foster-mother of Christ.
Bride the daughter of Dugall the brown,
Son of Aodh, son of Art, son of Conn,
Son of Crearar, son of Cis, son of Carmac, son of Carruin.

Every day and every night
That I say the genealogy of Bride,
I shall not be killed, I shall not be harried,
I shall not be put in cell, I shall not be wounded,
Neither shall Christ leave me in forgetfulness.

No fire, no sun, no moon shall burn me,
No lake, no water, nor sea shall drown me,
No arrow of fairy nor dart of fay shall wound me,
And I under the protection of my Holy Mary,
And my gentle foster-mother is my beloved Bride.

Carmina Gadelica (13)

Glorious Lord

Hail to you, glorious Lord!
May church and chancel praise you,
May chancel and church praise you,
May plain and hillside praise you,
May the three springs praise you,
Two higher than the wind and one above the earth,
May darkness and light praise you,
May the cedar and sweet fruit-tree praise you.
Abraham praised you, the founder of faith,
May life everlasting praise you,
May the birds and the bees praise you,
May the stubble and grass praise you.
Aaron and Moses praised you,
May male and female praise you,
May the seven days and the stars praise you,
May the lower and upper air praise you,
May books and letters praise you,
May the fish in the river praise you,
May thought and action praise you,
May the sand and the earth praise you,
May all the good things created praise you,
And I too shall praise you, Lord of glory,
Hail to you, glorious Lord!

Early Middle Welsh (16)

Praise to God

In the name of the Lord, mine to praise, of great praise,
I shall praise God, great the triumph of his love,
God who defends us, God who made us, God who saved us,
God our hope, perfect and honourable, beautiful his blessing.
We are in God's power, God above, Trinity's king.
God proved himself our liberation by his suffering,
God came to be imprisoned in humility.
Wise Lord, who will free us by Judgement Day,
Who will lead us to the feast through his mercy and sanctity
In Paradise, in pure release from the burden of sin,
Who will bring us salvation through penance and the five wounds.
Terrible grief, God defended us when he took on flesh.
Man would be lost if the perfect rite had not redeemed him.
Through the cross, blood-stained, came salvation to the world.
Christ, strong shepherd, his honour shall not fail.

Early Middle Welsh (16)

I am wind on sea
I am ocean wave
I am roar of sea
I am bull of seven fights
I am vulture on cliff
I am dewdrop
I am fairest of flowers
I am boar for boldness
I am salmon in pool
I am lake on plain
I am a mountain in a man
I am a word of skill
I am the point of a weapon
I am God who fashions fire for a head.

Amairgen (23)

Almighty Creator

Almighty Creator, it is you who have made
the land and sea . . .

The world cannot comprehend in song bright and melodious,
even though the grass and trees should sing,
all your wonders, O true Lord!

The Father created the world by a miracle;
it is difficult to express its measure.
Letters cannot contain it, letters cannot comprehend it.

Jesus created for the hosts of Christendom,
with miracles when he came,
resurrection through his nature.

He who made the wonder of the world,
will save us, has saved us.
It is not too great a toil to praise the Trinity.

Clear and high in the perfect assembly,
Let us praise above the nine grades of angels
The sublime and blessed Trinity.

Purely, humbly, in skilful verse,
I should love to give praise to the Trinity,
according to the greatness of his power.

God has required of the host in this world
who are his, that they should at times,
all together, fear the Trinity.

The one who has power, wisdom and dominion
above heaven, below heaven, completely;
it is not too great a toil to praise the Son of Mary.

Old Welsh, c. ninth century (16)

Patrick's Devotion

Now Patrick hath been likened to the Patriarchs: to wit, first he was a true pilgrim, like Abraham; meek, forgiving, like Moses; a psalmist of God's praise was he, like David son of Jesse; a student of wisdom like Solomon; a chosen vessel for proclaiming truth, like apostle Paul; a man full of grace and favour of the Holy Ghost, like John son of Zebedee; a lion in strength and boldness to bring the sinful and wicked of the world to faith and belief; a serpent in cunning and prudence for noticing every onslaught; a dove, mild and gentle in heart's desire and perfect word and righteous deed; a laborious servant to the Creator as to godliness and humility, and teaching of all good things, as many relate.

Now, this was the rule of his devotion: to wit, he used to sing all the psalms with their hymns and canticles and apocalypse, and two hundred other prayers every day. He used to baptize, to preach, and to celebrate the canonical hours according to their due order: he used to offer Christ's Body and Blood. He used to make the sign of the cross over his face a hundred times from one canonical hour to another. In the first watch of the night he used to sing a hundred psalms and make two hundred genuflections. In the second watch he used to be in cold water; the third watch in contemplation; the fourth watch on bare clay, with a stone under his head and a wet mantle about him. He used to ordain, anoint, consecrate, and bless. He used to cure lepers, the blind, the lame, the deaf, the dumb, and folk of every disease besides. He used to cast out devils; he used to raise the dead to life.

from the Leabhar Breac Homily on St Patrick

Alcuin his Epitaph

Here halt, I pray you, make a little stay,
O wayfarer, to read what I have writ,
And know by my fate what thy fate shall be.
What thou art now, wayfarer, world-renowned,
I was: what I am now, so shalt thou be.
The world's delight I followed with a heart
Unsatisfied: ashes am I, and dust.

Wherefore bethink thee rather of thy soul
Than of thy flesh; – this dieth, that abides.
Dost thou make wide thy fields? in this small house
Peace holds me now: no greater house for thee.
Wouldst have thy body clothed in royal red?
The worm is hungry for that body's meat.
Even as the flowers die in a cruel wind,
Even so, O flesh, shall perish all thy pride.

Now in thy turn, wayfarer, for this song
That I have made for thee, I pray you, say:
'Lord Christ, have mercy on Thy servant here,'
And may no hand disturb this sepulchre,
Until the trumpet rings from heaven's height,
'O thou that liest in the dust, arise,
The Judge of the unnumbered hosts is here!'

Alcuin was my name: learning I loved.
O thou that readest this, pray for my soul.

(trans. Helen Waddell) (12)

The Crucifixion

At the cry of the first bird
They began to crucify Thee, O cheek like a swan
It were not right ever to cease lamenting –
It was like the parting of day from night.

Ah! though sore the suffering
Put upon the body of Mary's Son –
Sorer to Him was the grief
That was upon her for His sake.

from the Leabhar Breac

God's Aid

God to enfold me,
God to surround me,
God in my speaking,
God in my thinking.

God in my sleeping,
God in my waking,
God in my watching,
God in my hoping.

God in my life,
God in my lips,
God in my soul,
God in my heart.

God in my sufficing,
God in my slumber,
God in mine ever-living soul,
God in mine eternity.

Carmina Gadelica (13)

The World

Take no oath, take no oath
by the sod you stand upon:
you walk it short while
but your burial is long.

Pay no heed, pay no heed
to the world and its way,
give no love, give no love
to what lasts but a day.

Have no care, have no care
for the meaningless earth,
lay no hold, lay no hold
on its gaiety and mirth.

A man fair of face
was here yesterday;
now he is nothing
but blood beneath clay.

The world is running out
like the ebbing sea:
fly far from it
and seek safety.

Carmina Gadelica (13)

Praise to the Trinity

Almighty Creator, who hast made all things,
The world cannot express all thy glories,
Even though the grass and the trees should sing.

The Father has wrought so great a multitude of wonders
That they cannot be equalled.
No letters can contain them, no letters can express them.

He who made the wonder of the world
Will save us, has saved us.
It is not too great a toil to praise the Trinity.

Purely, humbly, in skilful verse
I should delight to give praise to the Trinity.

Welsh

That I may Dwell in the Land of Heaven

To the Trinity I make my prayer,
O Lord, grant me the skill to sing your praise,
For the way of this world is perilous,
Our deeds and decisions a wild tumult.
Among the family of the saints, in their society,
King of Heaven, may I be ready to praise you.
Before my soul parts from my body,
Grant me, for my sins, the means to worship you,
To sing entreaty before your glory.
May I be part of the merciful Trinity,
My plea to you is like a battle cry,
Nine orders of heaven, he made the hosts,
The tenth is the blessed company of the saints,
Wonderful glory of the peoples,
A great host, their noble victory is clear,
A company who see God . . .
In heaven, on earth, at my end,
In times of joy and sorrow, in tribulation,
In my body, in my soul, in austerity,
Long preparation before the approach of glory,
I shall beseech you, Lord of the land of peace,
That my soul may dwell
For all eternity, in the highest place,
In the land of heaven, I shall not be refused.

Middle Welsh, twelfth century (7)

A Celtic Primer

Behold the Lightener of the stars
On the crests of the clouds,
And the choralists of the sky
Lauding Him.

Coming down with acclaim
From the Father above,
Harp and lyre of song
Sounding to Him.

Christ, Thou refuge of my love,
Why should I not raise thy fame!
Angels and saints melodious
Singing to Thee.

Thou Son of the Mary of graces,
Of exceeding white purity of beauty,
Joy were it to me to be in the fields
Of Thy riches.

O Christ my beloved,
O Christ of the Holy Blood,
By day and by night
I praise Thee.

(10)

Invocation of St Michael

O Angel!
Carry, O Michael so powerful,
My case to the Lord.

Are you listening?
Ask of the God of forgiveness
The remission of all my sins.

Do not delay,
Carry my fervent desire
Before the King, the Great King.

To my soul
Bring help, bring comfort
At the moment of my departure from earth.

In strength,
To meet my pining soul,
Come with multitudes of Angels.

O Champion
Against the evil, foul and troublesome world
Truly come and help me.

Do not shower
contempt on what I say;
Do not abandon me while I live.

You I choose
To free this soul of mine,
My mind, my reason, my body.

O Advocate
Triumphant and victorious in war,
O Angelic slayer of anti-Christ.

Maél Iśu óa Brocháin
Monk of Armagh, eleventh century (5)

Michael Militant

O Michael Militant,
Thou king of the angels,
Shield thy people
With the power of thy sword,
Shield thy people
With the power of thy sword.

Spread thy wing
Over sea and land,
East and west,
And shield us from the foe,
East and west,
And shield us from the foe.

Brighten thy feast
From heaven above;
Be with us in the pilgrimage
And in the twistings of the fight;
Be with us in the pilgrimage
And in the twistings of the fight.

A Celtic Primer

Thou chief of chiefs,
Thou chief of the needy,
Be with us in the journey
And in the gleam of the river;
Be with us in the journey
And in the gleam of the river.

Thou chief of chiefs,
Thou chief of the angels,
Spread thy wing
Over sea and land,
For thine is their fullness,
Thine is their fullness,
Thine own is their fullness,
Thine own is their fullness.

Gaelic (13)

Now we must praise the Guardian of heaven,
The might of the Lord and his wisdom of mind,
The work of the Father of glory, maker of all wonders.
He, Holy Creator, first fashioned heaven
As a roof for the sons of men.
Then the eternal Guardian of mankind
Adorned the earth below, a land for men,
Almighty King and everlasting Lord.

Caedmon

A Prayer to the Virgin

Gentle Mary, noble maiden, give us help!
Shrine of our Lord's body, casket of the mysteries!

Queen of queens, pure holy maiden,
Pray for us that our wretched transgression be forgiven for Thy sake.

Merciful one, forgiving one, with the grace of the Holy Spirit,
Pray with us the true-judging King of the goodly ambrosial clan.

Branch of Jesse's tree in the beauteous hazel-wood,
Pray for me until I obtain forgiveness of my foul sins.

Mary, splendid diadem, Thou that hast saved our race,
Glorious noble torch, orchard of Kings!

Brilliant one, transplendent one, with the deed of pure chastity,
Fair golden illumined ark, holy daughter from Heaven!

Mother of righteousness, Thou that excellest all else,
Pray with me Thy first-born to save me on the day of Doom.

Noble rare star, tree under blossom,
Powerful choice lamp, sun that warmeth every one.

Ladder of the great track by which every saint ascends,
Mayst Thou be our safeguard towards the glorious Kingdom.

Fair fragrant seat chosen by the King,
The noble guest who was in Thy womb three times three months.

Glorious royal porch through which He was incarnated,
The splendid chosen sun, Jesus, Son of the living God.

For the sake of the fair babe that was conceived in Thy womb,
For the sake of the holy child that is High-King in every place,

For the sake of His cross that is higher than any cross,
For the sake of His burial when He was buried in a stone-tomb,

For the sake of His resurrection when He arose before every one,
For the sake of the holy household from every place to Doom,

Be Thou our safeguard in the Kingdom of the good Lord,
That we may meet with dear Jesus – that is our prayer – hail!

Irish (20)

Cantemus in omni die

Let us sing every day,
harmonising in turns,
together proclaiming to God
a hymn worthy of holy Mary.

In two-fold chorus, from side to side,
let us praise Mary,
so that the voice strikes every ear
with alternating praise.

A Celtic Primer

Mary of the Tribe of Judah,
Mother of the Most High Lord,
gave fitting care
to languishing mankind.

Gabriel first brought the Word
from the Father's bosom
which was conceived and received
in the Mother's womb.

She is the most high, she the holy
venerable Virgin
who by faith did not draw back,
but stood forth firmly.

None has been found, before or since,
like this mother –
not out of all the descendants
of the human race.

By a woman and a tree
the world first perished;
by the power of a woman
it has returned to salvation.

Mary, amazing mother,
gave birth to her Father,
through whom the whole wide world,
washed by water, has believed.

She conceived the pearl
– they are not empty dreams –
for which sensible Christians
have sold all they have.

The mother of Christ had made
a tunic of a seamless weave;
Christ's death accomplished,
it remained thus by casting of lots.

Let us put on the armour of light,
the breastplate and helmet,
that we might be perfected by God,
taken up by Mary.

Truly, truly, we implore,
by the merits of the Child-bearer,
that the flame of the dread fire
be not able to ensnare us.

Let us call on the name of Christ,
below the angel witnesses,
that we may delight and be inscribed
in letters in the heavens.

Cú Chuimne, Latin
(trans. Clancy and Markus) (15)

If you want to understand
the Creator
seek to understand
Created things.

Columbanus

The Holy Man

He is a bird round which a trap is closed,
A leaking ship unfit for a wild sea,
An empty vessel and a withered tree,
Who lays aside God's wishes unimposed.
He is the sun's bright rays, pure gold and fine,
A silver chalice overfilled with wine,
Holy and happy, beautiful in love –
Who does the will of God in Heav'n above.

Anon.

The Blackbird

Ah, blackbird, thou art satisfied
Where thy nest is in the bush:
Hermit that clinkest no bell,
Sweet, soft, peaceful is thy note.

from the Leabhar Breac (23)

To the new Moon

Greeting to you, new moon, kindly jewel of guidance! I bend my knees to you, I offer you my love.
I bend my knees to you, I raise my hands to you, I lift up my eyes to you, new moon of the seasons.
Greeting to you, new moon, darling of my love! Greeting to you, new moon, darling of graces.
You journey on your course, you steer the flood-tides, you light up your face for us, new moon of the seasons.
Queen of guidance, queen of good luck, queen of my love, new moon of the seasons!

Scottish Gaelic

To the Moon

Greeting to you, gem of the night!
Beauty of the skies, gem of the night!
Mother of the stars, gem of the night!
Foster-child of the sun, gem of the night!
Majesty of the stars, gem of the night!

Scottish Gaelic

The Mountain Stream

Mountain stream, clear and limpid, wandering down towards the valley, whispering songs among the rushes – oh, that I were as the stream!
Mountain heather all in flower – longing fills me, at the sight, to stay upon the hills in the wind and the heather.
Small birds of the high mountain that soar up on the healthy wind, flitting from one peak to the other – oh, that I were as the bird!
Son of the mountain am I, far from home making my song; but my heart is in the mountain, with the heather and small birds.

Welsh, John Ceiriog Hughes (1833–87)

Winter and Summer

All the sweetness of nature was buried in black winter's grave, and the wind sings a sad lament with its cold plaintive cry; but oh, the teeming summer will come, bringing life in its arms, and will strew rosy flowers on the face of hill and dale.

In lovely harmony the wood has put on its green mantle, and summer is on its throne, playing its string-music; the willow, whose harp hung silent when it was withered in winter, now gives forth its melody – Hush! Listen! The world is alive.

Welsh, Thomas Telynog Evans (1840–65)

Jesu who Ought to be Praised

It were as easy for Jesu
To renew the withered tree
As to wither the new
Were it His will so to do.
Jesu! Jesu! Jesu!
Jesu who ought to be praised.

There is no life in the sea,
There is no creature in the river,
There is naught in the firmament,
But proclaims His goodness.
Jesu! Jesu! Jesu!
Jesu who ought to be praised.

There is no bird on the wing,
There is no star in the sky,
There is nothing beneath the sun,
But proclaims His goodness.
Jesu! Jesu! Jesu!
Jesu who ought to be praised.

Gaelic (13)

A Celtic Primer

Easter Sunday

Last night did Christ the Sun rise from the dark,
The mystic harvest of the fields of God,
And now the little wandering tribes of bees
Are brawling in the scarlet flowers abroad.
The winds are soft with birdsong; all night long
Darkling the nightingale her descant told,
And now inside church doors the happy folk
The Alleluia chant a hundredfold.
O father of thy folk, be thine by right
The Easter joy, the threshold of the light.

Latin

To the Sun

Greeting to you, sun of the seasons, as you travel the skies
on high, with your strong steps on the wing of the heights;
you are the happy mother of the stars.

You sink down in the perilous ocean without harm and
without hurt, you rise up on the quiet wave like a young queen in flower.

Gaelic (13)

Cosmic Crucifixion

The sun hid its own light; it mourned its Lord; a sudden darkness went over the
blue heavens, the wild and furious sea roared.
The whole world was dark; the land lay under gloomy trembling; at the death
of noble Jesus great rocks burst asunder.
Jerusalem swiftly released the dead from ancient burial; when Christ suffered
slaying the veil of the temple was rent.
A stream of blood gushed forth – severe excess – so that the bark of every tree
was red; there was blood on the breasts of the world, in the tree-tops of every
great forest.
It would have been fitting for God's elements, the beautiful sea, the blue heaven,
the present earth, that they should change their aspect when keening their hero.

The body of Christ pierced by points warranted severe lamentation; – it would be fitting – that they should keen in a stronger manner the man by whom they were created.

The king was patient at the crucifixion of his only-begotten, for had his good elements known, they would have keened sweetly.

That the sky did not fall on them, that the great fire did not burn them, that the ocean did not drown them! Their reproaches would not have been light.

That the heavy earth did not swallow them, the miserable pack who committed a great crime! That the hasty people led by Annas and Caiaphas should not have been turned to ashes!

That there were not birds in the stead nor wild beasts on Pilate's land, because without great fear, he beat Christ with the scourge.

Blathmac, eighth century

Winter

Keen is the wind, bare the hill, it is difficult to find shelter; the ford is marred, the lake freezes, a man could stand on a single stalk.

Wave after wave covers the shore; very loud are the outcries before the heights of the hill; scarcely can one stand up outside.

Cold is the bed of the lake before the tumult of winter; the reeds are withered, the stalks are broken, the wind is fierce, the wood is bare.

Cold is the bed of the fish in the shelter of the ice, the stag is thin, the reeds are bearded, short is the evening, the trees are bowed.

Snow falls, white is the surface, warriors do not go on their foray; cold are the lakes, their colour is without warmth.

Snow falls, white is the hoarfrost; idle is the shield on the old man's shoulder; very great the wind, it freezes the grass.

Snow falls on the top of the ice, the wind sweeps the crest of the close trees; fine is the shield on the brave man's shoulder.

Snow falls, it covers the valley; the warriors hasten to battle, I shall not go, a wound does not allow me.

Snow falls on the hillside, the horse is a prisoner, the cattle are lean; it is not like a summer day today . . .

Welsh, eleventh century, author unknown

The Mass of the Grove

I was in a pleasant place today
Beneath mantles of fine, green hazel,
Listening at break of day
To the skilful cock thrush
Singing a splendid englyn
of fluent signs and lessons.
He is a stranger here, of wise nature,
Love's brown go-between from afar,
From fair Carmarthenshire he came
At my golden girl's command.
Full of words, without password,
He makes his way to Nentyrch valley;
It was Morfudd who sent him,
Foster son of May, skilled in the arts of song,
Swathed in the vestments
Of flowers of the sweet boughs of May,
His chasuble was of the wings,
Green mantles of the wind.
By the great God, there was here
Only gold for the altar's canopy.
In bright language I heard
A long and faultless chanting,
An unfaltering reading to the people
Of the gospel without haste,
And on the hill for us there
Was raised a well-formed leaf as wafer,
And the slender, eloquent nightingale
From the corner of a nearby grove,
Poetess of the valley, rings out to the many
The Sanctus bell in her clear whistle,
Raising the sacrifice on high
To the sky above the bush,
With adoration to God the Father,
And with a chalice of ecstasy and love.
This psalmody pleases me:
Bred it was by a gentle grove of birch trees.

Dafydd ap Gwilym, fourteenth century, Welsh (16)

The Hermit's Song

I wish, O Son of the living God, O ancient, eternal king,
For a hidden little hut in the wilderness that it may be my dwelling.

An all-grey little lake to be by its side.
A clear pool to wash away sins through the grace of the Holy Spirit.

Quite near, a beautiful wood around it on every side,
To nurse many-voiced birds, hiding it with its shelter.

A southern aspect for warmth, a little brook across its floor,
A choice land with many gracious gifts such as be good for every plant.

A few men of sense – we will tell their number –
Humble and obedient, to pray to the King:

Four times three, three times four, fit for every need,
Twice six in the church, both north and south:

Six pairs beside myself,
Praying for ever the King who makes the sun shine.

A pleasant church with linen altar-cloth, a dwelling for God of Heaven;
Then, shining candles above the pure white Scriptures.

One house for all to go for the care of the body,
Without ribaldry, without boasting, without thought of evil.

This is the husbandry I would take, I would choose, and will not hide it:
Fragrant leek, hens, speckled salmon, trout, bees.

Raiment and food enough for me from the King of fair fame,
And I to be sitting for a while praying God in every place.

Ancient Irish

Straying Thoughts

My thought it is a wanton ranger,
It skips away;
I fear 'twill bring my soul in danger
On Judgment Day.

A Celtic Primer

For when the holy psalms are singing
Away it flies,
Gambolling, stumbling, lightly springing
Before God's eyes.

'Mongst giddypated folk it rambles,
Girls light of mind;
Through forests and through cities gambols
Swifter than wind.

Now in rich raths with jewels glowing
'Mid goodly men;
Now to the ragged pauper going
'Tis fled again.

Without a boat it skims the ocean,
'Tis swift to fly
Heavenward with unimpeded motion
From earth to sky.

Through all the courses of all folly
It runs, and then
Lightly, untouched of melancholy
Comes home again.

Vain is the hope to hold or bind it,
The unfettered thought
Wanton, unresting, idle-minded,
Sets chains at nought.

The sword's keen edge, the whip's sharp chiding
It scorns, grown bold;
Like an eel's tail it wriggles, sliding
Out of my hold.

No bolt, no bar, no lock, no fetter,
No prison cell
Can stay its course; they serve no better,
Pits deep as Hell.

O fair, chaste Christ! who in all places
Seest all men's eyes
Check by the Spirit's sevenfold graces
Thought's wandering wise.

Terrible Lord of earth and heaven!
Rule Thou my heart!
My faith, my love to Thee be given,
My every part!

So in thy companies to-morrow
I too may go;
Loyal and leal are they. My sorrow!
I am not so.

Early Irish (1)

Hospitality

O king of stars!
Whether my house be dark or bright,
Never shall it be closed against any one,
Lest Christ close His house against me.

If there be a guest in your house
And you conceal aught from him,
'Tis not the guest that will be without it,
But Jesus, Mary's Son.

Moling

Praising God

Let's praise God
at the beginning
and the end of time.
Whoever seeks him out
He'll not deny,
not refuse.
The son of Mary
queen-bee of kings,
Mary mother of Christ,
famed of maidens.
The sun will shift
from the east to the north:
out of your great mercy
implore your Son
to put an end to our sinning.

A Celtic Primer

God above us,
God before us.
God rules.
May the King of Heaven
give now the portion of mercy.
Regal bosom,
let there be peace between us
without denial.
May we undo what
we have done,
before going to my earth,
my verdant grave,
all dark without a candle
to my tumulus,
my nook,
my cranny,
my resting place.

After horses
and drinking new mead,
feasting,
making love to women,
I don't sleep,
I think –
about my end:
we are in a land
where pleasance
is troubled . . . .
like leaves,
we,
from the tip
of withered trees.

Woe to the miser
who amasses great riches
and doesn't
give to the glory of God.
Even though he's let off
in the bustle of the present,
in danger he will be
in the end.

The foolhardy doesn't know,
he doesn't tremble
in his time.
He doesn't get up early,
he doesn't greet you,
he doesn't stay put,
he doesn't chant a prayer,
doesn't beg for mercy.
He pays bitterly in the end
for his pride
and pomp
and sway . . .
nurtured the body
   for toads
   and snakes
   and monsters,
   evil done.

And death
will come to the door,
greedily collect,
take away.
Upon you
descend
old age
senility;
hearing
sight
bite
fade
away . . .
the skin of your fingers
shrivels,
this
has ageing
greying
wrought.

May Saint Michael beg for us
mercy's portion
from the King of Heaven.

   Black Book of Carmarthen (22)

To The Trinity

Trinity in heaven,
I extol you.
One in Three,
one unit of energy.
In divine right
one miracle,
one God to be praised.

Great King
I praise you,
great is your manhood.
Praise to you is true,
I am your extoller.
To be laureate
at Eloi's behest
is indeed benefit.
Greetings, Christ,
father and son
and the spirit of God.

I extol God
who is one and two,
who is three –
no lie,
and doubting him
no walkover –
he who made fruit and flow
and the world's miscellany:
God whose name is two,
whose word is divine,
God whose name is three,
whose energy is divine;
God whose name is one,
the God of Paul and Anthony.

One I extol
who is two and one,
who is three together,
who is God himself;
the one who made

Tuesdays and Mondays
man and woman
that shallows and depths
are not one;
who made hot and cold,
sun and moon,
a letter in wax
flame in a wick
love in sensibility,
and a maiden,
beloved, gentle:
did the sacking of five castles
for their fornication.

Black Book of Carmarthen (22)

Saint Mary

Saint Mary, Mother of God,
Preserve for me a child's heart,
Pure and transparent as a spring,
A heart simple and straight,
That will never taste unhappiness.
A devoted heart,
Tender and grateful,
A heart loyal and generous,
That will not forget goodness,
And will not hold on to evil.
Make for me a humble and patient heart,
Loving without expecting a return.
Content to leave in a beloved heart
The first place for your Son.
A lofty and invincible heart,
That no ignorance will be able to close,
That no insensitivity will be able to expend.
A heart wrought with the glory of Christ,
Pierced with His love,
Whose wound would not heal
Except in Heaven.

Anjela Duval, Breton, twentieth century (7)

A Marvellous Hour

The day is now over.
The hour's come I was waiting for.
After labour so material,
How sweet a spiritual hour.

I'm bathed here in tranquillity.
I hear no sound around me.
But the sound of the pendulum,
Counting out the drops of time.

The hour of prayer, hour of study.
Hour of dreaming, of fantasy,
Hour divine, full of ecstasy.

In this hour there's so much happiness!
Only one thing's missing to perfect it:
– In the hearth the singing of a cricket! . . .

Anjela Duval (7)

Christ's Bounties

O Son of God, do a miracle for me
and change my heart; taking flesh
to redeem me was more difficult
than the transformation of my sinfulness.

To help me you were scourged
by the Jews; dear child of Mary,
You are the refined molten
metal of our forge.

It is You who have made the
sun bright, together with the ice;
it is You who created the rivers
and the salmon that swim therein.

It is a care skill, O Christ,
that the nut-tree should be flowering;
your craft too brings forth the kernel,
O fairest ear of wheat.

Though the children of Eve do not deserve
the bounty of bird and salmon,
it was the Immortal One
on the Cross who made them both.

He makes the sloe to blossom
through the blackthorn, and
the nut-tree to flower;
What miracle is greater than this?

Irish, fifteenth century

Glorificamus Te

I offer Thee
Every flower that ever grew,
Every bird that ever flew,
Every wind that ever blew,
Good God!

Every thunder rolling,
Every church bell tolling,
Every leaf and sod!
Laudamus Te!

I offer Thee
Every wave that ever moved,
Every heart that ever loved,
Thee, my Father's Well-Beloved.
Dear Lord.

Every river dashing,
Every lightning flashing,
Like the angel's sword.
Benedicimus Te!

I offer Thee
Every cloud that ever swept
O'er the skies and broke and wept
In rain, and with the flowerlets slept.
My King.

A Celtic Primer

Each communicant praying,
Every angel staying
Before Thy throne to sing.
Adoramus Te!

I offer Thee
Every flake of virgin snow,
Every spring of earth below,
Every human joy and woe,
My Love!

O Lord! And all the glorious
Self o'er death victorious,
Throned in Heaven above.
Glorificamus Te!

Early Irish

Dawn Song

Would your soft cooing
Each morning in the chestnut tree
Be for me, russet dove?

No! I'd be crazy to think so!
Your song is a hymn
To the One who gave you
That nostalgic voice.

Your soft cooing
Is a dawn-song to your loving mate
And to your baby birds
And to all your winged friends.

. . . Who would sing for me?
An old woman without a relative or a mate!
Yet my heart is brimming with songs
For I love every Creature.

Anjela Duval, Breton, twentieth century (7)

To a Song Thrush

Frail bird of taught loveliness
You enrich and you astound us.
We wonder long at your song,
Your artistry and your voice.
In you I see, I believe,
A splendid and unique work of God,
He is glorious and glorified
Showing his virtue in the smallest creature.
How many bright wonders (clear note of loveliness)
Does this world contain?
How many parts, how many mirrors of his splendid work
Offer themselves a hundred times to our gaze?
For the book of his art is a speaking light
Of lines abundantly full,
And every day one chapter after another
Comes among us to teach us of him.

The smallest part of the work of his most lovely hand
Becomes our teacher, lordly and true.
A winged and lively bird,
Who gives an impromptu sermon
Who teaches us much
Of our Lord, who is Master,
Of his power and his wealth
And of his wisdom great and true.

If our Lord is great, and great is his praise
From just this one small part of earth
Then what of the image of his greatness
Which springs from his work in its fullness?
Through the image of the ascending steps
Of that gracious work, which he has made.
(Below and above the firmament the number of his
Marvels is without number.)

What of the greatness
Which is that pure loveliness
Of our God himself?

Thomas Jones, Welsh, eighteenth century (28)

A Celtic Primer

Words

Always the arriving winds of words
Pour like Atlantic gales over these ears,
These reefs, these foils and fenders, these shrinking
And sea-scaled edges of the brain-land.
Rebutted and rebounding, on they post
Past my remembrance, falling all unplanned.
But some day out of darkness they'll come forth,
Arrowed and narrowed into my tongue's tip,

And speak for me – their most astonished host.

W. R. Rogers, Northern Irish, twentieth century (16)

Your Pain is Yours

You may share
With one you care for
Your goods
Your knowledge
Your love
Your happiness
There's one thing you won't share:
Your pain
For that's been cut
To just your measure.

Anjela Duval (16)

Prayer for a New Year

Lord! Father of the Universe
And Father of all Creatures
Spirit and Matter
Today hear if she asks
The least of your children
Who loves you from the depths of her heart
Her happiness to live for ever . . .
Before you like a child before his father
With neither pain nor suspicion
I start a new Year
In the beginning of the springtime.

What will I be? I am in your hands.
Respectful? . . .Yes. Obedient? Hardly . . .
But may Your Will be done
And may a morsel of wisdom descend on my old age
So that my time will not be empty or vain
Give me Love and Enlightenment
Sufficient to share with others who
Stumble and grope on the Way
The Way so narrow that leads to Eternity . . .
Amen.

Anjela Duval (16)

The Creation

When the Spirit makes thin the canvas we see that the universe is a creation,
That the worker, because he is a child of God, is a person,
And we see The Christ rising from his Cross and Grave like the glory of
The sun in the ailing snow to light up the seventh Heaven.

Gwenallt, Welsh, twentieth century (8)

Gloria

The whole world is full of glory:

Here is the glory of created things,
the earth and the sky,
the sun and the moon,
the stars and the vast expanses:

Here is the fellowship
with all that was created,
the air and the wind,
cloud and rain,
sunshine and snow:

All life like the bubbling of a flowing river
and the dark currents of the depths of the sea
is full of glory.

A Celtic Primer

The white waves of the breath of peace
on the mountains,
and the light striding
in the distances of the sea.

The explosion of the dawn wood-pigeons
and the fire of the sunset doves,
sheep and cattle at their grazing,
the joy of countless creeping things
as they blossom,
spider and ant
of nimble disposition
proclaim the riches of goodness.

*

To curse life is to err.

*

The meadows and the yellow corn,
the slopes of the grape clusters,
the sweetness of the apple tree's fruit:

The provision on the tray
of the warm comely seasons
a part of each hard beginning:

The discretion that insists on respect
for all our partners –
all the creatures of our day
and our life in the world for ever.

*

Every land, every language,
became bread and wine:

Every labour,
railway stations,
bus stops
at the beginning of journeys,
every aviation:

Every art
under its own fig tree –
the vision of a man and a maid.

*

Lest treating
the misunderstanding between man
and his world, becomes
a giving way to meaninglessness:

And perchance we shall see the dancing
in the halls of the atoms
and the meddling with their temperament
as an art of the soul.

*

The coal in the bowels of the vale,
the clear water of the valleys
and the energy of machines' atmosphere:

The secret of fresh airs –
old meanings a cold well:

The delicate breeze
like the sun on the seagull's belly
awakening wings.

*

All beneficiaries
(unless we spit
the original terror of sin
on it all)
resounded the Gloria of praise.

Euros Bowen,
Detholion, Yr Academi Gymreig, 1984
(trans. Cynthia and Saunders Davies) (8)

In the Days of Caesar

In the days of Caesar, and the time of counting the subjects
A song that was obscure was sung to his naïve strength.
In Bethlehem Ephrata a group of shepherds discovered
The great music that is beyond its reason and number.
Those who left the ninety nine
For the sake of the one that was lost – distinctly heard
The day singing before dawn broke

About the birth of the shepherd of men, about the birth of the Lamb of God.
Little ones, and my little nation, can you not guess
The secret within you, that no Caesar can press into his order?
And will not the Hunter come to us in the desert,
Will not the Gatherer who brings us to new birth come,
And unite us within ourselves as a song above Bethlehem?
The Chief Bard of Heaven seeks us to be words for his song.

Waldo Williams,
Dail Pren, Gwasg Gomer, 1956
(trans. Cynthia and Saunders Davies) (8)

The Christ of Nature

He loved cherry sunsets growing heavy on the branches of the evening;
He loved bud coloured dawns opening from the east's earth.

He loved the sea, green in its happiness, seeking the shore;
He loved to see it languishing back stonily from its crest to its groove.

He loved the character of birds, the flock that trusted in His Father;
He loved lambs, the most skilfully fashioned: the lambs,
the most innocent in their nature.

He loved the beasts of the borders: the ones that dwelt in the wild;
He loved their sure dependence on that which the wilderness
provided.

He loved wheat shivering as it became golden and heavy headed with
nourishment;
He loved the fortressed mountain country, the desolation where peace grew.

He loved the earth, loved it as a lover, because it is God's earth;
He loved it, because it was created by His Father from nothingness to be
Life's temple.

Donald Evans,
Cread Crist, Cyhoeddiadau Barddus, 1986
(trans. Cynthia and Saunders Davies) (8)

The Birth

How strange, I believe, would our
Glossy stories be to Mary and Joseph,
About the choir of angels and a star, and the three
Gifts of the wise men under its rays.
There was only the birth of a little man, and giving to the earth
The honour of standing under his feet, giving rebirth to the wind
As his breath, the night to be his cradle,
And the day to be a field for his feats and a road for his roving.
Nothing more than two people's all – is there not
Some sure intuition in holy anxiety,
And they, without knowing of the Via Dolorosa,
Foresaw the Man's compassion,
And were caught up for a moment into the pure joy
Beyond the splendour of legend and song.

Waldo Williams, Dail Pres, Gwasg Gomer, 1956
(trans. Cynthia and Saunders Davies) (8)

The Christ

And He was the Word. Perhaps the swaddling-clothes
were not worthy of the Incarnation in Bethlehem town,
but between the ass and the bullock was the one of most exalted pedigree,
and amongst the cow-collars and hay racks, the Christ from heaven.

A Virgin gave birth to God, and although the secret was given to her,
Mary, the interpreter of the Word, was mute without speech:
in her flesh lay the whole universe, in her womb the one of unspotted lineage
until the Son came to the stable and to his cradle of coarse grass.

He was a translation into our syntax, so that our comprehension would not be
clouded,
God's inspiration in our mortal metres,
the Purpose in humanity's vocabulary, brother, flesh, mission,
eternity in the guise of our vocabulary, One and Three.

and the uncomprehending Wise men, coming to honour him,
above the chaste bastardy of the Christ dumbly marvelling.

Alan Llwyd, Cerddi'r Cyfannu, Christopher Davies, 1980
(trans. Cynthia and Saunders Davies) (8)

A Celtic Primer

The Christ
Explosion

Through Jesus, our greatest treasure,
came an explosion of true love.
He shattered the splendid walls
of the proud fortresses of the world's great ones.

He put his hand in the hand of the weak
and brought peace to humble dwellings.
Where there was hatred came the grace of the cross,
where there was injustice reconciliation shone.

This man, above all other,
owns the heart of life:
He, our incomparable support, loves us –
to praise him is delight.

The clever critics wound us,
the prosperous men belittle him.
He is the one – humble brother –
who becomes humanity's sun.

Gwilym R. Jones,
Mae gen I lyn a cherddi eraill, Cyhoeddiadau Barddas, 1986 (8)

Mary's Meditation

Here tonight I remember the wooden manger.
To my nostrils comes the familiar smell of wooden shreds and chips,
The smell of Joseph – that I smelt on the skin of his arms and in his hair
When we kissed in the workshop, our tears like the eaves' raindrops;
There were nails in the wood. What to these, when their points are sharp,
Is the soft protection afforded by the brittle flesh of feet and hands?
A material nail does not sense the divinity of flesh
And blood even if the sun of heaven and its edges weep.
I sang a sacred lullaby in the dung and the straw,
With a hammer of pain under my breast fiercely knocking;
As the carpenter's betrothed I knew that the flesh has its lattice,
But what maiden would not stoop with the Spirit embracing her?
And the shameful miracle, that grew through the months of trial,
Is tonight blessed, stored with the things of the heart.

J. Eirian Davies, Cyfrol o Gerddi, Gwasg Gee (8)

The Free Man

Christ is the Free Man. Look at him, my soul, at his nakedness, his blood, his sweat. The Eternal Prisoner! The soldiers beat him, cursing and laughing drunkenly. They feel that they represent a higher civilization than his, a richer culture and an infinitely better race. In each blow there is contempt and greed. Are not the Roman soldiers masters of the world?

Even in his anguish and shame Christ takes pity on the soldiers in their captivity.

He is the Free Man. Gaze on him, my soul. Does he have wealth, worldly power, an influential position in the organization of the country? No. He has nothing but a body now and the soldiers treat that body as they please. Flesh, blood, skin, bones, hair – he has only these things now, and the kingdom of Hell wants to take these things from him.

Look at him, my soul. He is a Free Man; the only free man in Jerusalem.

Pilate's empire is a prison; Caiaphas' religion is a prison; Judas' dream is a prison; Peter's confusion is a prison; Herod's ambition is a prison; having been freed from his cell Barabbas' rebellious movement is a prison. Christ alone is free.

My soul stand with him. There, by his side, under the lash of the soldiers, freedom is to be found.

Pennar Davies,
Cudd Fy Meiau, Gwasg Ty John Penry, 1957
(trans. Cynthia and Saunders Davies) (8)

It is better to be in prison with Christ than to be free without him . . .
Many of God's saints were killed, but not one of them was ever conquered.

Rhys Prydderch,
yn E. Evans [gol.] Gemau Deothineb, 1937
(trans. Cynthia and Saunders Davies) (8)

Yes, he was destroyed;
Yes he was nailed and torn
on a rough tree against the open sky,
and the rough nails were driven
blood red through his palms.
Mary and her family were hammered
with Him to the husky, angry sound
of Romans and a savage crowd,

and through the holes in his pure palms,
through the rents of his body, the whole universe fell
into the endless void,
through the hands into the bottomless void.

Yes, he was left
to wilt gently like a flower,
but there
he was blossoming in the bowels of the darkness,
and the empty cave,
with the echo through its hollowness once more;

yes, he discarded, in the mute pit,
his apparel of clay, until
the sound of his grave cover was heard, moving under the power of his sanctity.

And the grave and mourning were victory;
death was a sea of light
in the pit of his departure.

Alan Llwyd,
yn y Dirfawr Wag, Cyhoeddiadau Barddas, 1988 (8)

The Holy Spirit

When the true shepherd speaks, and man hears him, the heart burns within, the
flesh trembles, the mind lights like a candle, the conscience ferments like wine in
a crock, and the will bows to the truth, and that small, powerful, heavenly voice
raises up the dead from his own grave to live, to don the crown, and wonderfully
changes the whole of life to live like the Lamb of God.

Morgan Llwyd,
Gweithiau Morgan Llwyd, Cyfroll, Jarvis a Foster (8)

The Creator

Infinite and wise is God,
The God who does not reveal
The mysteries of his little insects,
And his minutest creations
That our eyes cannot see.

Wise and infinite is the God
who does not reveal
The mysteries of his worlds and constellations,
And his greatest creations
That our imaginations cannot grasp.
And because we cannot see,
Because we cannot understand,
Because we cannot grasp
All his mysteries,
We can but marvel,
And muse,
And humbly bow to worship Him.

W. Leslie Richards,
Cerddi'r Cyfnos, Gwasg Gee, 1986
(trans. Cynthia and Saunders Davies) (8)

You are what you are

'You who give life to great and to small
You in each life are life every hour.'

You are the agitator who churns the nerves
And the bottomless peace in the core of our being.

You are the darkness that understanding cannot darken
And the light that penetrates through every mystery.

You are the beyond who is an unattainable horizon
And the nearness who is the breath of life.

You are the Prosecutor who challenges each assertion
And the Advocate who strengthens our faith.

You are the conscience who stains every effort
And the mercy who forgives all our untruths.

You are the unknown that mocks the theologian
And the crystal riches that overflow the heart.

You are the hurricane that splinters the rocks
And the fortress that's strong in every tempest.

You are the death that ends our sufferings
And the real life that conquers death.

A Celtic Primer

You are the judgement that sifts the nations
And the faithful love that orders the world.

You are the zeal of the rebel who plunders
And the compassion that reconciles in the midst of violence.

In you all things live, move and have their being,
In you is the war and peace of our essence.

D. R. Thomas,
Gwynfyd a Gwae, Gwasg Gomer, 1987
(trans. Cynthia and Saunders Davies) (8)

Work of the Foreigner

Strip. Despoil our Country
Sweep away the sacred oaks of the Druids
The birches of the Celts and the yew-trees
– And the chestnuts of our youth –
In which our birds sang.
Start fires in the moor
In the heath. In the broom waving
Like seas of golden water
And write on the bare back
Of the old Country, in every foreign language
Poems of mourning
Ugly poems.
With their stiff letters
Rigid as their steel faces:
Long rows of lead soldiers
Tedious songs of their resin trees
With strange names!
And soon . . . if we don't pay attention
On the great organ
Of their dark and sad forests
– Fertilised with the ashes of our trees –
The Atlantic Wind
Will play while singing
. . . The Requiem of our Country.

Anjela Duval, Breton, twentieth century (16)

Misunderstanding

What's in it for you to stir up
My too tender heart?
Why do you inflame
My too active brain with madness?
You know very well
– or don't you know? –
– In spite of an invincible love –
There are too many differences between us
Between city-dwellers and peasants.

Their mockery has wounded me
And my audacity has wounded them
– Why that misunderstanding
Eternally between us?
– Why mock us
Scorn us
Make fun of us
Although we love you
The sap of your living heart
Of your bare earth – of my Country!
My Brittany. My love. My Life.
They love you too – they say –
– Yes then! Your brilliant multicoloured skirt
Your green woods. Your streams.
Your golden heath. Your alluring seas.
Your birds and your flowers.
But they should be repulsed
To hold between their white fingers
A handful of Soil of their Country
Soaked so often with the sweat
– and blood –
Of generations of Bretons.

Because of love for you
Sacred Soil of my Country
We suffer that disrespect
– done to you –
To be despised for loving you too much
Brittany, my only love

For you all my strength until the last spark
Until the hour when you will open my arms
On my rageless and lifeless body
While my ardent Soul passes
Toward the Paradise of our Race.

Anjela Duval (16)

In The Forest

On the soft carpet of the forest
To go on velvet footsteps
To sit at your feet
In the dappled sunlight, in silence
Far from the sounds of humans
To listen to the rustling of your leaves . . .
And to caress alternatively
With my hand and my look . . .
In a soft voice I call you
Using your magical names:
White-oak. Forest-aspen.
Maple. Hornbeam.
Black-alder. Willow. White Birch.

My thousand mute friends.

Anjela Duval (16)

The Chapel in Carmarthenshire

The Sabbaths in Zion were so well-mannered,
The Chapel was so natural in the countryside;
The Chapel that was alive with the Gospel
And warm with the hymns of Pantycelyn, Dafydd Jones of Caeo,
Thomas Lewis of Tal-y-llychau and the County's hymnwriters.
Outside it were the farmers' vehicles
And in the stable built onto it horses would stamp
In the middle of prayers and sermons;
And around it the fields in August
Were laden with corn and oats and barley.

There was only a wall between the Saviour in the chapel
And the Creator of the world outside.
The Chapel in the industrial South was so different,
Competing with the steel works, the tinplate works and the pit.

Yet despite this, the Chapel gave without discrimination,
Both in the rural rain and greenness, and the noise and fog,
Water on a forehead, the ring on a finger and the resurrection above the coffin.

Gwenallt, Gwreiddiau, 1959
(trans. Patrick Thomas) (25)

The Old Hymns

They sang above my cradle,
Over my boyhood and my youth,
Like a choir of Christian birds:
They and their song carried Calvary
And the cross to the centre of the workplaces;
Bethlehem and the cradle to the centre of the coal-tips;
The empty grave among the wagons,
And brought the river Jordan without vitriol in its water.

I hunted these birds from the forest,
Aiming my scientific gun;
Chased them from the brushwood and the undergrowth
With my positive, materialist cudgel:
But I would hear their song from other forests
Like a choir of soft, dark, foul-dunged owls.

In the drought and wilderness of the forest
They continued to sing under the roots of the trees,
Under the threshold of reason and doorstep of understanding,
Still singing although I didn't hear them;
But I know now that they persisted in singing
Perseveringly, assiduously, inexorably.

And when the light came back to the forest
They rose up from amongst the roots to the branches and the tree tops
To sing again, and their song had matured in the night:
Bringing the cradle, the Cross, the empty grave and Pentecost
Back again, fierily new;

A Celtic Primer

And under the drops of blood and water
Kissing His victorious feet,
Without daring from guilt to look at the terrible holiness of His face.

Gwenallt, Gwreiddiau, 1959 (trans. Patrick Thomas) (25)

Rhydcymerau

The saplings of the third world war were planted
On the land of Esgeir-ceir and fields of Tir-bach
Near Rhydcymerau.

I remember my grandmother in Esgeir-ceir
Sitting by the fire and pleating her apron;
The skin of her face as dry and yellow as the Peniarth manuscript,
And the Welsh on her aged lips the Welsh of Pantycelyn.
She was part of the Puritanical Wales of the last century.
My grandfather, although I never saw him,
Was 'a character'; a little creature, lively, tough, limping,
And fond of his pint;
He was an eighteenth century vagabond.
They raised nine children,
Poets, elders and Sunday School teachers,
Leaders in the small circles that they moved in.

Uncle Dafydd used to farm Tir-bach,
A country poet and a local rhymester,
His song to the little cockerel was famous thereabouts:
'The little cockerel scratching
    This end, that end of the garden.'
We used to go to him on our summer holidays
To tend the sheep and fashion lines of alliterative poetry,
Englynion and eight line verses to the eight-seven measure.
He raised eight children.
The eldest son was a minister with the Calvinistic Methodists,
And he too wrote poetry.
Our family was a nestful of poets.

And now there are only trees there,
With their impudent roots sucking the old earth:
Trees where there was a community,

Forest where there were farms,
The ragged slang of the Southern English where there was poetry and theology,
The bark of foxes where children and lambs once cried.
And in the darkness at its centre
Is the den of the English Minotaur;
And on trees, as on crosses,
The skeletons of poets, chapel elders, ministers and Sunday School teachers
Bleaching in the sun,
And being washed by the rain and dried by the wind.

Gwenallt, Eples, 1951
(trans. Patrick Thomas) (25)

Good Friday

I went for a walk on Good Friday afternoon
Through the fields of a farm to see the lambs,
To see the first lambs of the season,
Skin wrapped scraps of innocence and mischief.
And there were twelve sheep and lambs there
And a ram, who had set themselves out, each one,
As if an artist had been there arranging them
Before painting their picture.

Suddenly the bearded Shepherd came among them,
And I didn't know where He came from;
From a painting by an artist in Ravenna,
From an Oratorio by Bach,
From a chapter in John's Gospel,
Or from heaven.

Gradually His shepherd's crook became a Cross,
And I heard the thorns shouting in His head,
And the nails crying out in His hands and feet:
And then I saw the twelve, lambs and sheep
And an unnecessary, unentangled ram,
Red with the blood.

Gwenallt, Gwreiddiau, 1959
(trans. Patrick Thomas) (25)

A Celtic Primer

Easter Sunday

Holy Week is the world's sacred Winter:
The earth is a widow, the skies are sere,
There's a sound of scourging and nailing in the vinegary wind;
And the darkness chokes the Son of Man.

But spring, two springs, are coming to the world
From the depths on the third morning:
The lily, the primrose and the daffodil
Will follow the Saviour from the Egypt of soil.

The rejoicing is green and white, the praise is yellow
Because the new Adam has risen alive from the grave;
And the ivy, tying itself round the tree like the old serpent,
Is for us eternal life with God.

Gwenallt, Gwreiddiau, 1959 (trans. Patrick Thomas) (25)

The Church of the Pater Noster

On the Mount of Olives is the church of the Pater Noster;
A Church on the spot where, according to tradition,
Our Lord taught His Prayer to his disciples,
His own pattern of Prayer.
The Lord's Prayer is there in forty four languages;
And the first language is Syriac,
A language which is not much different, so they say,
From Aramaic, the language our Saviour spoke.
Amongst them was the prayer in Welsh,
The Welsh Pater Noster;
Welsh in the Church on the Mount of Olives;
The greatest privilege it has had.
Thank God for Welsh,
One of Europe's most Christian languages,
One of the dialects of the Trinity.
Its vocabulary is Christmas;
Its syntax is Calvary;
Its grammar is the grammar of the Empty Grave;
And its phonetics are Hosannas.

Gwenallt, Y Coed, 1969 (trans. Patrick Thomas) (25)

The Mournes

I shall not go to heaven when I die.
But if they let me be
I think I'll take a road I used to know
That goes by Slieve-na-garagh and the sea.
And all day breasting me the wind will blow,
And I'll hear nothing but the peewit's cry
And the sea talking in the caves below.
I think it will be winter when I die
(For no one from the North could die in spring)
And all the heather will be dead and grey,
And the bog-cotton will have blown away,
And there will be no yellow on the whin.

But I shall smell the peat,
And when it's almost dark I'll set my feet
Where a white track goes glimmering to the hills,
And see, far up, a light
– Would you think heaven could be so small a thing
As a lit window on the hills at night? –
And come in stumbling from the gloom,
Half-blind, into a firelit room.
Turn, and see you,
And there abide.

If it were true,
And I thought that they would let me be,
I almost wish it were tonight I died.

Helen Waddell (29)

My Blessed Saviour Jesus

O, my blessed Saviour Jesus,
Only friend of my frail soul,
In the midst of tribulations
Hold my spirit lest it fall;
When I'm cast in all directions
On the world's most fickle waves,
Give me help that I may anchor
To the only hold that saves.

I may lean upon relations
But I'll lose them all anon,
I can turn to lean on friendships
But they likewise soon are gone.
When I lean on ease and comfort
They can never stable be,
But to lean my weight on Jesus
Will support and succour me.

When'er I seek a foothold
On the shaky things around,
My stage is always crumbling
In fragments to the ground;
But if I can find a vantage
In the tempest in its rage
On th'eternal Rock of Ages
That is safe from age to age.

Old Welsh Hymn – 'O fy Iesu Bendigedig'
(trans. Ven. Samuel Jones, Llanllwni) (8)

A Birthday

Will you see the infancy of this sublime and celestial greatness?
I was a stranger, which at my entrance into the world was saluted and surrounded with innumerable joys; my knowledge was Divine.

I was entertain'd like an Angel with the works of God in their splendour and glory. Heaven and earth did sing my Creator's praises, and could not make more melody to Adam than to me. Certainly Adam in Paradise had not more sweet and curious apprehensions of the world than I.

All appear'd new, and strange at first, inexpressibly rare and delightful and beautiful. All things were spotless and pure and glorious. The corn was orient and immortal wheat, which never should be reap'd nor was ever sown. I thought it had stood from everlasting to everlasting. The green trees, when I saw them first, transported and ravished me, their sweetness and unusual beauty made my heart to leap, and almost mad with ecstasy, they were such strange and wonderful things.

O what venerable creatures did the aged seem! Immortal Cherubims! And the young men glittering and sparkling Angels, and maids strange seraphic pieces of life and beauty! I knew not that they were born or should die; but all things abided eternally. I knew not that there were sins or complaints or laws. I dream'd not of poverties, contentions or vices. All tears and quarrels were hidden from mine eyes. I saw all in the peace of Eden. Everything was at rest, free and immortal.

Third-century Meditation, author unknown

Here's my story; the stag cries,
Winter snarls as summer dies.

The wind bullies the low sun
In poor light; the seas moan.

Shapeless bracken is turning red,
The wild-goose raises its desperate head.

Birds' wings freeze where fields are hoary.
The world is ice. That's my story.

(trans. Brendan Kennelly)

I see his blood upon the rose
And in the stars the glory of his eyes;
His body gleams amid eternal snows,
His tears fall from the skies.

I see his face in every flower;
The thunder and the singing of the birds
Are but his voice – and carven by his power,
Rocks are his written words.

All pathways by his feet are worn,
His strong heart stirs the ever beating sea,
His crown of thorns is twined in every thorn
His cross is every tree.

Joseph Mary Plunkett, 1916

Learned music sings the lark,
I leave my cell to listen;
His open beak spills music, hark!
Where heaven's bright cloudlets glisten.

A Celtic Primer

And so I'll sing my morning psalm
That God bright heaven may give me,
And keep me in eternal calm
And from all sin relieve me.

Mediaeval Irish
(trans. Robin Flower) (1)

The God of All Things

Our God is the God of all things,
the God of heaven and earth,
the God of the sea and the streams,
the God of the sun, moon and stars,
the God of the great high mountains and the deep glens,
the God above heaven, in heaven and under heaven.
And he has a household – heaven and earth,
and the sea and all that they contain.

Ancient Irish
(trans. Whitley Stokes) (14)

I read or write, I teach or wonder what is truth,
I call upon my God by night and day.
I eat and freely drink, I make my rhymes,
And snoring sleep, or vigil keep and pray.
And very ware of all my shame I am;
O Mary, Christ, have mercy on your man.

Sedulius
(trans. Helen Waddell) (12)

To Saint David

Desiring good to my soul,
I am getting old, this was necessary,
to go to the place where Christ was crucified
although my two sad black feet
are stuck here in fetters,
feet do not wish to go there.
It is just as beneficial for me
to go three times to Menevia

as to go, fine dignity,
in the summers as far as Rome.
I knew where I would wish to be,
it is a virtuous residence,
in the manor of David of Menevia,
it is a fine spot, by the cross;
in Glyn Rhosyn is the beautiful [place],
and olive trees and vines
and excellence of music and manner
and the sound of men and a clock
and lively harmony,
shining brilliance,
between an entire organ and bells,
and a great heavy golden thuribulum
emitting incense to give a sweet odour.
Fine heaven of heavens open to all,
it's a good town after the fashion of Rome,
fair smooth paradise of Wales,
choice sovereign town laid out like paradise.

Saint Patrick was reluctant
because of God's displeasure, angry time,
because this was commanded, it was an insult,
that he should go from the place which he had made,
away from Menevia
before David's birth, he's good.
He was a saint from heaven to us
inherent before his birth;
he was a pure saint when he was born
because of the splitting of the stone, marvellous his faith;
he restored his sight
to the sick man's eyes, overcoming bad disease,
his godfather, worldly family,
without eyes or nose, great was the praise;
Saint was his father, it was undeniable
that he was the chief of the saints;
a beneficial bright-eyed saint
was Non his good pure mother
daughter of Ynyr of great family,
fine nun, it is a wonderful tale.
One good went into his mouth, cold bread and cress

and black water as long as he lived,
manner of a gift, of the same kind
as went into bright fine Non's mouth
since he was conceived, he is sovereign.

All the saints of the world, joint journey,
came to the fine senate long ago
to listen on the same day
to his sermon and some of his faith;
there rose up, it was no misfortune,
a hill under David of Brefi's feet
where he taught a splendid host,
where he delivered a fine sermon
six thousand, seven score thousand saints
and one thousand, what a congregation!
It was given to him to be, praise of purity,
head of all the saints of the world.
He blessed fairly,
the cantref of heaven was his refuge,
the warm fresh bath,
it will not cease, it will remain for ever.
Firmly did he permit,
good grace of the black Lent,
to the Britons above all others,
honour of the *brut*, the herring.
God transformed, harsh angry rage,
two wolves of devilish nature,
two old men who were from the land of magic,
cunning Gwydre and Odrud,
for committing, evil exploit long ago,
some sin which they willed;
and their mother – why should she be? –
was a wolverine, a curse on her;
and good David released them
from their long suffering and from their exile.
God stocked his altar,
his net performed a great miracle;
he drove the wild birds in flight
to the houses, my fair lord;
and the spirited, swift, hard-antlered stags,
wonderful servants, served him.

On Tuesday the first day of March in the grave
to die he went to lie.
There were on his grave, good end,
fine clergy singing a gloria,
angels of heaven on the bank of a stream
after his funeral.
The soul of a man who is buried
in the cemetery of David of Menevia
above all other land, it is not vain,
will not be condemned to the pit of hell;
no filthy devil will ever tread
on his land for all the world's wealth.

If there were in a book of paper
every day as on a long summer's day
one of the same nature as a public notary
with pen and ink with a steel tip
writing, it was profit,
his famous life,
hardly, however good he were,
would he ever manage to write
in three days and a full year
all the miracles which he performed.

Iolo Goch, Welsh, fourteenth century
(trans. Dafydd Johnston) (26)

A Prayer

Christ hear us, sovereign Lord,
lest I should suffer some oppression;
lamb-lion, alpha and omega,
god-man eternally true,
redeeming king you must dispense
true council to us against death.

He was not sown, he was not born
he was not clearly seen,
he is not seen on sea or land,
he tormented, he certain,
he is the retribution for the apple,
one whose properties are changeable,

A Celtic Primer

he high, he quiet,
he low, he clumsy,
he well-known through his will,
he swift, he wants no rewards,
coming and going very quickly
here and there by his steps,
he will be no older in the year,
no man knows, he will be no younger,
and he trembles and he does not freeze,
and he pulls and he is silent;
not sluggish where he comes, sparks do not burn him,
cold does not hinder him, weapons do not kill him,
no coward dares face him, no brave man waits for him,
flowing water does not drown him, swords do not stand against him,
he does not run hard, he does not rest,
he is not contained, no diseases carry him off,
not dead not alive, I know not what he is,
one does not feel him under cold protruding ribs,
a shower does not wet him, no eye sees him,
our pure father who listens to us.

True king of heaven for your peace,
for your suffering, for your passion,
for your agonies for mankind,
for your crown, best nobleman,
for your torment, for your distress,
bright scarlet language, and your wounds,
for your fast for the people of the world,
for your penance, for your pains,
for your virtue and the ten commandments,
man of pure nature, for your true blood,
for all your saints, for your wound,
for your pierced breast, for your honours,
for your torment and your bloody breast,
man of pure faith, for your true blood,
for your tribulation on Friday,
and your true light and your wounds,
for your praise, heavenly king,
valiant teacher, and your surpassing qualities
give me understanding to withstand evil,
pure wise lord, for your true blood:

this I wish, this I will get,
this I seek, fine objectives,
the protection of the true cross and protection of Idloes,
and giving me life, me and mine,
the protection of Maria and the protection of Anna,
and the saints of Asaph and the saintesses,
the protection of the saints of Bardsey and of Cybi,
and of David, Nudd of the South,
and of Ieuan and of Cadfan,
and of Sanan, Nudd of the saints,
the protection of Michael and Gabriel,
and of Uriel, the best protection,
the protection of the saints of the world be with me
to safeguard me against the snares.

Iolo Goch (26)

Ode to Mary

Wisely did Jesus choose you,
lovely jewel, as his mother.
The Lord said 'ave'
against the retribution for Eve's apple.

Eve did not take the forbidden
apple without encountering trouble;
evil does not go without heavy retribution
any more than good goes without payment.

Fair was the enlivening payment from the word of the Trinity,
from the coronet of the chair,
when Christ became – sweet cherished Lord,
lamb of God the highest – Mary's son.

Mary look upon me o empress,
you are the highest of maidens, sovereign Mary,
Mary you are blameless, queen Mary,
noble bright-faced Mary, mistress Mary,
have mercy on me, manner of a hen-eagle;
you are the virgins' songbook and their own benefactor,
glass window of heaven and its peacock,

A Celtic Primer

you are the angels' moon and their lioness,
and mother to God comprehending,
and daughter to your one brother, declaration of greatest fortune,
and you are sister to your one son and kinsman,
very closely, princess,
is your son related to you, no wonder.
It was a good womb-load, [yours] was the condition of a countess,
my soul, from the angel whom the spirit
sent to you, warm messenger,
he with a sweet word made you pregnant,
and God went into your bosom
as the sunbeam goes through glass,
like a cluster of splendid grace,
three ripe nuts, into three did it turn,
father, he excelled through love,
holy, tender, sweet, warm son,
spirit of purity, pure fair prophecy.
It is proverbial how easily the lord of perfect benefit
was delivered without birth pains,
without any wound from bearing him, prioress of heaven,
without any fornication with anyone intimately,
or disgrace from any man, there was no contact.
After the birth of the boy, well did he act,
a round constant star appeared
to the three holy kings, this was what happened,
to bring you an offering against misfortune,
gold and frankincense and myrrh, the saint is not angry.
Joseph from the manger, true was the declaration,
it is remembered, was the first who lifted him.
John the Baptist, may he save us,
the sinless mighty godfather bathed him
through faith and baptism, he did not mind,
in the water of the Jordan, there did he swim.
Well did you suckle him like a goddess
on your dear breast, queen on high.
From there you were a sorceress,
you fled with him towards a land,
to Egypt to escape punishment and persecution.
Marvellous was the power of Mary the companion,
a virgin bearing child, Mary my lady,

a virgin before bearing, tender nun,
a virgin whilst bearing, lying-in of a beneficial name,
still virginal and a mistress.
You are alive in heaven like an abbess
in your bodily form, radiant body beneficial like the sun,
with the brotherly man who married you,
and fittingly did he choose you.

Iolo Goch (26)

To Jesus Christ

Of great age are you, [Lord] Jesus, Spirit of the glorious God,
You [once] suffered a great penance –
A weapon wound, [and] savage stretching of your arms
Upon a wooden cross for the Five Ages of the world.

The world, it heard about your provident begetting
Of a thin-browed maid, who'd known no man;
[And] after you were, Deus, born it was early
That they called Thee from that place, Domine, Dominus.
Three kings of honour, solace and magnificence
Came to that kingdom, [all] judicious men;
They brought three gifts, to give them bounteously –
By Thy might and Mary – gold, frankincense, [and] myrrh.
True Father, Son of goodly grace, and Spirit,
True leader of salvation, and a radiant dawn!
Woe is me, God in Three, is it not arrogance for man
To betray Thy honour, so virtuous a wonder?
Judas' folly, it was such lack of wit in him
To yield Thee up to strangers: a payment passing understanding.
Excess, an act that was gratuitous, and terror for no end
Was it to wrench your limbs, [O] worthy Lord.
To sit in judgement was Pilate placed above Thee,
A vagabond, son of one begging for his bread.
About you, without shame, came Jews with fulsome lips,
[All] thieves of great deceit.
Nine went to bind Thee, in Thy mighty sanctity
To buy [our] penance [there] on that pine wood.
With your cruel bonds so grievous [and] so tight –
The weeping Mary, she cried out aloud.
[And] yet, despite the Cross, the end was gracious,

You came forth from the grave, as Matthew says.
When we may see your blessed Passion for us,
How can we not ponder on your redeeming suffering? –
Your feet full of blood, your mind [yet] not malicious,
Your hands, [my] God, that for me were wounded;
Marks of death upon your comely brow,
Pain from the lance, and lips becoming pale.
Thereafter, for your deep, infected wounding
A myriad ought to call Thee Sanctus.
For your Passion, [your] hard purpose – was not
Your coming, [O] God suffering, good for us?
Afterwards your death was not, for any, evil;
For Joseph, it was good you lived, O Jesus.

Dafydd ap Gwilym, fourteenth century (trans. Gwyn Thomas) (27)

Stanzas on The Mass

Anima Christi, sanctifica me.
Illustrious, compassionate spirit, Three and One,
The glory of prophets,
Fair soul of the comely-cross Christi,
Like a jewel within me, oh cleanse me.

Corpus Christi, salva me.
Body of Christ, so sad for vaunting sin,
[That is], if sought, communion flesh
That nurtures wholesome, pure spirit;
As you're alive, keep me alive.

Sanguis Christi, inebria me
Blood of Christ lest I, for what is in me,
Shall grievously be set apart and lost,
Arise, God's radiant glory,
And from the sin of sottishness preserve me.

Aqua lateris Christi, lava me.
Water of the side of Christ's undaunted dolorous wound,
Cross-joyous defender,
Sacred heart, without forsaking,
Resolutely cleanse life, cleanse me.

Passio Christi, comforta me
Passion of heaven's Christ, lord of the world's prophets,

Your five wounds were harsh,
A prayer of great vigour [and] good talent:
Great goodman, fortify me.

O bone Iesu, exaudi me.
Merciful, gracious Jesus, move towards me,
Answer of light;
Dawn of all altars of greatest esteem,
Listen to me and don't denounce me.

Et ne permittas me separari a te.
And, thou my life, set me (with grace increasing)
Near to you, world's virtue;
Like a tree, providing goodly strength,
Without stint is the glory I'll give thee.

Et cum angelis tuis laudem te.
With thy host, Lord of true power, of angels,
In the light that never will be lost,
In heaven it shall be proclaimed
How near is salvation, [and Lord] let that be true!

Amen.
Let it be true that we'll be brought to heaven's fair kingdom
With obedient homage,
A land which nurtures high [and] lasting grace,
A feast [where there will be] no vanity.

(26)

The Goodness of the Trinity

Good was the trinity which made, without privation,
A heaven and earth for us.
Good was the father, above all, to give
Us Anna, chaste of countenance.
Good was Anna of righteous growth,
For bearing Mary, a maid of true perfection.
Good was Mary, chaste of intercession,
For bearing Christ to lay waste the devil.
Good was the Lord God, in unfailing joy,
That with His cross did bring Five Ages from their pain.
Well may the Son of Mary (whose word is recognized)
Bring us, all men, to heaven.

(26)

A Celtic Primer

A
CELTIC
EUCHARIST

THE EUCHARIST IS A CONCENTRATE OF GOD'S PRESENCE IN ALL THINGS

BRENDANUS

INTRODUCTION

The question could be asked whether a 'Celtic Eucharist' consisting of ancient texts is of any use or relevance in today's world. I would answer that it is not my intention to 'mimic' an ancient Eucharist, but to link our cultural experience into the living tradition of the Church. Liturgy exists in the here and now. The Liturgy is the sacred work of the people of God, and it is to carve the kingdom of God from the raw material of creation. Its real significance is to make all things whole, to bring all things into Oneness in heaven and on earth through the symbols of the elements.

The Eucharist may be celebrated at twelve noon today, but that same liturgy has to link us back in time, even joining in the echo of worship which existed before history began. It may be seen as a pageant, or simple memorial of the First Liturgy, but it is more than that; it must bring the Apostolic City into the now, and then onwards joining with the Heavenly City. The dialogue with the past locates our present in the mainstream of Tradition, and is the guarantee of the Presence now. My 'now' exists because of tradition and within the Tradition.

In Scotland, as a child, I heard from my Grandmother about the holiness of the Eucharist, and I learned even more from her body language when present at its celebration. Now I know for myself what the Eucharist is. I am with Christ in Lampeter, Wales, when celebrating the Eucharist in the now, not with the Apostles or literally 'then' in the past, but when I look back I know that I am part of the Apostolic Tradition. As I look forward to the Eschaton, my concern with the present is taken into the future. I am part of the constant ongoing celebration of the eternal liturgy in heaven and on earth.

A liturgy is good because it is effective. The question is, does it reflect the Tradition and does it reflect the living reality of today as well as of the past? In our case, does the Celtic Eucharist reflect the Celtic Tradition? In other words, is this the way our Celtic ancestors would have worshipped, albeit in the modern idiom? I believe that it is in the essence of the self-same Tradition.

The Eucharist set out here is, albeit in a modern idiom, very similar to the liturgy celebrated in a Celi De community in the early ninth century. The texts compiled here are adopted from the mainstream early Irish tradition (see notes). They fit easily into the framework of modern worship and are offered as a resource to those who are searching for an authentic 'Celtic Liturgy' in praise of the Lord of the Elements, containing all the elements of our Christian roots. I have simply followed the practice of many Celtic scribes, in that I have collected together the prayers and texts which are useful for this particular Celtic Eucharist. It is by no means exhaustive.

Suggestions for Celebrating this Eucharist

The Optional Texts

The following sections are optional and may be left out should the celebrant so wish. The whole Liturgy need not be too wordy and pause for silence in appropriate places is to be encouraged.

The Entrance Rite

The Lorica Litany may be chanted in procession. It is a prayer for divine protection and favour.

The Ceremony of Light

This is designed for use at an evening Eucharist; it may follow the Lorica or take its place.

A Celtic Hymn

This may be chanted to typical Magnificat chant.

The Creed

Tirechán's Creed is best recited by a lone voice and may be left out if the Lorica, Ceremony of Light and a Celtic Hymn are used.

Notes for the Celebrant

This Celtic Eucharist is designed to be used alongside a modern lectionary, and may equally well be placed with the Roman, Irish, Scottish, Welsh or *Common Worship* lectionaries. If the celebrant wishes to use a Bible for the Old Testament, Epistle or Gospel readings, then the additional prayers in this book may be used to advantage. They are culled from various Celtic and scriptural sources for ease of use as opening sentences and prayers, prayers over the gifts, communion sentences and closing prayers.

It may also be noticed that the Litany of the Trinity after the Ministry of the Word is used as the Rite of Penance. This is in keeping with the Celtic Rite of practice; indeed the Kyrie ('Lord have mercy') in modern liturgies is a direct descendant of such a litany as that of the *Stowe Missal*.

It seems right to me that, after the heart has been opened by hearing the Word of God, compunction ensues and the need to ask forgiveness of God and neighbour in the sign of peace is in order before we approach the divine table.

The important thing is to use your common sense and sense of liturgical rhythm. The optional texts indicated above are there to enhance the spirit and liturgical practice of the whole work. This is a Eucharist which needs to be celebrated sensitively, gently and in a contemplative manner, with appropriate pauses for silence.

Alternative prayers and sentences are included in the Appendix.

With the saints
      I risked approaching
God's altar, bearing
      my burden.
It is a table to feed the
      starving poor.
It is a table to strengthen
      the weak.
There I could, as it were,
      touch
The broken body of holy
      Jesus.
Suddenly my heart melted
Like wax before
      the flame.

NICANDER

(Revd Morris Williams,
nineteenth century)

THE ENTRANCE RITE

Lorica Litany

St Patrick's Breastplate or Deer's Cry

This may be chanted in procession or a hymn version may be sung by the congregation

Cantor:
Today I shield myself with threefold pówer,
People:
Invocation *of* the Trinity.
Belief in the threeness, profession of the óneness.
In union with *the* Creator.

Today I shield myself with the power of Christ's baptism,
his hanging and búrial.
His rising again and his ascension,
his descent for *the* last judgement.

Today I shield myself with the loving power of the Chérubim.
Obedience of angels, service *of* archangels.
Hope of rising to my reward, prayers of the pátriarchs.
Sayings of the prophets, teachings of the apostles,
faith of confessors, deeds of *right*eous people.

Today I shield myself with power of heaven, light of the sún.
Brilliance of the moon, splend*our* of fire.
Speed of lightning, swiftness of wínd.
Depths of sea, firmness of earth, hard*ness* of rock.

Today I shield myself with God's power to diréct me,
God's strength *to* uphold me.
God's good sense to gúide me,
God's ear to *list*en for me.
God's speaking to spéak for me,
God's *hand* to guard me.
God's path opening befóre me,
God's shield *to* protect me.
From the snares of démons,
The inducements of *my* own vices.
The proclivities of human náture,
And those who *wish* me evil.
I summon these powers to cóme
between me and every cruel and merciless power
that threatens my body *and* my soul.

Christ be my protection todáy
ag*ainst* violence,
against íllness,
ag*ainst* drowning,
against mortal wóunding,
so that I may come to my ulti*mate* reward.

Christ be wíth me
Christ *be* before me,
Christ be behínd me,
Christ *be* inside me,
Christ be benéath me,
Christ *be* above me,
Christ on my ríght hand,
Christ *on* my left hand,
Christ when I líe down,
Christ *when* I sit down,
Christ when Iríse up,
Christ *all* around me.
Christ in the heart of everyone who behólds me;
Christ in every eye that sees me;
and Christ in every *ear* that hears me.

Today I shield myself with threefold power,
invocation of the Trínity.

Belief in the threeness, profession of the oneness,
in union with *the* Creator.

The Lord is salvátion;
Christ *is* salvation,
The Lord is salvátion;
May your salvation, O Lord, be *always* with us.

(32)

CEREMONY OF LIGHT

For optional evening use.

Thy word is a lantern unto my feet,
and a light unto my path.

Prayer bell or gong

Celebrant: At eventide there shall be light.

Lighting of the lamp

Reader: Blessed are you, O Lord our God,
King of the Universe,
at your word you bring on the evening twilight.
You create day and night;
you roll away light before the darkness,
and the darkness before the light;
you make the day to pass,
and the night to approach,
and divide the day from the night.
Blessed are you, O Lord,
for you bring on the evening twilight.

Celebrant: Lighten our darkness
we beseech you O Lord,
and of your great mercy defend us
from all perils and dangers of this night,
for the love of your only Son,
Our Saviour, Jesus Christ.
Amen.

Reader: Daylight has ended
Night is upon us
yet unto Thee
sustainer of all things
Darkness and Light,
all times and all seasons
all are as one
O Lord of Creation.

Phos Hilarion

O Gracious Light, pure brightness of the everliving / Father in / heaven,
O Jesus / Christ, / holy / and blessed!
Now as we come to the setting of the sun,
and our eyes behold the / evening / Light,
we sing your praises, O God: Father, / Son and / Holy Spirit.
You are worthy at all times to be praised by / happy / voices,*
O Son / of / God, O / Giver of / Life,
and to be / glorified / through / all / the / worlds.

O Gracious light, pure brightness of the everliving father in heaven,

O Jesus Christ, holy and blessed

Now as we come to the setting of the sun, and our eyes behold the

evening light,

We sing your praises, O God: Father, Son and Holy Spirit

You are worthy at all times to be praised by happy voices,

O Son of God, O Giver of life, and to be glorified through

all the worlds.

Pause

Celebrant: At this evening hour
may the understanding of all our hearts
be opened to that Light
which enlightens everyone
who comes into the world.
For this is the Light which gives us
true knowledge of the Name over all
by which God is known.

A Celtic Hymn for the Lighting of the Vesper Light

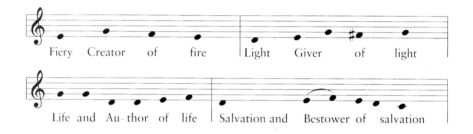

Fiery / creator / of / fire,
Light / Giver / of / light,
Life and / Author / of / life,
Salvation and / Bestower / of / salvation.

In case / the lamps / should / abandon
The / joys / of / this / night,
You who do / not desire / our death,
Give / light / to / our / breast.

To those / wandering / from / Egypt,
You bestow / the / double / grace,
You show / the veil / of / cloud,
And give / the / nocturnal / light.

With a / pillar of / cloud in the / day,
You protect / the / people / as they / go,
With a / pillar of / fire at / evening,
You dispel / the / night / with / light.

A Celtic Primer

You call out to / your servant / from the / flame,
You do not / spurn / the bush / of / thorns,
And though you are / consuming / fire,
You do not / burn / what / you / illumine.

Now it is / time that the / cloudy / bee-bread
Should be consumed, all / impurity / boiled / away
And the waxen / flesh should / shine
With the glow / of / the / Holy / Spirit.

You store now / in the / recesses of / the comb
The sweet food / of / the divine / honey,
And purify the / inmost cells / of the / heart,
You have / filled / them / with / your / word;

That the swarm / of the / new / brood,
Chosen / by / your mouth / and / spirit,
May leave their / burdens and / win / heaven
On / wings / now / free / from / care.

(33)

*If the Lorica has not been sung the Celebrant may begin the Eucharist here with
the sentence and the following greeting:*

In the name of God: Father, Son and Holy Spirit,
Amen.
Grace and peace be with you,
and also with you.

If the Lorica has been sung the Eucharist continues here.

Gloria

Glory to God in the highest,
and peace to his people on earth.
Lord God, heavenly King,
Almighty God and Father,
we worship you, we give you thanks,
we praise you for your glory.

Lord Jesus Christ, only Son of the Father,
Lord God, Lamb of God,
you take away the sin of the world:
have mercy on us;
you are seated at the right hand of the Father:
receive our prayer.

For you alone are the Holy One,
you alone are the Lord,
you alone are the Most High,
Jesus Christ, with the Holy Spirit,
in the glory of God the Father.
Amen.

(34)

The Collect of the Day

Let us pray.

The Ministry of the Word

Old and New Testament readings shall be announced:

A reading from the . . .

They shall end with the words:

This is the Word of the Lord.
Thanks be to God.

The Gospel alone may be proclaimed
(if the Lorica and ceremony of Light are used)

The Lord be with you,
and also with you.

Hear the Holy Gospel according to Saint . . .
Glory to Christ our Saviour.

This is the Gospel of the Lord.
Praise to Christ our Lord.

The Homily or Address

The Creed

(May be recited by a lone voice)

Our God is the God of all humans,
the God of heaven and earth,
the God of sea and rivers,
the God of the sun and moon,

the God of all the heavenly bodies,
the God of the lofty mountains,
the God of the lowly valleys.
God is above the heavens;
and he is beneath the heavens.
Heaven and earth and sea,
and everything that is in them,
such he has as his abode.
He inspires all things,
he gives life to all things,
he stands above all things,
and he stands beneath all things.
He enlightens the light of the sun,
he strengthens the light of the night and the stars,
he makes wells in the arid land and dry islands in the sea,
and he places the stars in the service of the greater lights.
He has a Son who is co-eternal with himself;
and similar in all respects to himself;
and neither is the Son younger than the Father,
nor is the Father older than the Son;
and the Holy Spirit breathes in them.
And the Father and the Son and Holy Spirit are inseparable.
[Amen.]

(35)

Or

A Declaration of Faith
Patrick's Confession

There is not, nor ever was, any other God – there was none before him and there shall not be any after him – besides him who is God the Father unbegotten: without a source, from him everything else takes its beginning. He is, as we say, the one who keeps hold of all things.

And his Son, Jesus Christ, whom we declare to have always existed with the Father.

He was with the Father spiritually before the world came into being; begotten of the Father before the beginning of anything in a way that is beyond our speech.

A Celtic Primer

And 'through him all things were made', all things visible and invisible. He was made man, and having conquered death was taken back into the heavens to the Father.

'And he has bestowed on him all power above every name in heaven and on earth and under the earth, so that every tongue may confess that our Lord and God is Jesus Christ'.

In him we believe, looking forward to his coming in the very near future when he will judge the living and the dead, and 'will repay each according to his works'.

And 'the Father has plentifully poured upon us the Holy Spirit', the gift and pledge of immortality, who makes those who believe and listen into 'sons of God' the Father and 'fellow heirs with Christ'.

This is whom we profess and worship, One God in Trinity of sacred name.

(35)

Bidding Prayer of St Martin

Celebrant:
With all our hearts and minds we pray to the Lord, who looks upon the earth and makes it tremble.

Reader:
For peace and tranquillity in our time and for your holy Catholic Church from one end of the earth to the other.*
For N our Bishop and Shepherd and for all bishops, presbyters and deacons, and all who administer in your Church.*
For this place and for all who dwell in it.*
For all who are in authority; for the bereaved, the dispossessed and those who seek refuge.*
For those who travel; those who do penance; those who learn the faith.*
For those who in your holy Church bring forth the fruits of compassion.*
For ourselves; through the prayers of your holy apostles and martyrs, grant us, Lord, your forgiveness.*
Grant us, Lord, a Christian and a peaceful end.*
Grant us, Lord, your holy bond of love; to abide for ever among us.*
Guard, Lord, the holiness and purity of our Catholic faith.*

(36)

Merciful Father
Accept these prayers
For the sake of your Son,
Our Saviour Jesus Christ
Amen.

Either
A pause for silent prayer
Or
Lord, in your mercy,
Hear our prayer.

Litany of the Trinity

(*May be sung Litany style*)

Have mercy upon us O God the Father Almíghty,
O *God* of Hosts,
O Hígh God,
O Lord of *all* the world,
O inéffable God,
O Creator *of* the Elements.

Have mercy upon us, O Almighty God,
Jesus Christ, Son of the Living Gód,
O *Son* twice-born,
O Only-begotten of God the Fáther,
O First born of the *Virgin* Mary,
O beginning of áll things,
O completion *of* the world,
O Wórd of God,
O Way to the hea*ven*ly Kingdom,
O life of áll things,
O Intelligence of the *mystic* world.

Have mercy upon us, O God Almíghty,
O *Holy* Spirit;
O Spirit that is highest of all spírits,
O Fin*ger* of God,

O Protection of all Christians,
O Comforter *of* the sorrowful,
O Clément one,
O merciful *Int*ercessor,
O Imparter of true wísdom,
O Author of the *Holy* Scriptures,
O Ruler of spéech,
O Sp*irit* of wisdom,
O Spirit of understánding,
O Sp*irit* of counsel,
O Spirit of stréngth,
O Sp*irit* of knowledge,
O Spirit from whom is ordered every lofty thíng.
O Holy Spirit you rule all created things,
visible *and* invisible,
Have mer*cy* upon us.

O Almighty God, the heavenly Fáther,
and the only-beg*ott*en Son,
Have mercy upón us.
Have mer*cy* upon us,
O Father, O Son, O Holy Spírit.
Have mercy upon us, O *only* God,
O God of heaven, have mercy upón us.
Have mercy upon *us*, O God,
from whom and through whom
is the rule of all created things for you, O God,
To whom be glory and honour
for eve*r* and ever.
Amen.

(37)

Absolution

May almighty God have mercy on us,
forgive us our sins,
and bring us to everlasting life. **Amen.**

Holy Sprinkling *(optional)*

A Celtic Eucharist

THE PEACE

Celebrant: Lord, peace you commanded, peace you gave us, peace you have left us. Grant us your peace from heaven and order this day and all the days of our life in your peace. We ask this through Christ our Lord.
Amen.

Stowe

Or

Lord Jesus Christ, you said to your apostles 'I leave you peace, my peace I give you'. Look not on our sins but on the faith of your Church, and grant us the peace and unity of your Kingdom, where you live for ever and ever.
Amen.

The Peace of the Lord be with you always;
and with your spirit.
Let us offer one another a sign of peace.

THE OFFERTORY

Celebrant: Thank you, O Lord God Almighty,
Thank you for the earth and the waters,
Thank you for the sky, the air and the sun,
Thank you for all living creatures.

Come, O Lord, in the Bread of Life.

Praise be to you, O Lord God Almighty,
For our homes, our families,
Our friends, and loved ones.
Praise be to you for all the people
Around us everywhere in this wounded world.

Come, O Lord, in the Cup of Healing.

The Prayer over the Gifts

A mention of the departed may be included:

We offer this spiritual sacrifice for [N and for] all who sleep, who have gone before us in the peace of the Lord Jesus, from Adam to the present day: you named them and you know their names.

The Great Thanksgiving

The Lord be with you,
And with your spirit.
Lift up your hearts.
We lift them up to the Lord.
Let us give thanks to the Lord our God.
It is right to give our thanks and praise.

The Stowe Preface

Father, all powerful and ever living God,
We do well always and everywhere to give you thanks through Jesus Christ our Lord.
You [O Father], with your only begotten Son and the Holy Spirit are God.
You are God, one immortal;
Incorruptible and unmoving;
Invisible and faithful;
Wonderful and worthy of praise;
Strong and worthy of honour;
You are God, most high and magnificent;
Living and true;
Wise and powerful;
Holy and splendid;
Great and good;
You are God, awesome and peace-loving;
Beautiful and righteous;
Pure and kind;
Blessed and just;
Tender and holy;
You are God, not in the singularity of one person,
But in the Trinity of substance.

A Celtic Eucharist   229

We believe you;
We bless you;
We adore you
And praise your name for evermore.
We praise you
Through Christ who is the salvation of the universe;
Through Christ who is the life of human beings;
Through Christ who is the resurrection of the dead.

Through him the angels praise your majesty;
the dominations adore;
the powers of the heaven of heavens tremble;
the virtues and the blessed seraphim
concelebrate in exultation;
so grant, we pray you,
that our voices may be admitted to that of the chorus,
in humble declaration of your glory,
as we say/sing:

Holy, holy, holy Lord,
God of power and might,
heaven and earth are full of your glory.
Hosanna in the highest.

Blessed is he who comes in the name of the Lord.
Hosanna in the highest.

(38)

Eucharistic Prayer I
(The Gelasian)

Most merciful Father, we humbly pray and implore you, through Jesus Christ your Son, our Lord, to be pleased to receive and bless + these gifts, these holy unblemished offerings.

We offer them to you in the first place for your holy Church throughout the whole world. Be pleased to keep her in peace, to watch over her, and to gather her in unity and to guide her, and also for [N] your servant our bishop, and all the bishops and all right believing teachers of the Catholic apostolic faith.

Remember, Lord, your servants and handmaids [N and N] and all here present whose faith and devotion are known to you. We offer for them, or they themselves offer, this sacrifice of praise for themselves and all their own, for the redeeming of their souls, for their hope of safety and salvation; and they now send up their prayers to you, the eternal, living and true God.

Being in fellowship we reverently bring to mind, firstly the glorious Mary, ever virgin, Mother of our God and Lord Jesus Christ, and then your blessed apostles and martyrs; Peter and Paul, Andrew, James, Bartholomew, Matthew, Simon and Jude, David, Ninian and Patrick, Columba, Teilo, Brigid, Deiniol and Samson, Asaph, Illtud, Dyfrig, Petroc, Padarn and all your saints: grant by their merits and prayers that at all times we may be defended and helped by your protection. Through the same Christ our Lord.
Amen.

Be pleased, O God, to bless + this offering, to accept it fully, to make it perfect and worthy to please you, so that it may become for us the Body and Blood of your dearly beloved Son, our Lord Jesus Christ.

Who, the day before he suffered, took bread into his holy and venerable hands, and with his eyes lifted up to heaven, to you, God, his almighty Father, giving thanks to you, he blessed, broke and gave it to his disciples saying: Take and eat you all of this, for this is my body.

In like manner, after he had supped, taking also this chalice into his holy and venerable hands, again giving thanks to you, he blessed and gave it to his disciples, saying: Take and drink you all of this for this is the chalice of my blood, of the new and eternal testament: the mystery of faith: which shall be shed for you and for many for the remission of sins. As often as you shall do these things, you shall do them in memory of me.

Wherefore, Lord, in memory of the blessed passion of the same Christ, your Son, our Lord, of his resurrection from the dead and of his ascension to heavenly glory, we your servants and with all your holy people offer to your sovereign majesty, from among your gifts bestowed upon us, a victim perfect, holy and spotless, the holy bread of everlasting life and the chalice of everlasting salvation.

Be pleased to look upon these offerings with a favourable and gracious countenance; accept them as you were pleased to accept the offerings of your servant Abel the righteous, the sacrifice of our father Abraham, and that of Melchisedech, your high priest, a holy sacrifice, a spotless victim.

We humbly implore you, almighty God, that these offerings be carried by the hands of your holy angel to your altar on high, in the sight of your divine majesty, that all who are partakers at the altar of the precious Body and Blood of your Son may be filled with all heavenly grace and blessing. Through the same Christ our Lord.
Amen.

Remember also, Lord, your servants and handmaids [N and N] who are gone hence before us, marked with the sign of faith, and sleep the sleep of peace. To them, Lord, and to all that rest in Christ grant, we implore you, a place of happiness, light and peace. Through the same Christ our Lord.
Amen.

To us also, your sinful servants, who hope in the multitude of your mercies, be pleased to grant some place and fellowship with your holy apostles and martyrs and all your saints. We pray you admit us into their company, not weighing our own merits but bestowing on us your own free pardon. Through Christ our Lord.

Through him, O Lord, you ever create these good things, and you hallow, quicken and bless + them as gifts for us.

By him and with him and in him are ever given to you, God the Father Almighty, in the unity of the Holy Spirit all honour and glory for ever and ever.
Amen.

(39)

Eucharistic Prayer II
(Gallican Rite)

The Gallican Preface

It is right, just and fitting, here and everywhere, to give you thanks, Lord, holy Father, eternal God; you saved us from everlasting death and the last darkness of hell, and gave mortal matter, put together from the liquid mud, to your Son and to eternity.

When you had overcome the chaos and confusion of the beginning and the darkness in which things swam, you gave wonderful forms to the amazed elements: the tender world blushed at the fires of the sun, and the rude earth wondered at the ways of the moon.

And lest there be no one to adorn the world and wonder at your Creation, you created humankind out of the clay and brought it to life in the Spirit.

Although we were formed in the likeness of your Son, we abandoned the commandments of your blessed majesty and were plunged, mortal once more, into the earth from whence we came, and mourned the loss of the eternal comfort of your gift. In your great goodness you sent the Word of salvation from heaven, that he should be made flesh by taking a human body, to care for the ancient wounds and for all that which the age had lost.

Therefore all the angels with all the saints praise him with unceasing voice, saying/singing:

Holy, holy, holy Lord,
God of power and might,
Heaven and earth are full of your glory.
Hosanna in the highest.

Blessed is he who comes in the name of the Lord.
Hosanna in the highest.

As the heavenly creatures resound on high the praise of your glory, your goodness wished that it should be known also to your servants; and this proclamation, made in the starry realms, to be as a gift, not only to be known but also to be imitated.

Therefore Jesus, the night before he suffered for the salvation of us all, in the midst of his apostles and disciples, took bread in his holy hands and looking up to you, God the father Almighty, gave thanks, blessed and broke it. Then giving it to his disciples said, 'Take, eat, this is my body which is given for you: do this for the life of the age.'

In like manner after supper taking the cup in his hands, and looking up to heaven to you, God the father Almighty, gave thanks, blessed it, and handed it to his apostles, saying: 'Take, drink from this, all of you; for this is the cup of my holy blood, of the new and eternal covenant, which is shed for you and for many for the forgiveness of sins. As often as you eat this bread and drink this cup, do it in remembrance of me, showing my passion to all and looking for my coming again.'

Therefore, most merciful Father, look upon the commandments of your Son, the mysteries of the Church, your gifts to those who believe: through Jesus Christ your Son, our God and Lord and Saviour, who, with you Lord and the Holy Spirit, reigns for ever, eternal Godhead, to the ages of ages.
Amen.

(40)

A Celtic Eucharist   233

Eucharistic Prayer III
(Hippolytus)

We give you thanks, O God, through your beloved servant Jesus Christ, whom at the end of time you sent to us as saviour and redeemer and the messenger of your will; who is your Word, inseparable from you, through whom you made all things, and in whom you are well pleased.

You sent him from heaven into the womb of the Virgin; and, dwelling in the womb, he was made flesh and was manifested as your Son, being born of the Holy Spirit and the Virgin. Having fulfilled your will, and winning for you a holy people he spread out his hands when he should suffer, that by his death he might set free from suffering those who believed in you. Jesus the Christ, when he was betrayed to his willing death, that he might bring to nought death and break the bonds of the devil, tread hell under foot, give light to the righteous, set the limit and manifest his resurrection, taking the loaf and giving thanks, said:

'Take, eat, this is my Body, which shall be broken for you.' Likewise also the cup, saying: 'This is my Blood which is shed for you; as often as you do this, do it in memory of me.'

Remembering therefore his death and resurrection, we offer to you this bread and this cup, giving you thanks as you have counted us worthy to stand before you and minister to you.

We pray you therefore to send your Holy Spirit upon these offerings gathered here, that all those who receive may be filled with your Holy Spirit for the confirmation of faith in truth, that they may praise and glorify you. Through your servant Jesus Christ, through whom to you be all honour and glory, with the Holy Spirit in your Holy Church, both now and to the ages of ages.
Amen.

(41)

The Holy Communion

As our Saviour taught us, we pray:

Our Father who art in heaven,
hallowed be thy name,
thy Kingdom come,
thy will be done,
on earth as it is in heaven.
Give us this day our daily bread.
And forgive us our trespasses,
as we forgive those who trespass against us.
And lead us not into temptation
but deliver us from evil.
For thine is the Kingdom,
the power, and the glory,
for ever and ever.
Amen.

Deliver us, we implore you Lord, from all evils, past, present and to come, and by the intercession of the blessed and glorious Mary, ever virgin, Mother of God, and of your blessed apostles Peter and Paul, and of Andrew and all the saints, mercifully give peace in our days; that through the help of your mercy we may always be free from sin and safe from all troubles. Through the same Jesus Christ, your Son, our Lord, who lives and reigns with you in the unity of the Holy Spirit, one God, for ever and ever.
Amen.

The Fraction of the Host
(From the *Stowe Missal*)

They recognized the Lord, Alleluia;
In the breaking of the loaf, Alleluia [Luke 24.35];
For the loaf that we break is the body
of our Lord Jesus Christ, Alleluia;
The cup which we bless is the blood
of our Lord Jesus Christ, Alleluia [1 Cor. 10.16–17]
For the remission of our sins, Alleluia [Matt. 26.28];

A Celtic Eucharist

O Lord, let your mercy come upon us, Alleluia;
In you O Lord have I put my trust, Alleluia [Ps. 31.1];
They recognized the Lord, Alleluia;
In the breaking of the loaf, Alleluia [Luke 24.35].

(42)

Celebrant: O Lord, we believe that in this breaking of your body and pouring out of your blood we become your redeemed people;
We confess that in taking the gifts of this pledge here, we lay hold
in hope of enjoying its true fruits in the heavenly places.

Agnus Dei

Jesus, Lamb of God: have mercy on us.
Jesus, bearer of our sins: have mercy on us.
Jesus, redeemer of the world: give us your peace.

Or

Lamb of God, you take away the sins of the world:
have mercy on us.
Lamb of God, you take away the sins of the world:
have mercy on us.
Lamb of God, you take away the sins of the world:
Grant us peace.

Celebrant: Jesus is the Lamb of God who takes away the sins of the world.
Happy are those who are called to his supper.
Lord, I am not worthy to receive you,
but only say the word and I shall be healed.

The Communion Antiphon

The Celebrant receives Holy Communion and says:
He gives heavenly bread to the hungry,
and to the thirsty water from the living spring.

Christ the Lord himself comes, who is Alpha and Omega.
He shall come again to judge us all.

Prayer of Elevation

Come, you holy ones, receive the body of Christ,
drinking the holy blood by which you were redeemed.

Stowe

Or

Praise to the Son of David.
If anyone is holy, let him come.
If anyone is not holy, let him repent.
Maranatha. (Come, Lord)
Amen.

Didache

The Sacrament is administered with these words:
The Body of Christ.
Amen.
The Blood of Christ.
Amen.

A Hymn may be sung during Communion.

Prayer after Communion
(see Appendix)

The Dismissal

The Lord be with you;
And with your spirit.

The Priest may say this or a different blessing:
(Alternative blessings may be found on page 250)
The peace of God which passes all understanding, keep your hearts and minds in
the knowledge and love of God, and of his Son, Jesus Christ our Lord: and the
blessing of God Almighty, the Father, the Son, and the Holy Spirit, be amongst
you and remain with you always.
Amen.

Let us go forth in peace;
In the name of Christ.
Amen.

Or

I bless you, in the name of the Father, the Son, and the Sacred Spirit, the One and the Three. May God give you to drink of his cup, the sun shine bright upon you, may the night call down peace, and when you come to his household may the door be open wide for you to go in to your joy.

Go in peace to love and serve the Lord.
In the name of Christ.
Amen.

Recessional Hymn

MAY THE ROAD RISE
    TO MEET YOU.
MAY THE WIND BE
    ALWAYS AT YOUR BACK.
MAY THE SUN SHINE
    WARM UPON YOUR FACE.
MAY THE RAINS FALL
    SOFT UPON YOUR FIELDS.
UNTIL WE MEET AGAIN.
MAY GOD HOLD YOU IN
    THE HOLLOW OF HIS HAND.

From the Gaelic
(taken from Celtic Blessings by Brendan O'Malley

Appendix: Alternative Prayers and Sentences

ADDITIONAL PRAYERS I

Sentence

You are my strength Lord, I will love you,
Under the shadow of your wings protect me.

The Prayers of Moucan
Welsh, eighth century

Opening Prayer

Kindle in our hearts, O God,
The flame of love that never ceases,
That it may burn in us, giving light to others.
May we shine for ever in your temple,
Set on fire with your eternal light,
Even your Son, Jesus Christ,
Our Saviour and Redeemer.
Amen.

St Columba

Prayer over the Gifts

Lord God,
May the gifts we offer increase our love for you
And bring us to eternal life.

Communion Sentence

He gives heavenly bread to the hungry,
And to the thirsty, water from the living spring.

A Celtic Eucharist

Prayer after Communion

We believe, O Lord, that in this breaking of your body and pouring out of your blood we become redeemed people. We confess that by our sharing of this sacrament we are strengthened to endure in hope until we lay hold and enjoy its true fruits in the heavenly places.

Stowe Missal

Additional Prayers II

Sentence

Let us adore the Lord,
Maker of marvellous works,
Bright heaven with its angels,
And on earth the white-waved sea.

Ancient Irish

Opening Prayer

O Lord Jesus Christ, you are the way, the truth and the life: suffer us not to stray from you, who are the way, nor to distrust you, who are the truth, nor to rest in any other thing than you, who are the life. Teach us by your Holy Spirit what to believe, what to do, and wherein to take our rest. We ask it for your Name's sake. Amen.

Erasmus

Prayer over the Gifts

Praise to you, O Christ,
King of eternal glory!
Man does not live on bread alone,
But on every word that comes from the mouth of God.
Praise to you, O Christ,
King of eternal glory!

A Celtic Primer

Communion Sentence

This is the living bread which comes down from heaven,
He who eats of it shall live for ever.

Prayer after Communion

Lord, may we be wakeful at sunrise to begin a new day for you;
Cheerful at sunset for having done our work for you;
Thankful at moonrise and under starshine for the beauty of your universe;
And may we add what little may be in us to add to your great world.
Amen.

The Abbot of Greve

ADDITIONAL PRAYERS III

Sentence

Brothers and sisters, be joyful, and keep your faith and belief, and do the little
things which you have heard and seen with me.

St David

Opening Prayer

O God, your name is blessed from the rising of the sun to its setting; fill our hearts
with knowledge of yourself and our mouths with your praise, that from East to
West all may sing your glory, with one voice and accord, in Jesus Christ, your
Son, our Lord. Amen.

Prayer over the Gifts

God our Creator,
May this bread and wine we offer
As a sign of love and worship
Lead us to eternal joy.

Communion Sentence

We know and believe in God's love for us.

Prayer after Communion

See that you are at peace among yourselves, my children,
And love one another in Jesus, the Christ, our Lord.

St Columba

ADDITIONAL PRAYERS IV

Sentence

Help us, Unity in trinity,
Trinity in Unity, take pity.

Laidcenn, Irish, seventh century

Opening Prayer

Let us pray to God the Father, God the Son,
And to God the Holy Spirit
Whose infinite greatness
Enfolds the whole world,
In persons three and one,
In essence simple and triune,
Suspending the earth above the waters,
Hanging the upper air with stars,
That he may be favourable to sinners
Who righteously justifies all who err,
Who ever-living lives.
May God be blessed for ages. Amen.

Moucan, Welsh, eighth century

A Celtic Primer

Prayer over the Gifts

Receive, Lord, we pray, the offerings which we make to you of what you have given us, so that by the power of your grace these holy mysteries may sanctify our present life and bring us to everlasting joys.

Prayer after Communion

Grant within us, Lord, the gift of your glory, that against all the evils of this present age, the power of the Eucharist we have received may be our protecting wall.

Stowe

ADDITIONAL PRAYERS V

Sentence

My soul's desire is to see the face of God,
and to rest in his house.

St Columba

Opening Prayer

Father, your love for us surpasses all our hopes and desires. Forgive our failings, keep us in your peace and lead us in the way of salvation.

Prayer over the Gifts

Lord, receive our gifts. Let our offerings enable us in the way of healing and holiness.

Communion Sentence

Dear Lord, you alone know what my soul truly desires, and you alone can sanctify those desires.

Prayer after Communion

May this sharing, Lord, in your Son's Body and Blood be the washing away of our sins, the strength of the weak, and our protection against the dangers of the world. May it set us free from evil and grant us our share in the joy of your Kingdom.

Stowe

ADDITIONAL PRAYERS VI

Sentence

The grace of God's love dwells in our hearts
as a jewel of gold is placed in a silver dish.

Iona, sixth century

Opening Prayer

God of all creation, we worship you as Lord. God, you are ever close to us, we rejoice to call you Father. From this world's uncertainty we look to you for strength. Keep us one in your peace, secure in your love.

Prayer over the Gifts

God of power, giver of all gifts, accept the offerings of your people, who offer them that you may make them a sacrament of our healing.

Sentence

My soul's desire is to enter the gates of heaven, and to gaze upon the light that shines forever.

Prayer after Communion

Lord, you satisfy our longings with this gift from heaven. Cleanse us from our secret faults and from the assaults of the evil one.

Stowe

Additional Prayers VII

Sentence

Let the summits of heaven praise you with roaming lightning,
O most loving Jesus, O righteous King of Kings.

Iona, sixth century

Opening Prayer

O Holy Jesus,
Gentle friend,
Morning star,
Midday sun adorned,
Fountain ever-new, ever-living, ever-lasting
Son of the merciful Father without mother in heaven,
Son of the Virgin Mary, without father on earth,
True and loving brother,
Give, grant, and impart to us your holy grace and your Holy Spirit, to protect and
preserve us from all our sins, present and future.

The Broom of Devotion, early Irish

Prayer over the Gifts

Lord, hear the prayer of your people and receive our gifts.
May the worship of each one here bring healing to all.

Prayer after Communion

We give thanks, Lord, Holy Father, Almighty God; we shared the Body and
Blood of Christ your Son and so you have fulfilled all our needs. Humbly we beg
your mercy, that this your sacrament may not bring us the punishment of our sins
but may speak to you for our forgiveness and salvation.

Additional Prayers VIII

Sentence

The King is knocking.
If you would have your share
of heaven on earth,
open the door of your heart
and let in the King.

Hebridean

Opening Prayer

You are our King. Yours is our flesh, our body, we love you blessed Christ, for our soul is yours. May we be in your royal dwelling all our days. May we eat the feast from your table. Do not leave us behind, O God our King.

Welsh

Prayer over the Gifts

Lord God, accept our prayers and offerings, convert the hearts of us all to yourself so that we, delivered from worldly covetousness, may rise to desire the things of heaven.

Prayer after Communion

God, we give you thanks because it is through you that we have celebrated these holy mysteries. We beg from you your gifts of holiness: have mercy on us, Lord, Saviour of the world, King for ever and ever.

Stowe

Blessing

The High-King's blessing be upon you,
may He be upon your daily trail;
the High-King's blessing be upon you,
that you be spared perils and pain.

Gaelic

A Celtic Primer

ALTERNATIVE DISMISSAL PRAYERS

Let us go forth,
In the goodness of our merciful Father,
In the gentleness of our brother Jesus,
In the radiance of his Holy Spirit,
In the faith of the apostles,
In the joyful praise of the angels,
In the holiness of the saints,
In the courage of the martyrs.

Celtic

I beseech you, Jesus, loving Saviour, to show yourself to all who seek you
so that we may know you and love you.
May we love you alone, desire you alone, and keep you always in our thoughts.
May love for you possess our hearts,
May affection for you fill our senses, so that we may love all else in you.
Jesus, King of Glory,
You know how to give greatly
And you have promised great things.
Nothing is greater than yourself.
We ask nothing else of you but yourself.
You are our life, our light, our food and our drink, our God and our all.

from an ancient Irish Prayer

The Celebrant may end with the blessing:
And may the blessing of Almighty God,
The Father, the Son and the Holy Spirit,
Come upon you and remain with you for ever.
Amen.

Celebrant: Go in peace to love and serve the Lord.
People: Thanks be to God.

ALTERNATIVE BLESSINGS

May Mary Virgin's Son Himself
Be a generous lamp to you,
To guide you over
The great and awful ocean of eternity
And the blessing of God Almighty. . .

Carmina Gadelica (13)

The love and affection of the angels be to you,
The love and affection of the saints be to you,
The love and affection of heaven be to you,
To guard you and to cherish you.
And the blessing of God Almighty . . .

Carmina Gadelica (13)

God's blessing be yours,
And well may it befall you;
Christ's blessing be yours,
And well be you entreated;
Spirit's blessing be yours,
And well spend your lives,
Each day that you rise up,
Each night that you lie down,
And the blessing of God Almighty . . .

Carmina Gadelica (13)

May the Creator bless you and keep you,
May the beloved compassion face you and have mercy upon you;
May the eternal Spirit's countenance be turned to you and give you peace;
May the Three in One bless you.

Hebridean

A Celtic Primer

May God give us light to guide us,
Courage to support us,
And love to unite us,
Now and evermore.
And may the blessing of God Almighty . . .

Celtic

May the Lord bless you and protect you.
May the Lord smile on you and show you his favour.
May the Lord befriend you and prosper you.
And may the blessing of God . . .

Celtic

God's grace distil on you,
Christ's grace distil on you,
Spirit's grace distil on you
Each day and each night
Of your portion in the world;
On each day and each night
Of your portion in the world.

Carmina Gadelica (13)

May the road rise to meet you,
May the wind be always at your back,
May the sun shine warm upon your face,
May the rain fall soft upon your fields,
And until we meet again,
May God hold you in the hollow of his hand.

Gaelic

The palmful of the God of Life
The palmful of the Christ of Love
The palmful of the Spirit of Peace
Triune of Grace
Bless you, in the Name . . .

Early Scottish

My Christ, my shield,
my encircler,
each day, each night,
each light, each dark,
be near me, uphold me,
my treasure, my triumph.

Iona

Salvation is of the Lord,
Salvation is of Christ.
May your blessing, Lord,
be upon your people,
Father, Son and Holy Spirit.
Amen.

adapted from Nuall Fir Fhio: 'Fer Fio's Cry'
(trans. John Carey) (18)

The holy lord of creation,
Christ, son of the holy Mary,
Jesus, beloved pillar –
may he go before the human race.
And the blessing . . .

from Felire Oengusso (18)

Blessing and brightness,
Wisdom, thanksgiving,
Great power and might
To the King who rules over all.

Glory and honour and goodwill,
Praise and the sublime song of minstrels,
Overflowing love from every heart
To the King of Heaven and Earth.

To the chosen Trinity has been joined
Before all, after all, universal
Blessing and everlasting blessing,
Blessing everlasting and blessing.

Irish, ninth century

A Celtic Primer

The Lord bless us, and preserve us from all evil,
and bring us to everlasting life;
and may the souls of the faithful,
through the mercy of God, rest in peace.

Sarum Primer

May the grace of the Lord Jesus sanctify us and keep us from all evil;
may he drive far from us all hurtful things, and purify both our souls and bodies;
may he bind us to himself by the bond of love,
and may his peace abound in our hearts.

Gregorian Sacramentary, sixth century

May God the Father bless us;
May Christ take care of us;
May the Holy Spirit enlighten us
all the days of our life.
The Lord be our Defender
and Keeper of body and soul
both now and for ever,
to the ages of ages.

Book of Cerne, tenth century

May the King shield you in the valleys,
May Christ aid you on the mountains,
May the Spirit bathe you on the slopes,
In hollow, on hill, on plain,
Mountain, valley and plain,
May the Three in One bless you . . .

Hebridean

May we all reach the Kingdom that is without end,
May we deserve it,
May we dwell there for ages unending.
Amen.

from the Rule of the Celi De

May the Three Who are over you,
The Three Who are below you,
The Three Who are above you here,
The Three Who are above you yonder,
The Three Who are in the earth,
The Three Who are in the air,
The Three Who are in the heaven,
The Three Who are in the great pouring sea –
bless you,
Father, Son and Holy Spirit.
Amen.

Gaelic

A Celtic Primer

THE PSALTER *(43)*

PSALM THEMES

Certain Psalms lend themselves to use as prayer and adoration, others to praise of God for his wonders as shown in nature, and there are Psalms of entreaty and thanksgiving.

The following table of Psalms is set out with Psalm numbers and a short reference to the content and context in which they may be used.

1	The two paths – happy the person who does not take the wrong road
2	God's chosen King
3	Morning Prayer for help
4	Evening Prayer for help
5	Prayer Psalm – give me a straight path to follow
6	Penitential Psalm
7	A prayer for justice
8	Praise of Creation
9	Thanksgiving to God for his justice
10	A prayer for the needy
11	Confidence in the Lord
12	A prayer for help
13	A cry for help
14	The wickedness of men
15	Prayer Psalm – who may dwell on thy holy mountain?
16	Prayer Psalm – I have set the Lord continually before me
17	The prayer of an innocent man
18	David's song of victory
19	Prayer Psalm – the heavens declare the glory of God
20	A prayer for victory
21	Praise for victory
22	A cry of anguish and a song of praise

23	The Lord is my shepherd
24	The Earth is the Lord's and all that is in it. A Temple Psalm useful on entering the church of destination
25	The Lord is my Light and my salvation. Trust in God
26	The prayer of a good man
27	A prayer of praise
28	A call for help
29	The voice of the Lord
30	Meditation Psalm – Can the dust give you thanks or declare your faithfulness?
31	A prayer of trust in God
32	Penitential Psalm – joy after forgiveness – blessed is he whose sin is forgiven – I will teach you and guide you in the way you should go
33	Hymn of praise. The main body of the Psalm, verses 4–18, shows why praise is due to God – his work in Creation, etc.
34	In praise of God's goodness
35	Lord, come to my rescue
36	The goodness of God
37	The destiny of the wicked and the good
38	Penitential Psalm
39	The confession of a suffering man
40	Joy in God's will
41	The prayer of a sick man
42	Thirst and longing for God – as a hind longs for the running streams
43	Lovely prayer – send forth thy light and thy truth to be my guide
44	A prayer for protection
45	A Royal wedding song
46	God is with us
47	God is king of all the earth; sing psalms with all your art
48	Zion, the city of God
49	The foolishness of trusting in riches
50	True worship
51	Prayer for forgiveness
52	God's judgement and grace
53	The Godlessness of men
54	A prayer in time of trouble

A Celtic Primer

55	Prayer of a persecuted man
56	A prayer of trust in God
57	Meditation Psalm for worship
58	A plea for justice
59	A prayer for safety
60	A prayer for deliverance
61	A prayer for protection
62	Prayer Psalm – my soul waits in silence for God, for from him comes my salvation – silence, stillness
63	Longing for God – a spiritual song of great devotion expressing a deep thirst for God
64	A prayer for protection
65	A harvest hymn praising God's wonderful creation
66	A song of praise and thanksgiving
67	A song of thanksgiving
68	A national song of triumph
69	A cry for help
70	A prayer for help
71	An old man's prayer
72	A prayer for the King
73	The justice of God
74	A prayer for national deliverance
75	God the Judge
76	God the Victor
77	Comfort in time of distress
78	God and his people
79	A prayer for the nation's deliverance
80	A prayer for the nation's restoration
81	Song for a festival
82	God the supreme ruler
83	A prayer against Israel's enemies
84	Pilgrim Psalm – 'How lovely is your dwelling place, O Lord God Almighty' – an appropriate Psalm for use when visiting Holy Wells!
85	Prayer for peace and justice
86	Prayer Psalm – Listen, O Lord to my prayer and hear my pleading

87	In praise of Jerusalem
88	A cry for help
89	A hymn to God's faithfulness
90	Of God and man
91	God our protector
92	A song of praise
93	The King of the Universe – the ocean lifts up its pounding waves! – a useful Psalm when walking the coastal path!
94	God the judge of all
95	O come and worship . . . the sea is his, he made it; Yahweh is revealed as Creator and Lord of the Universe – a good opening Psalm for pilgrimage
96	Creation Psalm. An open invitation to all nations and creation to sing a new song to the Lord
97	Psalm of the elements. God is King, let the earth rejoice, let coasts and islands rejoice
98	Creation Psalm – all the ends of the earth have seen the victory of our God
99	The Lord is King
100	Hymn of praise – an invitation to all the peoples of the world to praise God
101	A song of loyalty to God
102	Penitential Psalm
103	Joyful hymn of praise
104	In praise of the Creator
105	God and his people
106	The Lord's goodness to his people
107	In praise of God's goodness
108	Morning prayer for help
109	Lament of a man in trouble
110	The Lord and his chosen King
111	In praise of the Lord
112	In praise of the good person
113	Praise to the God of glory and mercy, a Psalm praising God's goodness and greatness
114	A Passover song
115	The one true God
116	Prayer Psalm – I am filled with love when God listens to the sound of my prayer
117	A summons to praise – God's loving kindness is available for all

118	A song of thanksgiving
119	In praise of God's law. The psalmist loves God's law because he loves God

The Pilgrim Songs or Songs of Ascent

120	Pilgrim Song. This Psalm is the first of a set of fifteen Psalms (120–134) sung by pilgrims as they journeyed to the holy city. The writer of this Psalm is glad to be away from the hostile surroundings of the past
121	Pilgrim Song. I lift up my eyes to the mountains; where shall I find help? A Psalm for use on pilgrimages which are not without danger
122	Pilgrim Song. I was glad when they said to me, 'Let us go to the house of the Lord!' – a Psalm for use both on arrival and departure at the sanctuary of the pilgrimage
123	Pilgrim Song. Looking upwards to God
124	Pilgrim Song. Thanksgiving of those who have been delivered
125	Pilgrim Song. An affirmation of trust in God's protection
126	Pilgrim Song. Those who sow in tears will reap with shouts of joy; homely and yet profound piety in this beautiful Psalm
127	Pilgrim Song. The labour of man without the help of God is worth nothing
128	Pilgrim Song. Blessed is everyone who fears the Lord, who walks in his ways! The blessing of domestic happiness
129	Pilgrim Song. Despite the curses as well as the blessings this Psalm is of trust in a God who will always continue to give protection to those who trust in him
130	Penitential Psalm and Pilgrim Song. Out of the depths. The sixth of the penitential Psalms of the ancient Church. A confessional Psalm of one who is able to rise from the uttermost depth of anguish engendered by sin to the assurance of the divine grace and forgiveness
131	Pilgrim song. A Psalm of great beauty and humility, perhaps written by a man in his later years who has now found peace in communion with God. This little Psalm has been described as 'a gem of exquisite beauty and surpassing loveliness'.
132	Pilgrim Song. Liturgical Psalm of dedication of the Temple
133	Pilgrim Song. The unity of the family. 'Behold how good and pleasant it is when brothers dwell in unity!'
134	Pilgrim Song. For the evening liturgy, related to a vigil service in the Jerusalem Temple. It may represent the blessing which is pronounced on pilgrims as they depart from Zion and is meant to accompany them on their journey, which is why this Psalm has been placed at the end of the Pilgrim Songs
135	A hymn of praise
136	A hymn of thanksgiving
137	A lament in exile

138	Prayer Psalm. The answering of prayer 'I will praise thee, O Lord, with my whole heart'.
139	Prayer Psalm. In praise of the all-knowing, all-present God where personal experience of the reality of God is embedded in the whole life of the poet. A contemplative Psalm coming from an intimate relationship with God
140	A prayer for protection
141	An evening prayer
142	A prayer for help
143	Penitential and Prayer Psalm. The last of the seven penitential Psalms of the Church. This Psalm represents the song of lament of a man aware of his own sinfulness in the presence of God
144	A King thanks God for victory
145	Praise to the kingship of God, as well as praise for the blessing of a rich harvest and for the mighty acts wrought by God!
146	Prayer Psalm – Praise the Lord, O my soul. This Psalm is a simple hymn expressing trust in God
147	God's goodness, power and love. A hymn to the all-powerful, gracious and mighty God
148	A cosmic hymn of praise – heaven, earth and all creation are called to glorify the Creator and Preserver of the world
149	A hymn of praise
150	The great Hallelujah. This last Psalm is a call to praise God, in which all the voices on earth and in heaven unite with the entire orchestra of the Temple music. It is the greatest symphony of praise to God ever composed on Earth

Let everything that hath breath praise the Lord! Hallelujah!

Psalm 1

1 Happy are they who have not walked
in the counsel of the wicked,*
nor lingered in the way of sinners,
nor sat in the seats of the scornful!
2 Their delight is in the law of the Lord,*
and they meditate on his law day and night.
3 They are like trees planted by streams of water,
bearing fruit in due season,
with leaves that do not wither;*
everything they do shall prosper.
4 It is not so with the wicked:*
they are like chaff which the wind blows away;
5 Therefore the wicked shall not stand upright
when judgement comes,*
nor the sinner in the council of the righteous.
6 For the Lord knows the way of the righteous,*
but the way of the wicked is doomed.

Psalm 2

1 Why are the nations in an uproar?*
Why do the peoples mutter empty threats?
2 Why do the kings of the earth rise up in revolt
and the princes plot together,*
against the Lord and against his anointed?
3 'Let us break their yoke', they say;*
'let us cast off their bonds from us.'
4 He whose throne is in heaven is laughing;*
the Lord has them in derision.
5 Then he speaks to them in his wrath*
and his rage fills them with terror.
6 'I myself have set my king*
upon my holy hill of Zion.'
7 Let me announce the decree of the Lord:*
he said to me, 'You are my Son;
this day have I begotten you.
8 'Ask of me and I will give you the nations for
your inheritance*
and the ends of the earth for your possession.

9   'You shall crush them with an iron rod*
     and shatter them like a piece of pottery.'
10   And now, you kings, be wise;*
     be warned, you rulers of the earth.
11   Submit to the Lord with fear,*
     and with trembling bow before him;
12   Lest he be angry and you perish;*
     for his wrath is quickly kindled.
13   Happy are they all*
     who take refuge in him!

Psalm 3

1   Lord, how many adversaries I have!*
     how many there are who rise up against me!
2   How many there are who say of me,*
     'There is no help for him in his God.'
3   But you, O Lord, are a shield about me;*
     you are my glory, the one who lifts up my head.
4   I call aloud upon the Lord*
     and he answers me from his holy hill;
5   I lie down and go to sleep;*
     I wake again, because the Lord sustains me.
6   I do not fear the multitudes of people*
     who set themselves against me all around.
7   Rise up, O Lord; set me free, O my God;*
     surely, you will strike all my enemies across the face,
     you will break the teeth of the wicked.
8   Deliverance belongs to the Lord.*
     Your blessing be upon your people!

Psalm 4

1   Answer me when I call, O God, defender of my cause;*
     you set me free when I am hard-pressed;
     have mercy on me and hear my prayer.
2   'You mortals, how long will you dishonour my glory;*
     how long will you worship dumb idols
     and run after false gods?'
3   Know that the Lord does wonders for the faithful;*
     when I call upon the Lord, he will hear me.
4   Tremble, then, and do not sin;*
     speak to your heart in silence upon your bed.
5   Offer the appointed sacrifices*

and put your trust in the Lord.

6   Many are saying, 'O that we might see better times!'*
Lift up the light of your countenance upon us, O Lord.

7   You have put gladness in my heart,*
more than when grain and wine and oil increase.

8   I lie down in peace; at once I fall asleep;*
for only you, Lord, make me dwell in safety.

Psalm 5

1   Give ear to my words, O Lord;*
consider my meditation.

2   Hearken to my cry for help, my King and my God,*
for I make my prayer to you.

3   In the morning, Lord, you hear my voice;*
early in the morning I make my appeal
and watch for you.

4   For you are not a God who takes pleasure in wickedness*
and evil cannot dwell with you.

5   Braggarts cannot stand in your sight;*
you hate all those who work wickedness.

6   You destroy those who speak lies;*
the bloodthirsty and deceitful, O Lord, you abhor.

7   But as for me, through the greatness of your mercy,
I will go into your house;*
I will bow down towards your holy temple in awe of you.

8   Lead me, O Lord, in your righteousness,
because of those who lie in wait for me;*
make your way straight before me.

9   For there is no truth in their mouth;*
there is destruction in their heart;

10   Their throat is an open grave;*
they flatter with their tongue.

11   Declare them guilty, O God;*
let them fall, because of their schemes.

12   Because of their many transgressions cast them out,*
for they have rebelled against you.

13   But all who take refuge in you will be glad;*
they will sing out their joy for ever.

14   You will shelter them,*
so that those who love your name may exult in you.

15   For you, O Lord, will bless the righteous;*
you will defend them with your favour as with a shield.

Psalm 6

1   Lord, do not rebuke me in your anger;*
do not punish me in your wrath.

2   Have pity on me, Lord, for I am weak;*
heal me, Lord, for my bones are racked.

3   My spirit shakes with terror;*
how long, O Lord, how long?

4   Turn, O Lord, and deliver me;*
save me for your mercy's sake.

5   For in death no one remembers you;*
and who will give you thanks in the grave?

6   I grow weary because of my groaning;*
every night I drench my bed
and flood my couch with tears.

7   My eyes are wasted with grief*
and worn away because of all my enemies.

8   Depart from me, all evildoers,*
for the Lord has heard the sound of my weeping.

9   The Lord has heard my supplication;*
the Lord accepts my prayer.

10   All my enemies shall be confounded and quake with fear;*
they shall turn back and suddenly be put to shame.

Psalm 7

1   O Lord my God, I take refuge in you;*
save and deliver me from all who pursue me;

2   Lest like a lion they tear me in pieces*
and snatch me away with none to deliver me.

3   O Lord my God, if I have done these things:*
if there is any wickedness in my hands,

4   If I have repaid my friend with evil,*
or plundered one who without cause is my enemy;

5   Then let my enemy pursue and overtake me,*
trample my life into the ground,
and lay my honour in the dust.

6   Stand up, O Lord, in your wrath;*
rise up against the fury of my enemies.

7   Awake, O my God, decree justice;*
let the assembly of the peoples gather round you.

8   Be seated on your lofty throne, O Most High;*
O Lord, judge the nations.

9   Give judgement for me

according to my righteousness, O Lord,*
and according to my innocence, O Most High.
10 Let the malice of the wicked come to an end,
but establish the righteous;*
for you test the mind and heart, O righteous God.
11 God is my shield and defence;*
he is the saviour of the true in heart.
12 God is a righteous judge;*
God sits in judgement every day.
13 If they will not repent, God will whet his sword;*
he will bend his bow and make it ready.
14 He has prepared his weapons of death;*
he makes his arrows shafts of fire.
15 Look at those who are in labour with wickedness,*
who conceive evil and give birth to a lie.
16 They dig a pit and make it deep*
and fall into the hole that they have made.
17 Their malice turns back upon their own head;*
their violence falls on their own scalp.
18 I will bear witness that the Lord is righteous;*
I will praise the name of the Lord Most High.

Psalm 8

1 O Lord our governor,*
how exalted is your name in all the world!
2 Out of the mouths of infants and children*
your majesty is praised above the heavens.
3 You have set up a stronghold against your adversaries,*
to quell the enemy and the avenger.
4 When I consider your heavens, the work of your fingers,*
the moon and the stars you have set in their courses,
5 What are mortals, that you should be mindful of them?*
mere human beings, that you should seek them out?
6 You have made them little lower than the angels;*
you adorn them with glory and honour.
7 You give them mastery over the works of your hands;*
and put all things under their feet,
8 All sheep and oxen,*
even the wild beasts of the field,
9 The birds of the air, the fish of the sea,*
and whatsoever walks in the paths of the sea.
10 O Lord our governor,*
how exalted is your name in all the world!

Psalm 9

1   I will give thanks to you, O Lord, with my whole heart;*
I will tell of all your marvellous works.

2   I will be glad and rejoice in you;*
I will sing to your name, O Most High.

3   When my enemies are driven back,*
they will stumble and perish at your presence.

4   For you have maintained my right and my cause;*
you sit upon your throne judging right.

5   You have rebuked the ungodly and destroyed the wicked;*
you have blotted out their name for ever and ever.

6   As for the enemy, they are finished, in perpetual ruin,*
their cities ploughed under,
the memory of them perished;

7   But the Lord is enthroned for ever;*
he has set up his throne for judgement.

8   It is he who rules the world with righteousness;*
he judges the peoples with equity.

9   The Lord will be a refuge for the oppressed,*
a refuge in time of trouble.

10   Those who know your name will put their trust in you,*
for you never forsake those who seek you, O Lord.

11   Sing praise to the Lord who dwells in Zion;*
proclaim to the peoples the things he has done.

12   The avenger of blood will remember them;*
he will not forget the cry of the afflicted.

13   Have pity on me, O Lord;*
see the misery I suffer from those who hate me,
O you who lift me up from the gate of death;

14   So that I may tell of all your praises
and rejoice in your salvation*
in the gates of the city of Zion.

15   The ungodly have fallen into the pit they dug,*
and in the snare they set is their own foot caught.

16   The Lord is known by his acts of justice;*
the wicked are trapped in the works of their own hands.

17   The wicked shall be given over to the grave,*
and also all the peoples that forget God.

18   For the needy shall not always be forgotten,*
and the hope of the poor shall not perish for ever.

19   Rise up, O Lord,
let not the ungodly have the upper hand;*
let them be judged before you.

20   Put fear upon them, O Lord;*
      let the ungodly know they are but mortal.

Psalm 10

1   Why do you stand so far off, O Lord,*
      and hide yourself in time of trouble?
2   The wicked arrogantly persecute the poor,*
      but they are trapped in the schemes they have devised.
3   The wicked boast of their heart's desire;*
      the covetous curse and revile the Lord.
4   The wicked are so proud that they care not for God;*
      their only thought is, 'God does not matter.'
5   Their ways are devious at all times;
      your judgements are far above out of their sight;*
      they defy all their enemies.
6   They say in their heart, 'I shall not be shaken;*
      no harm shall happen to me ever.'
7   Their mouth is full of cursing, deceit and oppression;*
      under their tongue are mischief and wrong.
8   They lurk in ambush in public squares
      and in secret places they murder the innocent;*
      they spy out the helpless.
9   They lie in wait, like a lion in a covert;
      they lie in wait to seize upon the lowly;*
      they seize the lowly and drag them away in their net.
10   The innocent are broken and humbled before them;*
      the helpless fall before their power.
11   They say in their heart, 'God has forgotten;*
      he hides his face; he will never notice.'
12   Rise up, O Lord;
      lift up your hand, O God;*
      do not forget the afflicted.
13   Why should the wicked revile God?*
      why should they say in their heart, 'You do not care'?
14   Surely, you behold trouble and misery;*
      you see it and take it into your own hand.
15   The helpless commit themselves to you,*
      for you are the helper of orphans.
16   Break the power of the wicked and evil;*
      search out their wickedness until you find none.
17   The Lord is king for ever and ever;*
      the ungodly shall perish from his land.
18   The Lord will hear the desire of the humble;*

you will strengthen their heart and your ears shall hear;
19 To give justice to the orphan and oppressed,*
so that mere mortals may strike terror no more.

Psalm 11

1 In the Lord have I taken refuge;*
how then can you say to me,
'Fly away like a bird to the hilltop;

2 'For see how the wicked bend the bow
and fit their arrows to the string,*
to shoot from ambush at the true of heart.

3 'When the foundations are being destroyed,*
what can the righteous do?'

4 The Lord is in his holy temple;*
the Lord's throne is in heaven.

5 His eyes behold the inhabited world;*
his piercing eye weighs our worth.

6 The Lord weighs the righteous as well as the wicked,*
but those who delight in violence he abhors.

7 Upon the wicked he shall rain coals of fire
and burning sulphur;*
a scorching wind shall be their lot.

8 For the Lord is righteous;
he delights in righteous deeds;*
and the just shall see his face.

Psalm 12

1 Help me, Lord, for there is no godly one left;*
the faithful have vanished from among us.

2 Everyone speaks falsely with their neighbour;*
with a smooth tongue they speak from a double heart.

3 O that the Lord would cut off all smooth tongues,*
and close the lips that utter proud boasts!

4 Those who say, 'With our tongue will we prevail;*
our lips are our own; who is lord over us?'

5 'Because the needy are oppressed,
and the poor cry out in misery,*
I will rise up', says the Lord,
'and give them the help they long for.'

6 The words of the Lord are pure words,*
like silver refined from ore
and purified seven times in the fire.

A Celtic Primer

7   O Lord, watch over us*
     and save us from this generation for ever.
8   The wicked prowl on every side,*
     and that which is worthless is highly prized by everyone.

Psalm 13

1   How long, O Lord;
     will you forget me for ever?*
     how long will you hide your face from me?
2   How long shall I have perplexity in my mind,
     and grief in my heart, day after day?*
     how long shall my enemy triumph over me?
3   Look upon me and answer me, O Lord my God;*
     give light to my eyes, lest I sleep in death;
4   Lest my enemy say, 'I have prevailed over him',*
     and my foes rejoice that I have fallen.
5   But I put my trust in your mercy;*
     my heart is joyful because of your saving help.
6   I will sing to the Lord,
     for he has dealt with me richly;*
     I will praise the name of the Lord Most High.

Psalm 14

1   The fool has said in his heart, 'There is no God.'*
     All are corrupt and commit abominable acts;
     there is none who does any good.
2   The Lord looks down from heaven upon us all,*
     to see if there is any who is wise,
     if there is one who seeks after God.
3   Everyone has proved faithless;
     all alike have turned bad;*
     there is none who does good; no, not one.
4   Have they no knowledge, all those evildoers*
     who eat up my people like bread
     and do not call upon the Lord?
5   See how they tremble with fear,*
     because God is in the company of the righteous.
6   Their aim is to confound the plans of the afflicted,*
     but the Lord is their refuge.
7   O that Israel's deliverance would come out of Zion!*
     when the Lord restores the fortunes of his people,
     Jacob will rejoice and Israel be glad.

The Psalter, including Psalm Themes for Prayer   269

Psalm 15

1   Lord, who may dwell in your tabernacle?*
     who may abide upon your holy hill?
2   Whoever leads a blameless life and does what is right,*
     who speaks the truth from his heart.
3   There is no guile upon his tongue;
     he does no evil to his friend;*
     he does not heap contempt upon his neighbour.
4   In his sight the wicked is rejected,*
     but he honours those who fear the Lord.
5   He has sworn to do no wrong*
     and does not take back his word.
6   He does not give his money in hope of gain,*
     nor does he take a bribe against the innocent.
7   Whoever does these things*
     shall never be overthrown.

Psalm 16

1   Protect me, O God, for I take refuge in you;*
     I have said to the Lord, 'You are my Lord,
     my good above all other.'
2   All my delight is upon the godly that are in the land,*
     upon those who are noble among the people.
3   But those who run after other gods*
     shall have their troubles multiplied.
4   Their libations of blood I will not offer,*
     nor take the names of their gods upon my lips.
5   O Lord, you are my portion and my cup;*
     it is you who uphold my lot.
6   My boundaries enclose a pleasant land;*
     indeed, I have a goodly heritage.
7   I will bless the Lord who gives me counsel;*
     my heart teaches me, night after night.
8   I have set the Lord always before me;*
     because he is at my right hand I shall not fall.
9   My heart, therefore, is glad and my spirit rejoices;*
     my body also shall rest in hope.
10   For you will not abandon me to the grave,*
     nor let your holy one see the Pit.
11   You will show me the path of life;*
     in your presence there is fullness of joy,
     and in your right hand are pleasures for evermore.

Psalm 17

1 Hear my plea of innocence, O Lord;
   give heed to my cry;*
   listen to my prayer,
   which does not come from lying lips.

2 Let my vindication come forth from your presence;*
   let your eyes be fixed on justice.

3 Weigh my heart, summon me by night,*
   melt me down; you will find no impurity in me.

4 I give no offence with my mouth as others do;*
   I have heeded the words of your lips.

5 My footsteps hold fast to the ways of your law;*
   in your paths my feet shall not stumble.

6 I call upon you, O God, for you will answer me;*
   incline your ear to me and hear my words.

7 Show me your marvellous loving-kindness,*
   O Saviour of those who take refuge at your right hand
   from those who rise up against them.

8 Keep me as the apple of your eye;*
   hide me under the shadow of your wings,

9 From the wicked who assault me,*
   from my deadly enemies who surround me.

10 They have closed their heart to pity,*
   and their mouth speaks proud things.

11 They press me hard,
   now they surround me,*
   watching how they may cast me to the ground,

12 Like a lion, greedy for its prey,*
   and like a young lion lurking in secret places.

13 Arise, O Lord; confront them and bring them down;*
   deliver me from the wicked by your sword.

14 Deliver me, O Lord, by your hand*
   from those whose portion in life is this world;

15 Whose bellies you fill with your treasure,*
   who are well supplied with children
   and leave their wealth to their little ones.

16 But at my vindication I shall see your face;*
   when I awake, I shall be satisfied,
   beholding your likeness.

Psalm 18, Part I

1   I love you, O Lord my strength,*
    O Lord my stronghold, my crag and my haven.
2   My God, my rock in whom I put my trust,*
    my shield, the horn of my salvation and my refuge;
    you are worthy of praise.
3   I will call upon the Lord,*
    and so shall I be saved from my enemies.
4   The breakers of death rolled over me,*
    and the torrents of oblivion made me afraid.
5   The cords of hell entangled me,*
    and the snares of death were set for me.
6   I called upon the Lord in my distress*
    and cried out to my God for help.
7   He heard my voice from his heavenly dwelling;*
    my cry of anguish came to his ears.
8   The earth reeled and rocked;*
    the roots of the mountains shook;
    they reeled because of his anger.
9   Smoke rose from his nostrils
    and a consuming fire out of his mouth;*
    hot burning coals blazed forth from him.
10 He parted the heavens and came down*
    with a storm cloud under his feet.
11 He mounted on cherubim and flew;*
    he swooped on the wings of the wind.
12 He wrapped darkness about him;*
    he made dark waters and thick clouds his pavilion.
13 From the brightness of his presence, through the clouds,*
    burst hailstones and coals of fire.
14 The Lord thundered out of heaven;*
    the Most High uttered his voice.
15 He loosed his arrows and scattered them;*
    he hurled thunderbolts and routed them.
16 The beds of the seas were uncovered,
    and the foundations of the world laid bare,*
    at your battle cry, O Lord,
    at the blast of the breath of your nostrils.
17 He reached down from on high and grasped me;*
    he drew me out of great waters.
18 He delivered me from my strong enemies
    and from those who hated me;*
    for they were too mighty for me.

A Celtic Primer

19　They confronted me in the day of my disaster;*
　　but the Lord was my support.

20　He brought me out into an open place;*
　　he rescued me because he delighted in me.

Psalm 18, Part II

21　The Lord rewarded me because of my righteous dealing;*
　　because my hands were clean he rewarded me;

22　For I have kept the ways of the Lord*
　　and have not offended against my God;

23　For all his judgements are before my eyes,*
　　and his decrees I have not put away from me;

24　For I have been blameless with him*
　　and have kept myself from iniquity;

25　Therefore the Lord rewarded me
　　according to my righteous dealing,*
　　because of the cleanness of my hands in his sight.

26　With the faithful you show yourself faithful, O God;*
　　with the forthright you show yourself forthright.

27　With the pure you show yourself pure,*
　　but with the crooked you are wily.

28　You will save a lowly people,*
　　but you will humble the haughty eyes.

29　You, O Lord, are my lamp;*
　　my God, you make my darkness bright.

30　With you I will break down an enclosure;*
　　with the help of my God I will scale any wall.

31　As for God, his ways are perfect;
　　the words of the Lord are tried in the fire;*
　　he is a shield to all who trust in him.

32　For who is God, but the Lord?*
　　who is the rock, except our God?

33　It is God who girds me about with strength*
　　and makes my way secure.

34　He makes me sure-footed like a deer*
　　and lets me stand firm on the heights.

35　He trains my hands for battle*
　　and my arms for bending even a bow of bronze.

36　You have given me your shield of victory;*
　　your right hand also sustains me;
　　your loving care makes me great.

37　You lengthen my stride beneath me,*
　　and my ankles do not give way.

38   I pursue my enemies and overtake them;*
       I will not turn back till I have destroyed them.
39   I strike them down and they cannot rise;*
       they fall defeated at my feet.
40   You have girded me with strength for the battle;*
       you have cast down my adversaries beneath me;
       you have put my enemies to flight.
41   I destroy those who hate me;
       they cry out, but there is none to help them;*
       they cry to the Lord, but he does not answer.
42   I beat them small like dust before the wind;*
       I trample them like mud in the streets.
43   You deliver me from the strife of the peoples;*
       you put me at the head of the nations.
44   A people I have not known shall serve me;
       no sooner shall they hear than they shall obey me;*
       strangers will cringe before me.
45   The foreign peoples will lose heart;*
       they shall come trembling out of their strongholds.
46   The Lord lives! Blessèd is my rock!*
       Exalted is the God of my salvation!
47   He is the God who gave me victory*
       and cast down the peoples beneath me.
48   You rescued me from the fury of my enemies;
       you exalted me above those who rose against me;*
       you saved me from my deadly foe;
49   Therefore will I extol you among the nations, O Lord,*
       and sing praises to your name.
50   He multiplies the victories of his king;*
       he shows loving-kindness to his anointed,
       to David and his descendants for ever.

Psalm 19

1   The heavens declare the glory of God,*
       and the firmament shows his handiwork.
2   One day tells its tale to another,*
       and one night imparts knowledge to another.
3   Although they have no words or language,*
       and their voices are not heard,
4   Their sound has gone out into all lands,*
       and their message to the ends of the world.
5   In the deep has he set a pavilion for the sun;*
       it comes forth like a bridegroom out of his chamber;

it rejoices like a champion to run its course.

6   It goes forth from the uttermost edge of the heavens
and runs about to the end of it again;*
nothing is hidden from its burning heat.

7   The law of the Lord is perfect
and revives the soul;*
the testimony of the Lord is sure
and gives wisdom to the innocent.

8   The statutes of the Lord are just
and rejoice the heart;*
the commandment of the Lord is clear
and gives light to the eyes.

9   The fear of the Lord is clean
and endures for ever;*
the judgements of the Lord are true
and righteous altogether.

10 More to be desired are they than gold,
more than much fine gold,*
sweeter far than honey,
than honey in the comb.

11 By them also is your servant enlightened,*
and in keeping them there is great reward.

12 Who can tell how often he offends?*
Cleanse me from my secret faults.

13 Above all, keep your servant from presumptuous sins;
let them not get dominion over me;*
then shall I be whole and sound,
and innocent of a great offence.

14 Let the words of my mouth and the meditation of my heart
be acceptable in your sight,*
O Lord, my strength and my redeemer.

Psalm 20

1   May the Lord answer you in the day of trouble,*
the name of the God of Jacob defend you;

2   Send you help from his holy place*
and strengthen you out of Zion;

3   Remember all your offerings*
and accept your burnt sacrifice;

4   Grant you your heart's desire*
and prosper all your plans.

5   We will shout for joy at your victory
and triumph in the name of our God;*

       may the Lord grant all your requests.

6   Now I know that the Lord gives victory
       to his anointed;*
       he will answer him out of his holy heaven,
       with the victorious strength of his right hand.

7   Some put their trust in chariots and some in horses,*
       but we will call upon the name of the Lord our God.

8   They collapse and fall down,*
       but we will arise and stand upright.

9   O Lord, give victory to the king*
       and answer us when we call.

Psalm 21

1   The king rejoices in your strength, O Lord;*
       how greatly he exults in your victory!

2   You have given him his heart's desire;*
       you have not denied him the request of his lips.

3   For you meet him with blessings of prosperity,*
       and set a crown of fine gold upon his head.

4   He asked you for life and you gave it to him;*
       length of days, for ever and ever.

5   His honour is great, because of your victory;*
       splendour and majesty have you bestowed upon him.

6   For you will give him everlasting felicity*
       and will make him glad with the joy of your presence.

7   For the king puts his trust in the Lord;*
       because of the loving-kindness of the Most High,
       he will not fall.

8   Your hand will lay hold upon all your enemies;*
       your right hand will seize all those who hate you.

9   You will make them like a fiery furnace*
       at the time of your appearing, O Lord;

10   You will swallow them up in your wrath,*
       and fire shall consume them.

11   You will destroy their offspring from the land*
       and their descendants
       from among the peoples of the earth.

12   Though they intend evil against you
       and devise wicked schemes,*
       yet they shall not prevail.

13   For you will put them to flight*
       and aim your arrows at them.

14   Be exalted, O Lord, in your might;*
       we will sing and praise your power.

PSALMS 22–37

Psalm 22

1 My God, my God, why have you forsaken me?*
   and are so far from my cry
   and from the words of my distress?

2 O my God, I cry in the daytime,
   but you do not answer;*
   by night as well, but I find no rest.

3 Yet you are the Holy One,*
   enthroned upon the praises of Israel.

4 Our forebears put their trust in you;*
   they trusted and you delivered them.

5 They cried out to you and were delivered;*
   they trusted in you and were not put to shame.

6 But as for me, I am a worm and no man,*
   scorned by all and despised by the people.

7 All who see me laugh me to scorn;*
   they curl their lips and wag their heads, saying,

8 'He trusted in the Lord; let him deliver him;*
   let him rescue him, if he delights in him.'

9 Yet you are he who took me out of the womb,*
   and kept me safe upon my mother's breast.

10 I have been entrusted to you ever since I was born;*
   you were my God
   when I was still in my mother's womb.

11 Be not far from me, for trouble is near,*
   and there is none to help.

12 Many young bulls encircle me;*
   strong bulls of Bashan surround me.

13 They open wide their jaws at me,*
   like a ravening and a roaring lion.

14 I am poured out like water;
   all my bones are out of joint;*
   my heart within my breast is melting wax.

15 My mouth is dried out like a pot-sherd;
   my tongue sticks to the roof of my mouth;*
   and you have laid me in the dust of the grave.

16 Packs of dogs close me in,
   and gangs of evildoers circle around me;*
   they pierce my hands and my feet;
   I can count all my bones.

17 They stare and gloat over me;*

they divide my garments among them;
they cast lots for my clothing.

18 Be not far away, O Lord;*
you are my strength; hasten to help me.

19 Save me from the sword,*
my life from the power of the dog.

20 Save me from the lion's mouth,*
my wretched body from the horns of wild bulls.

21 I will declare your name to my people;*
in the midst of the congregation I will praise you.

22 Praise the Lord, you that fear him;*
stand in awe of him, O offspring of Israel;
all you of Jacob's line, give glory.

23 For he does not despise nor abhor
the poor in their poverty;
neither does he hide his face from them;*
but when they cry to him he hears them.

24 My praise is of him in the great assembly;*
I will perform my vows
in the presence of those who worship him.

25 The poor shall eat and be satisfied,
and those who seek the Lord shall praise him:*
'May your heart live for ever!'

26 All the ends of the earth
shall remember and turn to the Lord,*
and all the families of the nations
shall bow before him.

27 For kingship belongs to the Lord;*
he rules over the nations.

28 To him alone all who sleep in the earth
bow down in worship;*
all who go down to the dust fall before him.

29 My soul shall live for him;
my descendants shall serve him;*
they shall be known as the Lord's for ever.

30 They shall come and make known to a people yet unborn*
the saving deeds that he has done.

Psalm 23

1 The Lord is my shepherd;*
I shall not be in want.

2 He makes me lie down in green pastures*
and leads me beside still waters.

A Celtic Primer

3   He revives my soul*
    and guides me along right pathways for his name's sake.
4   Though I walk through the valley of the shadow of death,
    I shall fear no evil;*
    for you are with me;
    your rod and your staff, they comfort me.
5   You spread a table before me
    in the presence of those who trouble me;*
    you have anointed my head with oil,
    and my cup is running over.
6   Surely your goodness and mercy shall follow me
    all the days of my life,*
    and I will dwell in the house of the Lord for ever.

Psalm 24

1   The earth is the Lord's and all that is in it,*
    the world and all who dwell therein.
2   For it is he who founded it upon the seas*
    and made it firm upon the rivers of the deep.
3   'Who can ascend the hill of the Lord?*
    and who can stand in his holy place?'
4   'Those who have clean hands and a pure heart,*
    who have not pledged themselves to falsehood,
    nor sworn by what is a fraud.
5   'They shall receive a blessing from the Lord*
    and a just reward from the God of their salvation.'
6   Such is the generation of those who seek him,*
    of those who seek your face, O God of Jacob.
7   Lift up your heads, O gates;
    lift them high, O everlasting doors;*
    and the King of glory shall come in.
8   'Who is this King of glory?'*
    'The Lord, strong and mighty,
    the Lord, mighty in battle.'
9   Lift up your heads, O gates;
    lift them high, O everlasting doors;*
    and the King of glory shall come in.
10 'Who is he, this King of glory?'*
    'The Lord of hosts,
    he is the King of glory.'

Psalm 25

1   To you, O Lord, I lift up my soul;
      my God, I put my trust in you;*
      let me not be humiliated,
      nor let my enemies triumph over me.

2   Let none who look to you be put to shame;*
      let the treacherous be disappointed in their schemes.

3   Show me your ways, O Lord,*
      and teach me your paths.

4   Lead me in your truth and teach me,*
      for you are the God of my salvation;
      in you have I trusted all the day long.

5   Remember, O Lord, your compassion and love,*
      for they are from everlasting.

6   Remember not the sins of my youth
      and my transgressions;*
      remember me according to your love
      and for the sake of your goodness, O Lord.

7   Gracious and upright is the Lord;*
      therefore he teaches sinners in his way.

8   He guides the humble in doing right*
      and teaches his way to the lowly.

9   All the paths of the Lord are love and faithfulness*
      to those who keep his covenant and his testimonies.

10   For your name's sake, O Lord,*
      forgive my sin, for it is great.

11   Who are they who fear the Lord?*
      he will teach them the way that they should choose.

12   They shall dwell in prosperity,*
      and their offspring shall inherit the land.

13   The Lord is a friend to those who fear him*
      and will show them his covenant.

14   My eyes are ever looking to the Lord,*
      for he shall pluck my feet out of the net.

15   Turn to me and have pity on me,*
      for I am left alone and in misery.

16   The sorrows of my heart have increased;*
      bring me out of my troubles.

17   Look upon my adversity and misery*
      and forgive me all my sin.

18   Look upon my enemies, for they are many,*
      and they bear a violent hatred against me.

19   Protect my life and deliver me;*

let me not be put to shame, for I have trusted in you.
20   Let integrity and uprightness preserve me,*
for my hope has been in you.
21   Deliver Israel, O God,*
out of all his troubles.

Psalm 26

1   Give judgement for me, O Lord,
for I have lived with integrity;*
I have trusted in the Lord and have not faltered.
2   Test me, O Lord, and try me;*
examine my heart and my mind.
3   For your love is before my eyes;*
I have walked faithfully with you.
4   I have not sat with the worthless,*
nor do I consort with the deceitful.
5   I have hated the company of evildoers;*
I will not sit down with the wicked.
6   I will wash my hands in innocence, O Lord,*
that I may go in procession round your altar,
7   Singing aloud a song of thanksgiving*
and recounting all your wonderful deeds.
8   Lord, I love the house in which you dwell*
and the place where your glory abides.
9   Do not sweep me away with sinners,*
nor my life with those who thirst for blood,
10   Whose hands are full of evil plots,*
and their right hand full of bribes.
11   As for me, I will live with integrity;*
redeem me, O Lord, and have pity on me.
12   My foot stands on level ground;*
in the full assembly I will bless the Lord.

Psalm 27

1   The Lord is my light and my salvation;
whom then shall I fear?*
the Lord is the strength of my life;
of whom then shall I be afraid?
2   When evildoers came upon me to eat up my flesh,*
it was they, my foes and my adversaries,
who stumbled and fell.
3   Though an army should encamp against me,*

yet my heart shall not be afraid;

4   And though war should rise up against me,*
     yet will I put my trust in him.

5   One thing have I asked of the Lord;
     one thing I seek;*
     that I may dwell in the house of the Lord
     all the days of my life;

6   To behold the fair beauty of the Lord*
     and to seek him in his temple.

7   For in the day of trouble
     he shall keep me safe in his shelter;*
     he shall hide me in the secrecy of his dwelling
     and set me high upon a rock.

8   Even now he lifts up my head*
     above my enemies round about me;

9   Therefore I will offer in his dwelling an oblation
     with sounds of great gladness;*
     I will sing and make music to the Lord.

10   Hearken to my voice, O Lord, when I call;*
     have mercy on me and answer me.

11   You speak in my heart and say, 'Seek my face.'*
     Your face, Lord, will I seek.

12   Hide not your face from me,*
     nor turn away your servant in displeasure.

13   You have been my helper;
     cast me not away;*
     do not forsake me, O God of my salvation.

14   Though my father and my mother forsake me,*
     the Lord will sustain me.

15   Show me your way, O Lord;*
     lead me on a level path, because of my enemies.

16   Deliver me not into the hand of my adversaries,*
     for false witnesses have risen up against me,
     and also those who speak malice.

17   What if I had not believed
     that I should see the goodness of the Lord*
     in the land of the living!

18   O tarry and await the Lord's pleasure;
     be strong and he shall comfort your heart;*
     wait patiently for the Lord.

Psalm 28

1   O Lord, I call to you;
    my rock, do not be deaf to my cry;*
    lest, if you do not hear me,
    I become like those who go down to the Pit.
2   Hear the voice of my prayer when I cry out to you,*
    when I lift up my hands to your holy of holies.
3   Do not snatch me away with the wicked
    or with the evildoers,*
    who speak peaceably with their neighbours,
    while strife is in their hearts.
4   Repay them according to their deeds,*
    and according to the wickedness of their actions.
5   According to the work of their hands repay them,*
    and give them their just deserts.
6   They have no understanding of the Lord's doings,
    nor of the works of his hands;*
    therefore he will break them down
    and not build them up.
7   Blessèd is the Lord!*
    for he has heard the voice of my prayer.
8   The Lord is my strength and my shield;*
    my heart trusts in him and I have been helped;
9   Therefore my heart dances for joy,*
    and in my song will I praise him.
10 The Lord is the strength of his people,*
    a safe refuge for his anointed.
11 Save your people and bless your inheritance;*
    shepherd them and carry them for ever.

Psalm 29

1   Ascribe to the Lord, you gods,*
    ascribe to the Lord glory and strength.
2   Ascribe to the Lord the glory due to his name;*
    worship the Lord in the beauty of holiness.
3   The voice of the Lord is upon the waters;
    the God of glory thunders;*
    the Lord is upon the mighty waters.
4   The voice of the Lord is a powerful voice;*
    the voice of the Lord is a voice of splendour.
5   The voice of the Lord breaks the cedar trees;*
    the Lord breaks the cedars of Lebanon;

6   He makes Lebanon skip like a calf,*
      and Mount Hermon like a young wild ox.

7   The voice of the Lord splits the flames of fire;
      the voice of the Lord shakes the wilderness;*
      the Lord shakes the wilderness of Kadesh.

8   The voice of the Lord makes the oak trees writhe*
      and strips the forests bare.

9   And in the temple of the Lord*
      all are crying, 'Glory!'

10   The Lord sits enthroned above the flood;*
      the Lord sits enthroned as king for evermore.

11   The Lord shall give strength to his people;*
      the Lord shall give his people the blessing of peace.

Psalm 30

1   I will exalt you, O Lord,
      because you have lifted me up*
      and have not let my enemies triumph over me.

2   O Lord my God, I cried out to you,*
      and you restored me to health.

3   You brought me up, O Lord, from the dead;*
      you restored my life as I was going down to the grave.

4   Sing to the Lord, you servants of his;*
      give thanks for the remembrance of his holiness.

5   For his wrath endures but the twinkling of an eye,*
      his favour for a lifetime.

6   Weeping may spend the night,*
      but joy comes in the morning.

7   While I felt secure, I said,
      'I shall never be disturbed.*
      You, Lord, with your favour,
      made me as strong as the mountains.'

8   Then you hid your face,*
      and I was filled with fear.

9   I cried to you, O Lord;*
      I pleaded with the Lord, saying,

10   'What profit is there in my blood,
      if I go down to the Pit?*
      will the dust praise you or declare your faithfulness?

11   'Hear, O Lord, and have mercy upon me;*
      O Lord, be my helper.'

12   You have turned my wailing into dancing;*
      you have put off my sack-cloth and clothed me with joy;

13   Therefore my heart sings to you without ceasing;*
     O Lord my God, I will give you thanks for ever.

Psalm 31

1   In you, O Lord, have I taken refuge;
     let me never be put to shame;*
     deliver me in your righteousness.
2   Incline your ear to me;*
     make haste to deliver me.
3   Be my strong rock, a castle to keep me safe,
     for you are my crag and my stronghold;*
     for the sake of your name, lead me and guide me.
4   Take me out of the net
     that they have secretly set for me,*
     for you are my tower of strength.
5   Into your hands I commend my spirit,*
     for you have redeemed me,
     O Lord, O God of truth.
6   I hate those who cling to worthless idols,*
     and I put my trust in the Lord.
7   I will rejoice and be glad because of your mercy;*
     for you have seen my affliction;
     you know my distress.
8   You have not shut me up in the power of the enemy;*
     you have set my feet in an open place.
9   Have mercy on me, O Lord, for I am in trouble;*
     my eye is consumed with sorrow,
     and also my throat and my belly.
10   For my life is wasted with grief,
     and my years with sighing;*
     my strength fails me because of affliction,
     and my bones are consumed.
11   I have become a reproach to all my enemies
     and even to my neighbours,
     a dismay to those of my acquaintance;*
     when they see me in the street they avoid me.
12   I am forgotten like the dead, out of mind;*
     I am as useless as a broken pot.
13   For I have heard the whispering of the crowd;
     fear is all around;*
     they put their heads together against me;
     they plot to take my life.
14   But as for me, I have trusted in you, O Lord.*

I have said, 'You are my God.

15 'My times are in your hand;*
rescue me from the hand of my enemies,
and from those who persecute me.

16 'Make your face to shine upon your servant,*
and in your loving-kindness save me.'

17 Lord, let me not be ashamed
for having called upon you;*
rather, let the wicked be put to shame;
let them be silent in the grave.

18 Let the lying lips be silenced
which speak against the righteous,*
haughtily, disdainfully and with contempt.

19 How great is your goodness, O Lord,
which you have laid up for those who fear you;*
which you have done in the sight of all
for those who put their trust in you.

20 You hide them in the covert of your presence
from those who slander them;*
you keep them in your shelter from the strife of tongues.

21 Blessèd be the Lord!*
for he has shown me the wonders of his love
in a besieged city.

22 Yet I said in my alarm,
'I have been cut off from the sight of your eyes.'*
Nevertheless, you heard the sound of my entreaty
when I cried out to you.

23 Love the Lord, all you who worship him;*
the Lord protects the faithful,
but repays to the full those who act haughtily.

24 Be strong and let your heart take courage,*
all you who wait for the Lord.

Psalm 32

1 Happy are they whose transgressions are forgiven,*
and whose sin is put away!

2 Happy are they to whom the Lord imputes no guilt,*
and in whose spirit there is no guile!

3 While I held my tongue, my bones withered away,*
because of my groaning all day long.

4 For your hand was heavy upon me day and night;*
my moisture was dried up as in the heat of summer.

5 Then I acknowledged my sin to you,*

and did not conceal my guilt.

6 I said, 'I will confess my transgressions to the Lord';*
   then you forgave me the guilt of my sin.

7 Therefore all the faithful will make their prayers to you
   in time of trouble;*
   when the great waters overflow, they shall not reach them.

8 You are my hiding-place;
   you preserve me from trouble;*
   you surround me with shouts of deliverance.

9 'I will instruct you and teach you
   in the way that you should go;*
   I will guide you with my eye.

10 'Do not be like horse or mule,
   which have no understanding;*
   who must be fitted with bit and bridle,
   or else they will not stay near you.'

11 Great are the tribulations of the wicked;*
   but mercy embraces those who trust in the Lord.

12 Be glad, you righteous, and rejoice in the Lord;*
   shout for joy, all who are true of heart.

Psalm 33

1 Rejoice in the Lord, you righteous;*
   it is good for the just to sing praises.

2 Praise the Lord with the harp;*
   play to him upon the psaltery and lyre.

3 Sing for him a new song;*
   sound a fanfare with all your skill upon the trumpet.

4 For the word of the Lord is right,*
   and all his works are sure.

5 He loves righteousness and justice;*
   the loving-kindness of the Lord fills the whole earth.

6 By the word of the Lord were the heavens made,*
   by the breath of his mouth all the heavenly hosts.

7 He gathers up the waters of the ocean
   as in a water-skin*
   and stores up the depths of the sea.

8 Let all the earth fear the Lord;*
   let all who dwell in the world stand in awe of him.

9 For he spoke and it came to pass;*
   he commanded and it stood fast.

10 The Lord brings the will of the nations to naught;*
   he thwarts the designs of the peoples.

11 But the Lord's will stands fast for ever,*
   and the designs of his heart from age to age.
12 Happy is the nation whose God is the Lord!*
   happy the people he has chosen to be his own!
13 The Lord looks down from heaven,*
   and beholds all the people in the world.
14 From where he sits enthroned he turns his gaze*
   on all who dwell on the earth.
15 He fashions all the hearts of them*
   and understands all their works.
16 There is no king that can be saved by a mighty army;*
   the strong are not delivered by great strength.
17 The horse is a vain hope for deliverance;*
   for all its strength it cannot save.
18 Behold, the eye of the Lord
   is upon those who fear him,*
   on those who wait upon his love,
19 To pluck their lives from death,*
   and to feed them in time of famine.
20 Our soul waits for the Lord;*
   he is our help and our shield.
21 Indeed, our heart rejoices in him,*
   for in his holy name we put our trust.
22 Let your loving-kindness, O Lord, be upon us,*
   as we have put our trust in you.

Psalm 34

1 I will bless the Lord at all times;*
   his praise shall ever be in my mouth.
2 I will glory in the Lord;*
   let the humble hear and rejoice.
3 Proclaim with me the greatness of the Lord;*
   let us exalt his name together.
4 I sought the Lord and he answered me*
   and delivered me out of all my terror.
5 Look upon him and be radiant,*
   and let not your faces be ashamed.
6 I called in my affliction and the Lord heard me*
   and saved me from all my troubles.
7 The angel of the Lord
   encompasses those who fear him,*
   and he will deliver them.
8 Taste and see that the Lord is good;*

happy are they who trust in him!

9   Fear the Lord, you that are his saints,*
for those who fear him lack nothing.

10   The young lions lack and suffer hunger,*
but those who seek the Lord
lack nothing that is good.

11   Come, children, and listen to me;*
I will teach you the fear of the Lord.

12   Who among you loves life*
and desires long life to enjoy prosperity?

13   Keep your tongue from evil-speaking*
and your lips from lying words.

14   Turn from evil and do good;*
seek peace and pursue it.

15   The eyes of the Lord are upon the righteous,*
and his ears are open to their cry.

16   The face of the Lord is against those who do evil,*
to root out the remembrance of them from the earth.

17   The righteous cry and the Lord hears them*
and delivers them from all their troubles.

18   The Lord is near to the brokenhearted*
and will save those whose spirits are crushed.

19   Many are the troubles of the righteous,*
but the Lord will deliver him out of them all.

20   He will keep safe all his bones;*
not one of them shall be broken.

21   Evil shall slay the wicked,*
and those who hate the righteous will be punished.

22   The Lord ransoms the life of his servants,*
and none will be punished who trust in him.

Psalm 35

1   Fight those who fight me, O Lord;*
attack those who are attacking me.

2   Take up shield and armour*
and rise up to help me.

3   Draw the sword and bar the way
against those who pursue me;*
say to my soul, 'I am your salvation.'

4   Let those who seek after my life be shamed and humbled;*
let those who plot my ruin fall back and be dismayed.

[5   Let them be like chaff before the wind,*
and let the angel of the Lord drive them away.

6   Let their way be dark and slippery,*
     and let the angel of the Lord pursue them.
7   For they have secretly spread a net for me without a cause;*
     without a cause they have dug a pit to take me alive.
8   Let ruin come upon them unawares;*
     let them be caught in the net they hid;
     let them fall into the pit they dug.]
9   Then I will be joyful in the Lord;*
     I will glory in his victory.
10   My very bones will say, 'Lord, who is like you?*
     You deliver the poor
     from those who are too strong for them,
     the poor and needy from those who rob them.'
11   Malicious witnesses rise up against me;*
     they charge me with matters I know nothing about.
12   They pay me evil in exchange for good;*
     my soul is full of despair.
13   But when they were sick I dressed in sack-cloth*
     and humbled myself by fasting;
14   I prayed with my whole heart,
     as one would for a friend or a brother;*
     I behaved like one who mourns for his mother,
     bowed down and grieving.
15   But when I stumbled,
     they were glad and gathered together;
     they gathered against me;*
     strangers whom I did not know
     tore me to pieces and would not stop.
16   They put me to the test and mocked me;*
     they gnashed at me with their teeth.
17   O Lord, how long will you look on?*
     rescue me from the roaring beasts,
     and my life from the young lions.
18   I will give you thanks in the great congregation;*
     I will praise you in the mighty throng.
19   Do not let my treacherous foes rejoice over me,*
     nor let those who hate me without a cause
     wink at each other.
20   For they do not plan for peace,*
     but invent deceitful schemes
     against the quiet in the land.
21   They opened their mouths at me and said,*
     'Aha! we saw it with our own eyes.'
22   You saw it, O Lord; do not be silent;*

A Celtic Primer

O Lord, be not far from me.

23 Awake, arise, to my cause!*
to my defence, my God and my Lord!

24 Give me justice, O Lord my God,
according to your righteousness;*
do not let them triumph over me.

25 Do not let them say in their hearts,
'Aha! just what we want!'*
Do not let them say, 'We have swallowed him up.'

26 Let all who rejoice at my ruin be ashamed and disgraced;*
let those who boast against me
be clothed with dismay and shame.

27 Let those who favour my cause
sing out with joy and be glad;*
let them say always, 'Great is the Lord,
who desires the prosperity of his servant.'

28 And my tongue shall be talking of your righteousness*
and of your praise all the day long.

Psalm 36

1 There is a voice of rebellion deep in the heart of the wicked;*
there is no fear of God before their eyes.

2 They flatter themselves in their own eyes*
that their hateful sin will not be found out.

3 The words of their mouths are wicked and deceitful;*
they have left off acting wisely and doing good.

4 They think up wickedness upon their beds
and have set themselves in no good way;*
they do not abhor that which is evil.

5 Your love, O Lord, reaches to the heavens,*
and your faithfulness to the clouds.

6 Your righteousness is like the strong mountains,
your justice like the great deep;*
you save both human and beast, O Lord.

7 How priceless is your love, O God!*
your people take refuge under the shadow of your wings.

8 They feast upon the abundance of your house;*
you give them drink from the river of your delights.

9 For with you is the well of life,*
and in your light we see light.

10 Continue your loving-kindness to those who know you,*
and your favour to those who are true of heart.

11 Let not the foot of the proud come near me,*

nor the hand of the wicked push me aside.

12   See how they are fallen, those who work wickedness!*
they are cast down and shall not be able to rise.

Psalm 37, Part I

1   Do not fret yourself because of evildoers;*
do not be jealous of those who do wrong.

2   For they shall soon wither like the grass,*
and like the green grass fade away.

3   Put your trust in the Lord and do good;*
dwell in the land and feed on its riches.

4   Take delight in the Lord,*
and he shall give you your heart's desire.

5   Commit your way to the Lord
and put your trust in him,*
and he will bring it to pass.

6   He will make your righteousness as clear as the light*
and your just dealing as the noonday.

7   Be still before the Lord*
and wait patiently for him.

8   Do not fret yourself over the one who prospers,*
the one who succeeds in evil schemes.

9   Refrain from anger, leave rage alone;*
do not fret yourself; it leads only to evil.

10   For evildoers shall be cut off,*
but those who wait upon the Lord
shall possess the land.

11   In a little while the wicked shall be no more;*
you shall search out their place,
but they will not be there.

12   But the lowly shall possess the land;*
they will delight in abundance of peace.

13   The wicked plot against the righteous*
and gnash at them with their teeth.

14   The Lord laughs at the wicked,*
because he sees that their day will come.

15   The wicked draw their sword and bend their bow
to strike down the poor and needy,*
to slaughter those who are upright in their ways.

16   Their sword shall go through their own heart,*
and their bow shall be broken.

17   The little that the righteous have*
is better than great riches of the wicked.

A Celtic Primer

18   For the power of the wicked shall be broken,*
       but the Lord upholds the righteous.

Psalm 37, Part II

19   The Lord cares for the lives of the godly,*
       and their inheritance shall last for ever.

20   They shall not be ashamed in bad times,*
       and in days of famine they shall have enough.

21   As for the wicked, they shall perish,*
       and the enemies of the Lord,
       like the glory of the meadows, shall vanish;
       they shall vanish like smoke.

22   The wicked borrow and do not repay,*
       but the righteous are generous in giving.

23   Those who are blessed by God shall possess the land,*
       but those who are cursed by him shall be destroyed.

24   Our steps are directed by the Lord;*
       he strengthens those in whose way he delights.

25   If they stumble, they shall not fall headlong,*
       for the Lord holds them by the hand.

26   I have been young and now I am old,*
       but never have I seen the righteous forsaken,
       or their children begging bread.

27   The righteous are always generous in their lending,*
       and their children shall be a blessing.

28   Turn from evil and do good,*
       and dwell in the land for ever.

29   For the Lord loves justice;*
       he does not forsake his faithful ones.

30   They shall be kept safe for ever,*
       but the offspring of the wicked shall be destroyed.

31   The righteous shall possess the land*
       and dwell in it for ever.

32   The mouth of the righteous utters wisdom,*
       and their tongue speaks what is right.

33   The law of their God is in their heart,*
       and their footsteps shall not falter.

34   The wicked spy on the righteous*
       and seek occasion to kill them.

35   The Lord will not abandon them to their hand,*
       nor let them be found guilty when brought to trial.

36   Wait upon the Lord and keep his way;*
       he will raise you up to possess the land,

and when the wicked are cut off, you will see it.

37 I have seen the wicked in their arrogance,*
 flourishing like a tree in full leaf.
38 I went by and, behold, they were not there;*
 I searched for them, but they could not be found.
39 Mark those who are honest; observe the upright;*
 for there is a future for the peaceable.
40 Transgressors shall be destroyed, one and all;*
 the future of the wicked is cut off.
41 But the deliverance of the righteous
 comes from the Lord;*
 he is their stronghold in time of trouble.
42 The Lord will help them and rescue them;*
 he will rescue them from the wicked and deliver them,
 because they seek refuge in him.

PSALMS 38–54

Psalm 38

1 O Lord, do not rebuke me in your anger;*
 do not punish me in your wrath.
2 For your arrows have already pierced me,*
 and your hand presses hard upon me.
3 There is no health in my flesh,
 because of your indignation;*
 there is no soundness in my body, because of my sin.
4 For my iniquities overwhelm me;*
 like a heavy burden they are too much for me to bear.
5 My wounds stink and fester*
 by reason of my foolishness.
6 I am utterly bowed down and prostrate;*
 I go about in mourning all the day long.
7 My loins are filled with searing pain;*
 there is no health in my body.
8 I am utterly numb and crushed;*
 I wail, because of the groaning of my heart.
9 O Lord, you know all my desires,*
 and my sighing is not hidden from you.
10 My heart is pounding, my strength has failed me,*
 and the brightness of my eyes is gone from me.
11 My friends and companions draw back from my affliction;*
 my neighbours stand afar off.

12 Those who seek after my life lay snares for me;*
   those who strive to hurt me speak of my ruin
   and plot treachery all the day long.
13 But I am like the deaf who do not hear,*
   like those who are mute and do not open their mouth.
14 I have become like one who does not hear*
   and from whose mouth comes no defence.
15 For in you, O Lord, have I fixed my hope;*
   you will answer me, O Lord my God.
16 For I said, 'Do not let them rejoice at my expense,*
   those who gloat over me when my foot slips.'
17 Truly, I am on the verge of falling,*
   and my pain is always with me.
18 I will confess my iniquity*
   and be sorry for my sin.
19 Those who are my enemies without cause are mighty,*
   and many in number are those who wrongfully hate me.
20 Those who repay evil for good slander me,*
   because I follow the course that is right.
21 O Lord, do not forsake me;*
   be not far from me, O my God.
22 Make haste to help me,*
   O Lord of my salvation.

Psalm 39

1 I said, 'I will keep watch upon my ways,*
  so that I do not offend with my tongue.
2 'I will put a muzzle on my mouth*
  while the wicked are in my presence.'
3 So I held my tongue and said nothing;*
  I refrained from rash words;
  but my pain became unbearable.
4 My heart was hot within me;
  while I pondered, the fire burst into flame;*
  I spoke out with my tongue:
5 Lord, let me know my end and the number of my days,*
  so that I may know how short my life is.
6 You have given me a mere handful of days,
  and my lifetime is as nothing in your sight;*
  truly, even those who stand erect are but a puff of wind.
7 We walk about like a shadow
  and in vain we are in turmoil;*
  we heap up riches and cannot tell who will gather them.

8   And now, what is my hope?*
     O Lord, my hope is in you.
9   Deliver me from all my transgressions*
     and do not make me the taunt of the fool.
10   I fell silent and did not open my mouth,*
     for surely it was you that did it.
11   Take your affliction from me;*
     I am worn down by the blows of your hand.
12   With rebukes for sin you punish us;
     like a moth you eat away all that is dear to us;*
     truly, everyone is but a puff of wind.
13   Hear my prayer, O Lord, and give ear to my cry;*
     hold not your peace at my tears.
14   For I am but a sojourner with you,*
     a wayfarer, as all my forebears were.
15   Turn your gaze from me, that I may be glad again,*
     before I go my way and am no more.

Psalm 40

1   I waited patiently upon the Lord;*
     he stooped to me and heard my cry.
2   He lifted me out of the desolate pit,
     out of the mire and clay;*
     he set my feet upon a high cliff and made my footing sure.
3   He put a new song in my mouth,
     a song of praise to our God;*
     many shall see and stand in awe
     and put their trust in the Lord.
4   Happy are they who trust in the Lord!*
     they do not resort to evil spirits or turn to false gods.
5   Great things are they that you have done, O Lord my God!
     how great your wonders and your plans for us!*
     there is none who can be compared with you.
6   O that I could make them known and tell them!*
     but they are more than I can count.
7   In sacrifice and offering you take no pleasure*
     you have given me ears to hear you;
8   Burnt-offering and sin-offering you have not required,*
     and so I said, 'Behold, I come.
9   'In the roll of the book it is written concerning me:*
     "I love to do your will, O my God; your law is deep in my heart."'
10   I proclaimed righteousness in the great congregation;*
     behold, I did not restrain my lips; and that, O Lord, you know.

11   Your righteousness have I not hidden in my heart;
          I have spoken of your faithfulness and your deliverance;*
          I have not concealed your love and faithfulness
          from the great congregation.

12   You are the Lord;
          do not withhold your compassion from me;*
          let your love and your faithfulness keep me safe for ever,

13   For innumerable troubles have crowded upon me;
          my sins have overtaken me and I cannot see;*
          they are more in number than the hairs of my head,
          and my heart fails me.

14   Be pleased, O Lord, to deliver me;*
          O Lord, make haste to help me.

15   Let them be ashamed and altogether dismayed
          who seek after my life to destroy it;*
          let them draw back and be disgraced
          who take pleasure in my misfortune.

16   Let those who say 'Aha!' and gloat over me be confounded,*
          because they are ashamed.

17   Let all who seek you rejoice in you and be glad;*
          let those who love your salvation continually say,
          'Great is the Lord!'

18   Though I am poor and afflicted,*
          the Lord will have regard for me.

19   You are my helper and my deliverer;*
          do not tarry, O my God.

Psalm 41

1   Happy are they who consider the poor and needy!*
          the Lord will deliver them in the time of trouble.

2   The Lord preserves them and keeps them alive,
          so that they may be happy in the land;*
          he does not hand them over to the will of their enemies.

3   The Lord sustains them on their sick-bed*
          and ministers to them in their illness.

4   I said, 'Lord, be merciful to me;*
          heal me, for I have sinned against you.'

5   My enemies are saying wicked things about me:*
          'When will he die and his name perish?'

6   Even if they come to see me, they speak empty words;*
          their heart collects false rumours;
          they go outside and spread them.

7   All my enemies whisper together about me*

and devise evil against me.

8   'A deadly thing', they say, 'has fastened on him;*
    he has taken to his bed and will never get up again.'

9   Even my best friend, whom I trusted,
    who broke bread with me,*
    has lifted up his heel and turned against me.

10 But you, O Lord, be merciful to me and raise me up,*
    and I shall repay them.

11 By this I know you are pleased with me,*
    that my enemy does not triumph over me.

12 In my integrity you hold me fast,*
    and shall set me before your face for ever.

13 Blessèd be the Lord God of Israel,*
    from age to age. Amen. Amen.

Psalm 42

1   As the deer longs for the water-brooks,*
    so longs my soul for you, O God.

2   My soul is athirst for God, athirst for the living God;*
    when shall I come to appear before the presence of God?

3   My tears have been my food day and night,*
    while all day long they say to me,
    'Where now is your God?'

4   I pour out my soul when I think on these things:*
    how I went with the multitude
    and led them into the house of God,

5   With the voice of praise and thanksgiving,*
    among those who keep holy-day.

6   Why are you so full of heaviness, O my soul?*
    and why are you so disquieted within me?

7   Put your trust in God;*
    for I will yet give thanks to him,
    who is the help of my countenance, and my God.

8   My soul is heavy within me;*
    therefore I will remember you from the land of Jordan,
    and from the peak of Mizar among the heights of Hermon.

9   One deep calls to another in the noise of your cataracts;*
    all your rapids and floods have gone over me.

10 The Lord grants his loving-kindness in the daytime;*
    in the night season his song is with me,
    a prayer to the God of my life.

11 I will say to the God of my strength,
    'Why have you forgotten me?*

and why do I go so heavily
while the enemy oppresses me?'
12 While my bones are being broken,*
my enemies mock me to my face;
13 All day long they mock me*
say to me, 'Where now is your God?'
14 Why are you so full of heaviness, O my soul?*
and why are you so disquieted within me?
15 Put your trust in God;*
for I will yet give thanks to him,
who is the help of my countenance, and my God.

If desired, Psalms 42 and 43 may be said as one psalm.

Psalm 43

1 Give judgement for me, O God,
and defend my cause against an ungodly people;*
deliver me from the deceitful and the wicked.
2 For you are the God of my strength;
why have you put me from you?*
and why do I go so heavily
while the enemy oppresses me?
3 Send out your light and your truth,
that they may lead me,*
and bring me to your holy hill
and to your dwelling;
4 That I may go to the altar of God,
to the God of my joy and gladness;*
and on the harp I will give thanks to you,
O God my God.
5 Why are you so full of heaviness, O my soul?*
and why are you so disquieted within me?
6 Put your trust in God;*
for I will yet give thanks to him,
who is the help of my countenance, and my God.

Psalm 44

1 We have heard with our ears, O God,
our forebears have told us,*
the deeds you did in their days,
in the days of old.
2 How with your hand you drove the peoples out

and planted our forebears in the land;*
how you destroyed nations and made your people flourish.

3   For they did not take the land by their sword,
nor did their arm win the victory for them;*
but your right hand, your arm,
and the light of your countenance,
because you favoured them.

4   You are my King and my God;*
you command victories for Jacob.

5   Through you we pushed back our adversaries;*
through your name we trampled on those
who rose up against us.

6   For I do not rely on my bow,*
and my sword does not give me the victory.

7   Surely, you gave us victory over our adversaries*
and put those who hate us to shame.

8   Every day we gloried in God,*
and we will praise your name for ever.

9   Nevertheless, you have rejected and humbled us*
and do not go forth with our armies.

10   You have made us fall back before our adversary,*
and our enemies have plundered us.

11   You have made us like sheep to be eaten*
and have scattered us among the nations.

12   You are selling your people for a trifle*
and are making no profit on the sale of them.

13   You have made us the scorn of our neighbours,*
a mockery and derision to those around us.

14   You have made us a byword among the nations,*
a laughing-stock among the peoples.

15   My humiliation is daily before me,*
and shame has covered my face;

16   Because of the taunts of the mockers and blasphemers,*
because of the enemy and avenger.

17   All this has come upon us;*
yet we have not forgotten you,
nor have we betrayed your covenant.

18   Our heart never turned back,*
nor did our footsteps stray from your path;

19   Though you thrust us down into a place of misery,*
and covered us over with deep darkness.

20   If we have forgotten the name of our God,*
or stretched out our hands to some strange god,

21   Will not God find it out?*

for he knows the secrets of the heart.

22 Indeed, for your sake we are killed all the day long;*
we are accounted as sheep for the slaughter.

23 Awake, O Lord! why are you sleeping?*
Arise! do not reject us for ever.

24 Why have you hidden your face*
and forgotten our affliction and oppression?

25 We sink down into the dust;*
our body cleaves to the ground.

26 Rise up and help us,*
and save us for the sake of your steadfast love.

Psalm 45

1 My heart is stirring with a noble song;
let me recite what I have fashioned for the king;*
my tongue shall be the pen of a skilled writer.

2 You are the fairest of men;*
grace flows from your lips,
because God has blessed you for ever.

3 Strap your sword upon your thigh, O mighty warrior,*
in your pride and in your majesty.

4 Ride out and conquer in the cause of truth*
and for the sake of justice.

5 Your right hand will show you marvellous things;*
your arrows are very sharp, O mighty warrior.

6 The peoples are falling at your feet,*
and the king's enemies are losing heart.

7 Your throne, O God, endures for ever and ever,*
a sceptre of righteousness is the sceptre of your kingdom;
you love righteousness and hate iniquity;

8 Therefore God, your God, has anointed you*
with the oil of gladness above your fellows.

9 All your garments are fragrant with myrrh, aloes and cassia,*
and the music of strings from ivory palaces makes you glad.

10 Kings' daughters stand among the ladies of the court;*
on your right hand is the queen,
adorned with the gold of Ophir.

11 'Hear, O daughter; consider and listen closely;*
forget your people and your family's house.

12 'The king will have pleasure in your beauty;*
he is your master; therefore do him honour.

13 'The people of Tyre are here with a gift;*
the rich among the people seek your favour.'

14   All glorious is the princess as she enters;*
      her gown is cloth-of-gold.
15   In embroidered apparel she is brought to the king;*
      after her the bridesmaids follow in procession.
16   With joy and gladness they are brought,*
      and enter into the palace of the king.
17   'In place of fathers, O king, you shall have sons;*
      you shall make them princes over all the earth.
18   'I will make your name to be remembered
      from one generation to another;*
      therefore nations will praise you for ever and ever.'

Psalm 46

1   God is our refuge and strength,*
      a very present help in trouble;
2   Therefore we will not fear, though the earth be moved,*
      and though the mountains be toppled
      into the depths of the sea;
3   Though its waters rage and foam,*
      and though the mountains tremble at its tumult.
4   The Lord of hosts is with us;*
      the God of Jacob is our stronghold.
5   There is a river whose streams
      make glad the city of God,*
      the holy habitation of the Most High.
6   God is in the midst of her;
      she shall not be overthrown;*
      God shall help her at the break of day.
7   The nations make much ado
      and the kingdoms are shaken;*
      God has spoken and the earth shall melt away.
8   The Lord of hosts is with us;*
      the God of Jacob is our stronghold.
9   Come now and look upon the works of the Lord,*
      what awesome things he has done on earth.
10   It is he who makes war to cease in all the world;*
      he breaks the bow and shatters the spear
      and burns the shields with fire.
11   'Be still, then, and know that I am God;*
      I will be exalted among the nations;
      I will be exalted in the earth.'
12   The Lord of hosts is with us;*
      the God of Jacob is our stronghold.

Psalm 47

1   Clap your hands, all you peoples;*
    shout to God with a cry of joy.
2   For the Lord Most High is to be feared;*
    he is the great king over all the earth.
3   He subdues the peoples under us,*
    and the nations under our feet.
4   He chooses our inheritance for us,*
    the pride of Jacob whom he loves.
5   God has gone up with a shout,*
    the Lord with the sound of the ram's-horn.
6   Sing praises to God, sing praises;*
    sing praises to our king, sing praises.
7   For God is king of all the earth;*
    sing praises with all your skill.
8   God reigns over the nations;*
    God sits upon his holy throne.
9   The nobles of the peoples have gathered together*
    with the people of the God of Abraham.
10 The rulers of the earth belong to God,*
    and he is highly exalted.

Psalm 48

1   Great is the Lord and highly to be praised;*
    in the city of our God is his holy hill.
2   Beautiful and lofty, the joy of all the earth,
    is the hill of Zion,*
    the very centre of the world
    and the city of the great king.
3   God is in her citadels;*
    he is known to be her sure refuge.
4   Behold, the kings of the earth assembled*
    and marched forward together.
5   They looked and were astounded;*
    they retreated and fled in terror.
6   Trembling seized them there;*
    they writhed like a woman in childbirth,
    like ships of the sea when the east wind shatters them.
7   As we have heard, so have we seen,
    in the city of the Lord of hosts, in the city of our God;*
    God has established her for ever.
8   We have waited in silence

on your loving-kindness, O God,*
in the midst of your temple.

9   Your praise, like your name, O God,
reaches to the world's end;*
your right hand is full of justice.

10   Let Mount Zion be glad
and the cities of Judah rejoice,*
because of your judgements.

11   Make the circuit of Zion; walk round about her;*
count the number of her towers.

12   Consider well her bulwarks; examine her strongholds;*
that you may tell those who come after.

13   This God is our God for ever and ever;*
he shall be our guide for evermore.

Psalm 49

1   Hear this, all you peoples;
hearken, all you who dwell in the world,*
you of high degree and low, rich and poor together.

2   My mouth shall speak of wisdom,*
and my heart shall meditate on understanding.

3   I will incline my ear to a proverb*
and set forth my riddle upon the harp.

4   Why should I be afraid in evil days,*
when the wickedness of those at my heels surrounds me,

5   The wickedness of those
who put their trust in their goods,*
and boast of their great riches?

6   We can never ransom ourselves,*
or deliver to God the price of our life;

7   For the ransom of our life is so great,*
that we should never have enough to pay it,

8   In order to live for ever and ever,*
and never see the grave.

9   For we see that the wise die also;
like the dull and stupid they perish*
and leave their wealth to those who come after them.

10   Their graves shall be their homes for ever,
their dwelling places from generation to generation,*
though they call the lands after their own names.

11   Even though honoured, they cannot live for ever;*
they are like the beasts that perish.

12   Such is the way of those

A Celtic Primer

who foolishly trust in themselves,*
and the end of those who delight in their own words.

13 Like a flock of sheep they are destined to die;
Death is their shepherd;*
they go down straightway to the grave.

14 Their form shall waste away,*
and the land of the dead shall be their home.

15 But God will ransom my life;*
he will snatch me from the grasp of death.

16 Do not be envious when some become rich,*
or when the grandeur of their house increases;

17 For they will carry nothing away at their death,*
nor will their grandeur follow them.

18 Though they thought highly of themselves
while they lived,*
and were praised for their success,

19 They shall join the company of their forebears,*
who will never see the light again.

20 Those who are honoured, but have no understanding,*
are like the beasts that perish.

Psalm 50

1 The Lord, the God of gods, has spoken;*
he has called the earth
from the rising of the sun to its setting.

2 Out of Zion, perfect in its beauty,*
God reveals himself in glory.

3 Our God will come and will not keep silence;*
before him there is a consuming flame,
and round about him a raging storm.

4 He calls the heavens and the earth from above*
to witness the judgement of his people.

5 'Gather before me my loyal followers,*
those who have made a covenant with me
and sealed it with sacrifice.'

6 Let the heavens declare the rightness of his cause;*
for God himself is judge.

7 Hear, O my people, and I will speak:
'O Israel, I will bear witness against you;*
for I am God, your God.

8 'I do not accuse you because of your sacrifices;*
your offerings are always before me.

9 'I will take no bull-calf from your stalls,*

nor he-goats out of your pens;
10 'For the beasts of the forest are mine,*
the herds in their thousands upon the hills.
11 'I know every bird in the sky,*
and the creatures of the fields are in my sight.
12 'If I were hungry, I would not tell you,*
for the whole world is mine and all that is in it.
13 'Do you think I eat the flesh of bulls,*
or drink the blood of goats?
14 'Offer to God a sacrifice of thanksgiving*
and make good your vows to the Most High.
15 'Call upon me in the day of trouble;*
I will deliver you and you shall honour me.'
16 But to the wicked God says:*
'Why do you recite my statutes,
and take my covenant upon your lips;
17 'Since you refuse discipline,*
and toss my words behind your back?
18 'When you see a thief, you make him your friend,*
and you cast in your lot with adulterers.
19 'You have loosed your lips for evil,*
and harnessed your tongue to a lie.
20 'You are always speaking evil of your brother*
and slandering your own mother's son.
21 'These things you have done and I kept still,*
and you thought that I am like you.
22 'I have made my accusation;*
I have put my case in order before your eyes.
23 'Consider this well, you who forget God,*
lest I rend you and there be none to deliver you.
24 'Whoever offers me the sacrifice of thanksgiving
honours me;*
but to those who keep in my way
will I show the salvation of God.'

Psalm 51

1 Have mercy on me, O God,
according to your loving-kindness;*
in your great compassion blot out my offences.
2 Wash me through and through from my wickedness*
and cleanse me from my sin.
3 For I know my transgressions,*
and my sin is ever before me.

4 Against you only have I sinned*
   and done what is evil in your sight.
5 And so you are justified when you speak*
   and upright in your judgement.
6 Indeed, I have been wicked from my birth,*
   a sinner from my mother's womb.
7 For behold, you look for truth deep within me,*
   and will make me understand wisdom secretly.
8 Purge me from my sin and I shall be pure;*
   wash me and I shall be clean indeed.
9 Make me hear of joy and gladness,*
   that the body you have broken may rejoice.
10 Hide your face from my sins*
   and blot out all my iniquities.
11 Create in me a clean heart, O God,*
   and renew a right spirit within me.
12 Cast me not away from your presence*
   and take not your holy Spirit from me.
13 Give me the joy of your saving help again*
   and sustain me with your bountiful Spirit.
14 I shall teach your ways to the wicked,*
   and sinners shall return to you.
15 Deliver me from death, O God,*
   and my tongue shall sing of your righteousness,
   O God of my salvation.
16 Open my lips, O Lord,*
   and my mouth shall proclaim your praise.
17 Had you desired it, I would have offered sacrifice,*
   but you take no delight in burnt-offerings.
18 The sacrifice of God is a troubled spirit;*
   a broken and contrite heart, O God, you will not despise.
19 Be favourable and gracious to Zion,*
   and rebuild the walls of Jerusalem.
20 Then you will be pleased with the appointed sacrifices,
   with burnt-offerings and oblations;*
   then shall they offer young bullocks upon your altar.

Psalm 52

1 You tyrant, why do you boast of wickedness*
   against the godly all day long?
2 You plot ruin; your tongue is like a sharpened razor,*
   O worker of deception.
3 You love evil more than good*

The Psalter, including Psalm Themes for Prayer

and lying more than speaking the truth.

4 You love all words that hurt,*
O you deceitful tongue.

[5 O that God would demolish you utterly,*
topple you and snatch you from your dwelling
and root you out of the land of the living!]

6 The righteous shall see and tremble,*
and they shall laugh, saying,

7 'This is the one who did not take God for a refuge,*
but trusted in great wealth and relied upon wickedness.'

8 But I am like a green olive tree in the house of God;*
I trust in the mercy of God for ever and ever.

9 I will give you thanks for what you have done*
and declare the goodness of your name
in the presence of the godly.

Psalm 53

1 The fool has said in his heart, 'There is no God.'*
All are corrupt and commit abominable acts;
there is none who does any good.

2 God looks down from heaven upon us all,*
to see if there is any who is wise,
if there is one who seeks after God.

3 Every one has proved faithless;
all alike have turned bad;*
there is none who does good; no, not one.

4 Have they no knowledge, those evildoers*
who eat up my people like bread
and do not call upon God?

5 See how greatly they tremble,
such trembling as never was;*
for God has scattered the bones of the enemy;
they are put to shame, because God has rejected them.

6 O that Israel's deliverance would come out of Zion!*
when God restores the fortunes of his people
Jacob will rejoice and Israel be glad.

Psalm 54

1 Save me, O God, by your name;*
in your might, defend my cause.

2 Hear my prayer, O God;*
give ear to the words of my mouth.

A Celtic Primer

3   For the arrogant have risen up against me,
    and the ruthless have sought my life,*
    those who have no regard for God.
4   Behold, God is my helper;*
    it is the Lord who sustains my life.
5   Render evil to those who spy on me;*
    in your faithfulness, destroy them.
6   I will offer you a freewill sacrifice*
    and praise your name, O Lord, for it is good.
7   For you have rescued me from every trouble,*
    and my eye has seen the ruin of my foes.

Psalms 55–71

Psalm 55

1   Hear my prayer, O God;*
    do not hide yourself from my petition.
2   Listen to me and answer me;*
    I have no peace, because of my cares.
3   I am shaken by the noise of the enemy*
    and by the pressure of the wicked;
4   For they have cast an evil spell upon me*
    and are set against me in fury.
5   My heart quakes within me,*
    and the terrors of death have fallen upon me.
6   Fear and trembling have come over me,*
    and horror overwhelms me.
7   And I said, 'O that I had wings like a dove!*
    I would fly away and be at rest.
8   'I would flee to a far-off place*
    and make my lodging in the wilderness.
9   'I would hasten to escape*
    from the stormy wind and tempest.'
10 Swallow them up, O Lord; confound their speech;*
    for I have seen violence and strife in the city.
11 Day and night the watch make their rounds   upon her walls,*
    but trouble and misery are in the midst of her.
12 There is corruption at her heart;*
    her streets are never free of oppression and deceit.
13 For had it been an adversary who taunted me,
    then I could have borne it;*
    or had it been an enemy who vaunted himself against me,

then I could have hidden from him.

14 But it was you, one after my own heart,*
my companion, my own familiar friend.

15 We took sweet counsel together,*
and walked with the throng in the house of God.

[16 Let death come upon them suddenly;
let them go down alive into the grave;*
for wickedness is in their dwellings, in their very midst.]

17 But I will call upon God,*
and the Lord will deliver me.

18 In the evening, in the morning and at noonday
I will complain and lament,*
and he will hear my voice.

19 He will bring me safely back from the battle
waged against me;*
for there are many who fight me.

20 God, who is enthroned of old,
will hear me and bring them down;*
they never change; they do not fear God.

21 My companion stretched forth his hand against his comrade;*
he has broken his covenant.

22 His speech is softer than butter,*
but war is in his heart.

23 His words are smoother than oil,*
but they are drawn swords.

24 Cast your burden upon the Lord and he will sustain you;*
he will never let the righteous stumble.

25 For you will bring the bloodthirsty and deceitful*
down to the pit of destruction, O God.

26 They shall not live out half their days,*
but I will put my trust in you.

Psalm 56

1 Have mercy on me, O God,
for my enemies are hounding me;*
all day long they assault and oppress me.

2 They hound me all the day long;*
truly there are many who fight against me, O Most High.

3 Whenever I am afraid,*
I will put my trust in you.

4 In God, whose word I praise,
in God I trust and will not be afraid,*
for what can flesh do to me?

5   All day long they damage my cause;*
     their only thought is to do me evil.

6   They band together; they lie in wait;*
     they spy upon my footsteps; because they seek my life.

7   Shall they escape despite their wickedness?*
     O God, in your anger, cast down the peoples.

8   You have noted my lamentation;
     put my tears into your bottle;*
     are they not recorded in your book?

9   Whenever I call upon you,
     my enemies will be put to flight;*
     this I know, for God is on my side.

10   In God the Lord, whose word I praise,
     in God I trust and will not be afraid,*
     for what can mortals do to me?

11   I am bound by the vow I made to you, O God;*
     I will present to you thank-offerings;

12   For you have rescued my soul from death
     and my feet from stumbling,*
     that I may walk before God in the light of the living.

Psalm 57

1   Be merciful to me, O God, be merciful,
     for I have taken refuge in you;*
     in the shadow of your wings will I take refuge
     until this time of trouble has gone by.

2   I will call upon the Most High God,*
     the God who maintains my cause.

3   He will send from heaven and save me;
     he will confound those who trample upon me;*
     God will send forth his love and his faithfulness.

4   I lie in the midst of lions that devour the people;*
     their teeth are spears and arrows,
     their tongue a sharp sword.

5   They have laid a net for my feet and I am bowed low;*
     they have dug a pit before me
     but have fallen into it themselves.

6   Exalt yourself above the heavens, O God,*
     and your glory over all the earth.

7   My heart is firmly fixed, O God, my heart is fixed;*
     I will sing and make melody.

8   Wake up, my spirit; awake, lute and harp;*
     I myself will waken the dawn.

9   I will confess you among the peoples, O Lord;*
      I will sing praise to you among the nations.

10   For your loving-kindness is greater than the heavens,*
      and your faithfulness reaches to the clouds.

11   Exalt yourself above the heavens, O God,*
      and your glory over all the earth.

Psalm 58

[1   Do you indeed decree righteousness, you rulers?*
      do you judge the peoples with equity?

2   No; you devise evil in your hearts,*
      and your hands deal out violence in the land.

3   The wicked are perverse from the womb;*
      liars go astray from their birth.

4   They are as venomous as a serpent,*
      they are like the deaf adder which stops its ears,

5   Which does not heed the voice of the charmer,*
      no matter how skilful his charming.

6   O God, break their teeth in their mouths;*
      pull the fangs of the young lions, O Lord.

7   Let them vanish like water that runs off;*
      let them wither like trodden grass.

8   Let them be like the snail that melts away,*
      like a stillborn child that never sees the sun.

9   Before they bear fruit, let them be cut down like a brier;*
      like thorns and thistles let them be swept away.

10   The righteous will be glad when they see the vengeance;*
      they will bathe their feet in the blood of the wicked.

11   And they will say,
      'Surely, there is a reward for the righteous;*
      surely, there is a God who rules in the earth.']

Psalm 59

1   Rescue me from my enemies, O God;*
      protect me from those who rise up against me.

2   Rescue me from evildoers*
      and save me from those who thirst for my blood.

3   See how they lie in wait for my life,
      how the mighty gather together against me;*
      not for any offence or fault of mine, O Lord.

4   Not because of any guilt of mine*
      they run and prepare themselves for battle.

A Celtic Primer

5   Rouse yourself, come to my side and see;*
     for you, Lord God of hosts, are Israel's God.
[6   Awake, and punish all the ungodly;*
     show no mercy to those who are faithless and evil.]
7   The ungodly go to and fro in the evening;*
     they snarl like dogs and run about the city.
8   Behold, they boast with their mouths,
     and taunts are on their lips;*
     'For who', they say, 'will hear us?'
9   But you, O Lord, you laugh at them;*
     you laugh all the ungodly to scorn.
10   My eyes are fixed on you, O my Strength;*
     for you, O God, are my stronghold.
11   My merciful God comes to meet me;*
     God will let me look in triumph on my enemies.
12   Slay them, O God, lest my people forget;*
     send them reeling by your might
     and put them down, O Lord our shield.
13   For the sins of their mouths, for the words of their lips,
     for the cursing and lies that they utter,*
     let them be caught in their pride.
[14 Make an end of them in your wrath;*
     make an end of them and they shall be no more.]
15   Let everyone know that God rules in Jacob,*
     and to the ends of the earth.
16   They go to and fro in the evening;*
     they snarl like dogs and run about the city.
17   They forage for food,*
     and if they are not filled, they howl.
18   For my part, I will sing of your strength;*
     I will celebrate your love in the morning;
19   For you have become my stronghold,*
     a refuge in the day of my trouble.
20   To you, O my Strength, will I sing;*
     for you, O God, are my stronghold
     and my merciful God.

Psalm 60

1   O God, you have cast us off and broken us;*
     you have been angry;
     O take us back to you again.
2   You have shaken the earth and split it open;*
     repair the cracks in it, for it totters.

3   You have made your people know hardship;*
      you have given us wine that makes us stagger.
4   You have set up a banner for those who fear you,*
      to be a refuge from the power of the bow.
5   Save us by your right hand and answer us,*
      that those who are dear to you may be delivered.
6   God spoke from his holy place and said:*
      'I will exult and parcel out Shechem;
      I will divide the valley of Succoth.
7   'Gilead is mine and Manasseh is mine;*
      Ephraim is my helmet and Judah my sceptre.
8   'Moab is my wash-basin,
      on Edom I throw down my sandal to claim it,*
      and over Philistia will I shout in triumph.'
9   Who will lead me into the strong city?*
      who will bring me into Edom?
10   Have you not cast us off, O God?*
      you no longer go out, O God, with our armies.
11   Grant us your help against the enemy,*
      for vain is human help.
12   With God we will do valiant deeds,*
      and he shall tread our enemies under foot.

Psalm 61

1   Hear my cry, O God,*
      and listen to my prayer.
2   I call upon you from the ends of the earth
      with heaviness in my heart;*
      set me upon the rock that is higher than I.
3   For you have been my refuge,*
      a strong tower against the enemy.
4   I will dwell in your house for ever;*
      I will take refuge under the cover of your wings.
5   For you, O God, have heard my vows;*
      you have granted me the heritage
      of those who fear your name.
6   Add length of days to the king's life;*
      let his years extend over many generations.
7   Let him sit enthroned before God for ever;*
      bid love and faithfulness watch over him.
8   So will I always sing the praise of your name,*
      and day by day I will fulfil my vows.

Psalm 62

1 For God alone my soul in silence waits;*
from him comes my salvation.

2 He alone is my rock and my salvation,*
my stronghold, so that I shall not be greatly shaken.

3 How long will you assail me to crush me,
all of you together,*
as if you were a leaning fence, a toppling wall?

4 They seek only to bring me down
from my place of honour;*
lies are their chief delight.

5 They bless with their lips,*
but in their hearts they curse.

6 For God alone my soul in silence waits;*
truly, my hope is in him.

7 He alone is my rock and my salvation,*
my stronghold, so that I shall not be shaken.

8 In God is my safety and my honour;*
God is my strong rock and my refuge.

9 Put your trust in him always, O people,*
pour out your hearts before him, for God is our refuge.

10 Those of high degree are but a fleeting breath,*
even those of low estate cannot be trusted.

11 On the scales they are lighter than a breath,*
all of them together.

12 Put no trust in extortion;
in robbery take no empty pride;*
though wealth increase, set not your heart upon it.

13 God has spoken once, twice have I heard it,*
that power belongs to God.

14 Steadfast love is yours, O Lord,*
for you repay everyone according to his deeds.

Psalm 63

1 O God, you are my God; eagerly I seek you;*
my soul thirsts for you, my flesh faints for you,
as in a barren and dry land where there is no water;

2 Therefore I have gazed upon you in your holy place,*
that I might behold your power and your glory.

3 For your loving-kindness is better than life itself;*
my lips shall give you praise.

4 So will I bless you as long as I live*

and lift up my hands in your name.
5   My soul is content, as with marrow and fatness,*
    and my mouth praises you with joyful lips,
6   When I remember you upon my bed,*
    and meditate on you in the night watches.
7   For you have been my helper,*
    and under the shadow of your wings I will rejoice.
8   My soul clings to you;*
    your right hand holds me fast.
9   May those who seek my life to destroy it*
    go down into the depths of the earth;
10 Let them fall upon the edge of the sword,*
    and let them be food for jackals.
11 But the king will rejoice in God;
    all those who swear by him will be glad,*
    for the mouth of those who speak lies shall be stopped.

Psalm 64

1   Hear my voice, O God, when I complain;*
    protect my life from fear of the enemy.
2   Hide me from the conspiracy of the wicked,*
    from the mob of evildoers.
3   They sharpen their tongue like a sword,*
    and aim their bitter words like arrows,
4   That they may shoot down the blameless from ambush;*
    they shoot without warning and are not afraid.
5   They hold fast to their evil course;*
    they plan how they may hide their snares.
6   They say, 'Who will see us?
    who will find out our crimes?*
    we have thought out a perfect plot.'
7   The human mind and heart are a mystery;*
    but God will loose an arrow at them,
    and suddenly they will be wounded.
8   He will make them trip over their tongues,*
    and all who see them will shake their heads.
9   Everyone will stand in awe and declare God's deeds;*
    they will recognise his works.
10 The righteous will rejoice in the Lord
    and put their trust in him,*
    and all who are true of heart will glory.

A Celtic Primer

Psalm 65

1 You are to be praised, O God, in Zion;*
   to you shall vows be performed in Jerusalem.
2 To you that hear prayer shall all flesh come,*
   because of their transgressions.
3 Our sins are stronger than we are,*
   but you will blot them out.
4 Happy are they whom you choose
   and draw to your courts to dwell there!*
   they will be satisfied by the beauty of your house,
   by the holiness of your temple.
5 Awesome things will you show us in your righteousness,
   O God of our salvation,*
   O Hope of all the ends of the earth
   and of the seas that are far away.
6 You make fast the mountains by your power;*
   they are girded about with might.
7 You still the roaring of the seas,*
   the roaring of their waves,
   and the clamour of the peoples.
8 Those who dwell at the ends of the earth
   will tremble at your marvellous signs;*
   you make the dawn and the dusk to sing for joy.
9 You visit the earth and water it abundantly;
   you make it very plenteous;*
   the river of God is full of water.
10 You prepare the grain,*
   for so you provide for the earth.
11 You drench the furrows and smooth out the ridges;*
   with heavy rain you soften the ground
   and bless its increase.
12 You crown the year with your goodness,*
   and your paths overflow with plenty.
13 May the fields of the wilderness be rich for grazing,*
   and the hills be clothed with joy.
14 May the meadows cover themselves with flocks
   and the valleys cloak themselves with grain;*
   let them shout for joy and sing.

Psalm 66

1 Be joyful in God, all you lands;*
   sing the glory of his name;

The Psalter, including Psalm Themes for Prayer

sing the glory of his praise.

2 Say to God, 'How awesome are your deeds!*
because of your great strength
your enemies cringe before you.

3 'All the earth bows down before you,*
sings to you, sings out your name.'

4 Come now and see the works of God,*
how wonderful he is in his doing towards all people.

5 He turned the sea into dry land,
so that they went through the water on foot,*
and there we rejoiced in him.

6 In his might he rules for ever;
his eyes keep watch over the nations;*
let no rebel rise up against him.

7 Bless our God, you peoples;*
make the voice of his praise to be heard;

8 Who holds our souls in life,*
and will not allow our feet to slip.

9 For you, O God, have proved us;*
you have tried us just as silver is tried.

10 You brought us into the snare;*
you laid heavy burdens upon our backs.

11 You let enemies ride over our heads;
we went through fire and water;*
but you brought us out into a place of refreshment.

12 I will enter your house with burnt-offerings
and will pay you my vows,*
which I promised with my lips
and spoke with my mouth when I was in trouble.

13 I will offer you sacrifices of fat beasts
with the smoke of rams;*
I will give you oxen and goats.

14 Come and listen, all you who fear God,*
and I will tell you what he has done for me.

15 I called out to him with my mouth,*
and his praise was on my tongue.

16 If I had found evil in my heart,*
the Lord would not have heard me;

17 But in truth God has heard me;*
he has attended to the voice of my prayer.

18 Blessèd be God, who has not rejected my prayer,*
nor withheld his love from me.

Psalm 67

1 May God be merciful to us and bless us,*
   show us the light of his countenance and come to us.
2 Let your ways be known upon earth,*
   your saving health among all nations.
3 Let the peoples praise you, O God;*
   let all the peoples praise you.
4 Let the nations be glad and sing for joy,*
   for you judge the peoples with equity
   and guide all the nations upon earth.
5 Let the peoples praise you, O God;*
   let all the peoples praise you.
6 The earth has brought forth her increase;*
   may God, our own God, give us his blessing.
7 May God give us his blessing,*
   and may all the ends of the earth stand in awe of him.

Psalm 68

1 Let God arise and let his enemies be scattered;*
   let those who hate him flee before him.
2 Let them vanish like smoke
   when the wind drives it away;*
   as the wax melts at the fire,
   so let the wicked perish at the presence of God.
3 But let the righteous be glad and rejoice before God;*
   let them also be merry and joyful.
4 Sing to God, sing praises to his name;
   exalt him who rides upon the heavens;*
   Yahweh is his name, rejoice before him!
5 Father of orphans, defender of widows,*
   God in his holy habitation!
6 God gives the solitary a home
   and brings forth prisoners into freedom;*
   but the rebels shall live in dry places.
7 O God, when you went forth before your people,*
   when you marched through the wilderness,
8 The earth shook and the skies poured down rain,
   at the presence of God, the God of Sinai,*
   at the presence of God, the God of Israel.
9 You sent a gracious rain, O God, upon your inheritance;*
   you refreshed the land when it was weary.
10 Your people found their home in it;*

in your goodness, O God,
you have made provision for the poor.

11 The Lord gave the word;*
great was the company of women who bore the tidings:

12 'Kings with their armies are fleeing away;*
the women at home are dividing the spoils.'

13 Though you lingered among the sheepfolds,*
you shall be like a dove
whose wings are covered with silver,
whose feathers are like green gold.

14 When the Almighty scattered kings,*
it was like snow falling in Zalmon.

15 O mighty mountain, O hill of Bashan!*
O rugged mountain, O hill of Bashan!

16 Why do you look with envy, O rugged mountain,
at the hill which God chose for his resting place?*
truly, the Lord will dwell there for ever.

17 The chariots of God are twenty thousand,
even thousands of thousands;*
the Lord comes in holiness from Sinai.

18 You have gone up on high and led captivity captive;
you have received gifts even from your enemies,*
that the Lord God might dwell among them.

19 Blessèd be the Lord day by day,*
the God of our salvation, who bears our burdens.

20 He is our God, the God of our salvation;*
God is the Lord, by whom we escape death.

[21 God shall crush the heads of his enemies,*
and the hairy scalp of those
who go on still in their wickedness.

22 The Lord has said, 'I will bring them back from Bashan;*
I will bring them back from the depths of the sea;

23 'That your foot may be dipped in blood,*
the tongues of your dogs in the blood of your enemies.']

24 Your procession is seen, O God,*
your procession into the sanctuary, my God and my King.

25 The singers go before, musicians follow after,*
in the midst of maidens playing upon the hand-drums.

26 Bless God in the congregation;*
bless the Lord, you that are of the fountain of Israel.

27 There is Benjamin, least of the tribes, at the head;
the princes of Judah in a company;*
and the princes of Zebulon and Naphtali.

28 Send forth your strength, O God;*

A Celtic Primer

establish, O God, what you have wrought for us.
29   Kings shall bring gifts to you,*
    for your temple's sake at Jerusalem.
30   Rebuke the wild beast of the reeds,*
    and the peoples, a herd of wild bulls with its calves.
31   Trample down those who lust after silver;*
    scatter the peoples that delight in war.
32   Let tribute be brought out of Egypt;*
    let Ethiopia stretch out her hands to God.
33   Sing to God, O kingdoms of the earth;*
    sing praises to the Lord.
34   He rides in the heavens, the ancient heavens;*
    he sends forth his voice, his mighty voice.
35   Ascribe power to God;*
    his majesty is over Israel;
    his strength is in the skies.
36   How wonderful is God in his holy places!*
    the God of Israel giving strength and power to his people!
    Blessèd be God!

Psalm 69

1   Save me, O God,*
    for the waters have risen up to my neck.
2   I am sinking in deep mire,*
    and there is no firm ground for my feet.
3   I have come into deep waters,*
    and the torrent washes over me.
4   I have grown weary with my crying;
    my throat is inflamed;*
    my eyes have failed from looking for my God.
5   Those who hate me without a cause
    are more than the hairs of my head;
    my lying foes who would destroy me are mighty.*
    Must I then give back what I never stole?
6   O God, you know my foolishness,*
    and my faults are not hidden from you.
7   Let not those who hope in you
    be put to shame through me, Lord God of hosts;*
    let not those who seek you be disgraced because of me,
    O God of Israel.
8   Surely, for your sake have I suffered reproach,*
    and shame has covered my face.
9   I have become a stranger to my own kindred,*

an alien to my mother's children.
10 Zeal for your house has eaten me up;*
   the scorn of those who scorn you has fallen upon me.
11 I humbled myself with fasting,*
   but that was turned to my reproach.
12 I put on sack-cloth also,*
   and became a byword among them.
13 Those who sit at the gate murmur against me,*
   and the drunkards make songs about me.
14 But as for me, this is my prayer to you,*
   at the time you have set, O Lord:
15 'In your great mercy, O God,*
   answer me with your unfailing help.
16 'Save me from the mire; do not let me sink;*
   let me be rescued from those who hate me
   and out of the deep waters.
17 'Let not the torrent of waters wash over me,
   neither let the deep swallow me up;*
   do not let the Pit shut its mouth upon me.
18 'Answer me, O Lord, for your love is kind;*
   in your great compassion, turn to me.
19 'Hide not your face from your servant;*
   be swift and answer me, for I am in distress.
20 'Draw near to me and redeem me;*
   because of my enemies deliver me.
21 'You know my reproach, my shame and my dishonour;*
   my adversaries are all in your sight.'
22 Reproach has broken my heart and it cannot be healed;*
   I looked for sympathy, but there was none,
   for comforters, but I could find no one.
23 They gave me gall to eat,*
   and when I was thirsty, they gave me vinegar to drink.
[24 Let the table before them be a trap*
   and their sacred feasts a snare.
25 Let their eyes be darkened, that they may not see,*
   and give them continual trembling in their loins.
26 Pour out your indignation upon them,*
   and let the fierceness of your anger overtake them.
27 Let their camp be desolate,*
   and let there be none to dwell in their tents.
28 For they persecute him whom you have stricken*
   and add to the pain of those whom you have pierced.
29 Lay to their charge guilt upon guilt,*
   and let them not receive your vindication.

30   Let them be wiped out of the book of the living*
      and not be written among the righteous.]
31   As for me, I am afflicted and in pain;*
      your help, O God, will lift me up on high.
32   I will praise the name of God in song;*
      I will proclaim his greatness with thanksgiving.
33   This will please the Lord more than an offering of oxen,*
      more than bullocks with horns and hoofs.
34   The afflicted shall see and be glad;*
      you who seek God, your heart shall live.
35   For the Lord listens to the needy,*
      and his prisoners he does not despise.
36   Let the heavens and the earth praise him,*
      the seas and all that moves in them;
37   For God will save Zion and rebuild the cities of Judah;*
      they shall live there and have it in possession.
38   The children of his servants will inherit it,*
      and those who love his name will dwell therein.

Psalm 70

1   Be pleased, O God, to deliver me;*
      O Lord, make haste to help me.
2   Let those who seek my life
      be ashamed and altogether dismayed;*
      let those who take pleasure in my misfortune
      draw back and be disgraced.
3   Let those who say to me 'Aha!'
      and gloat over me turn back,*
      because they are ashamed.
4   Let all who seek you rejoice and be glad in you;*
      let those who love your salvation say for ever,
      'Great is the Lord!'
5   But as for me, I am poor and needy;*
      come to me speedily, O God.
6   You are my helper and my deliverer;*
      O Lord, do not tarry.

Psalm 71

1   In you, O Lord, have I taken refuge;*
      let me never be ashamed.
2   In your righteousness, deliver me and set me free;*
      incline your ear to me and save me.

3   Be my strong rock, a castle to keep me safe;*
    you are my crag and my stronghold.
4   Deliver me, my God, from the hand of the wicked,*
    from the clutches of the evildoer and the oppressor.
5   For you are my hope, O Lord God,*
    my confidence since I was young.
6   I have been sustained by you ever since I was born;
    from my mother's womb you have been my strength;*
    my praise shall be always of you.
7   I have become a portent to many;*
    but you are my refuge and my strength.
8   Let my mouth be full of your praise*
    and your glory all the day long.
9   Do not cast me off in my old age;*
    forsake me not when my strength fails.
10 For my enemies are talking against me,*
    and those who lie in wait for my life
    take counsel together.
11 They say, 'God has forsaken him;
    go after him and seize him;*
    because there is none who will save.'
12 O God, be not far from me;*
    come quickly to help me, O my God.
13 Let those who set themselves against me
    be put to shame and be disgraced;*
    let those who seek to do me evil
    be covered with scorn and reproach.
14 But I shall always wait in patience,*
    and shall praise you more and more.
15 My mouth shall recount your mighty acts
    and saving deeds all day long;*
    though I cannot know the number of them.
16 I will begin with the mighty works of the Lord God;*
    I will recall your righteousness, yours alone.
17 O God, you have taught me since I was young,*
    and to this day I tell of your wonderful works.
18 And now that I am old and grey-headed, O God,
    do not forsake me,*
    till I make known your strength to this generation
    and your power to all who are to come.
19 Your righteousness, O God, reaches to the heavens;*
    you have done great things; who is like you, O God?
20 You have showed me great troubles and adversities,*
    but you will restore my life and bring me up again

A Celtic Primer

from the deep places of the earth.

21   You strengthen me more and more;*
     you enfold and comfort me,

22   Therefore I will praise you upon the lyre
     for your faithfulness, O my God;*
     I will sing to you with the harp, O Holy One of Israel.

23   My lips will sing with joy when I play to you,*
     and so will my soul, which you have redeemed.

24   My tongue will proclaim your righteousness all day long,*
     for they are ashamed and disgraced
     who sought to do me harm.

PSALMS 72–88

Psalm 72

1   Give the king your justice, O God,*
    and your righteousness to the king's son;

2   That he may rule your people righteously*
    and the poor with justice;

3   That the mountains may bring prosperity to the people,*
    and the little hills bring righteousness.

4   He shall defend the needy among the people;*
    he shall rescue the poor and crush the oppressor.

5   He shall live as long as the sun and moon endure,*
    from one generation to another.

6   He shall come down like rain upon the mown field,*
    like showers that water the earth.

7   In his time shall the righteous flourish;*
    there shall be abundance of peace
    till the moon shall be no more.

8   He shall rule from sea to sea,*
    and from the River to the ends of the earth.

9   His foes shall bow down before him,*
    and his enemies lick the dust.

10   The kings of Tarshish and of the isles shall pay tribute,*
    and the kings of Arabia and Saba offer gifts.

11   All kings shall bow down before him,*
    and all the nations do him service.

12   For he shall deliver the poor who cries out in distress,*
    and the oppressed who has no helper.

13   He shall have pity on the lowly and poor;*
    he shall preserve the lives of the needy.

14 He shall redeem their lives from oppression and violence,*
    and dear shall their blood be in his sight.
15 Long may he live,
    and may there be given to him gold from Arabia;*
    may prayer be made for him always,
    and may they bless him all the day long.
16 May there be abundance of grain on the earth,
    growing thick even on the hilltops;*
    may its fruit flourish like Lebanon,
    and its grain like grass upon the earth.
17 May his name remain for ever
    and be established as long as the sun endures;*
    may all the nations bless themselves in him
    and call him blessèd.
18 Blessèd be the Lord God, the God of Israel,*
    who alone does wondrous deeds!
19 And blessèd be his glorious name for ever!*
    and may all the earth be filled with his glory.
    Amen. Amen.

Psalm 73

1   Truly, God is good to Israel,*
    to those who are pure in heart.
2   But as for me, my feet had nearly slipped;*
    I had almost tripped and fallen;
3   Because I envied the proud*
    and saw the prosperity of the wicked:
4   For they suffer no pain,*
    and their bodies are sleek and sound;
5   In the misfortunes of others they have no share;*
    they are not afflicted as others are;
6   Therefore they wear their pride like a necklace*
    and wrap their violence about them like a cloak.
7   Their iniquity comes from gross minds,*
    and their hearts overflow with wicked thoughts.
8   They scoff and speak maliciously;*
    out of their haughtiness they plan oppression.
9   They set their mouths against the heavens,*
    and their evil speech runs through the world.
10 And so the people turn to them*
    and find in them no fault.
11 They say, 'How should God know?*
    is there knowledge in the Most High?'

A Celtic Primer

12   So then, these are the wicked;*
      always at ease, they increase their wealth.
13   In vain have I kept my heart clean,*
      and washed my hands in innocence.
14   I have been afflicted all day long,*
      and punished every morning.
15   Had I gone on speaking this way,*
      I should have betrayed the generation of your children.
16   When I tried to understand these things,*
      it was too hard for me;
17   Until I entered the sanctuary of God*
      and discerned the end of the wicked.
18   Surely, you set them in slippery places;*
      you cast them down in ruin.
19   O how suddenly do they come to destruction,*
      come to an end and perish from terror!
20   Like a dream when one awakens, O Lord,*
      when you arise you will make their image vanish.
21   When my mind became embittered,*
      I was sorely wounded in my heart.
22   I was stupid and had no understanding;*
      I was like a brute beast in your presence.
23   Yet I am always with you;*
      you hold me by my right hand.
24   You will guide me by your counsel,*
      and afterwards receive me with glory.
25   Whom have I in heaven but you?*
      and having you I desire nothing upon earth.
26   Though my flesh and my heart should waste away,*
      God is the strength of my heart and my portion for ever.
27   Truly, those who forsake you will perish;*
      you destroy all who are unfaithful.
28   But it is good for me to be near God;*
      I have made the Lord God my refuge.
29   I will speak of all your works*
      in the gates of the city of Zion.

Psalm 74

1   O God, why have you utterly cast us off?*
      why is your wrath so hot
      against the sheep of your pasture?
2   Remember your congregation that you purchased long ago,*
      the tribe you redeemed to be your inheritance,

and Mount Zion where you dwell.

3 Turn your steps towards the endless ruins;*
the enemy has laid waste everything in your sanctuary.

4 Your adversaries roared in your holy place;*
they set up their banners as tokens of victory.

5 They were like men coming up with axes
to a grove of trees;*
they broke down all your carved work
with hatchets and hammers.

6 They set fire to your holy place;*
they defiled the dwelling-place of your name
and razed it to the ground.

7 They said to themselves, 'Let us destroy them altogether.'*
They burned down all the meeting-places of God
in the land.

8 There are no signs for us to see;
there is no prophet left;*
there is not one among us who knows how long.

9 How long, O God, will the adversary scoff?*
will the enemy blaspheme your name for ever?

10 Why do you draw back your hand?*
why is your right hand hidden in your bosom?

11 Yet God is my king from ancient times,*
victorious in the midst of the earth.

12 You divided the sea by your might*
and shattered the heads of the dragons upon the waters;

13 You crushed the heads of Leviathan*
and gave him to the people of the desert for food.

14 You split open spring and torrent;*
you dried up ever-flowing rivers.

15 Yours is the day, yours also the night;*
you established the moon and the sun.

16 You fixed all the boundaries of the earth;*
you made both summer and winter.

17 Remember, O Lord, how the enemy scoffed,*
how a foolish people despised your name.

18 Do not hand over the life of your dove to wild beasts;*
never forget the lives of your poor.

19 Look upon your covenant;*
the dark places of the earth are haunts of violence.

20 Let not the oppressed turn away ashamed;*
let the poor and needy praise your name.

21 Arise, O God, maintain your cause;*
remember how fools revile you all day long.

A Celtic Primer

22 Forget not the clamour of your adversaries,*
    the unending tumult of those who rise up against you.

Psalm 75

1   We give you thanks, O God, we give you thanks,*
    calling upon your name
    and declaring all your wonderful deeds.
2   'I will appoint a time,' says God;*
    'I will judge with equity.
3   'Though the earth and all its inhabitants are quaking,*
    I will make its pillars fast.
4   'I will say to the boasters, "Boast no more",*
    and to the wicked, "Do not toss your horns;
5   '"Do not toss your horns so high,*
    nor speak with a proud neck."'
6   For judgement is neither from the east
    nor from the west,*
    nor yet from the wilderness or the mountains.
7   It is God who judges;*
    he puts down one and lifts up another.
8   For in the Lord's hand there is a cup,
    full of spiced and foaming wine, which he pours out,*
    and all the wicked of the earth
    shall drink and drain the dregs.
9   But I will rejoice for ever;*
    I will sing praises to the God of Jacob.
10 He shall break off all the horns of the wicked;*
    but the horns of the righteous shall be exalted.

Psalm 76

1   In Judah is God known;*
    his name is great in Israel.
2   At Salem is his tabernacle,*
    and his dwelling is in Zion.
3   There he broke the flashing arrows,*
    the shield, the sword and the weapons of battle.
4   How glorious you are!*
    more splendid than the everlasting mountains!
5   The strong of heart have been despoiled;
    they sink into sleep;*
    none of the warriors can lift a hand.
6   At your rebuke, O God of Jacob,*

both horse and rider lie stunned.

7   What terror you inspire!*
who can stand before you when you are angry?

8   From heaven you pronounced judgement;*
the earth was afraid and was still;

9   When God rose up to judgement*
and to save all the oppressed of the earth.

10   Truly, wrathful Edom will give you thanks,*
and the remnant of Hamath will keep your feasts.

11   Make a vow to the Lord your God and keep it;*
let all around him bring gifts
to him who is worthy to be feared.

12   He breaks the spirit of princes,*
and strikes terror in the kings of the earth.

Psalm 77

1   I will cry aloud to God;*
I will cry aloud and he will hear me.

2   In the day of my trouble I sought the Lord;*
my hands were stretched out by night and did not tire;
I refused to be comforted.

3   I think of God, I am restless,*
I ponder and my spirit faints.

4   You will not let my eyelids close;*
I am troubled and I cannot speak.

5   I consider the days of old;*
I remember the years long past;

6   I commune with my heart in the night;*
I ponder and search my mind.

7   Will the Lord cast me off for ever?*
will he no more show his favour?

8   Has his loving-kindness come to an end for ever?*
has his promise failed for evermore?

9   Has God forgotten to be gracious?*
has he, in his anger, withheld his compassion?

10   And I said, 'My grief is this:*
the right hand of the Most High has lost its power.'

11   I will remember the works of the Lord,*
and call to mind your wonders of old time.

12   I will meditate on all your acts*
and ponder your mighty deeds.

13   Your way, O God, is holy;*
who is so great a god as our God?

14   You are the God who works wonders*
      and have declared your power among the peoples.
15   By your strength you have redeemed your people,*
      the children of Jacob and Joseph.
16   The waters saw you, O God;
      the waters saw you and trembled;*
      the very depths were shaken.
17   The clouds poured out water; the skies thundered;*
      your arrows flashed to and fro;
18   The sound of your thunder was in the whirlwind;
      your lightnings lit up the world;*
      the earth trembled and shook.
19   Your way was in the sea,
      and your paths in the great waters,*
      yet your footsteps were not seen.
20   You led your people like a flock*
      by the hand of Moses and Aaron.

Psalm 78, Part I

1   Hear my teaching, O my people;*
      incline your ears to the words of my mouth.
2   I will open my mouth in a parable;*
      I will declare the mysteries of ancient times.
3   That which we have heard and known,
      and what our forebears have told us,*
      we will not hide from their children.
4   We will recount to generations to come
      the praiseworthy deeds and the power of the Lord,*
      and the wonderful works he has done.
5   He gave his decrees to Jacob
      and established a law for Israel,*
      which he commanded them to teach their children;
6   That the generations to come might know,
      and the children yet unborn;*
      that they in their turn might tell it to their children;
7   So that they might put their trust in God,*
      and not forget the deeds of God,
      but keep his commandments;
8   And not be like their forebears,
      a stubborn and rebellious generation,*
      a generation whose heart was not steadfast,
      and whose spirit was not faithful to God.
9   The people of Ephraim, armed with the bow,*

turned back in the day of battle;
10   They did not keep the covenant of God,*
     and refused to walk in his law;
11   They forgot what he had done,*
     and the wonders he had shown them.
12   He worked marvels in the sight of their forebears,*
     in the land of Egypt, in the field of Zoan.
13   He split open the sea and let them pass through;*
     he made the waters stand up like walls.
14   He led them with a cloud by day,*
     and all the night through with a glow of fire.
15   He split the hard rocks in the wilderness*
     and gave them drink as from the great deep.
16   He brought streams out of the cliff,*
     and the waters gushed out like rivers.
17   But they went on sinning against him,*
     rebelling in the desert against the Most High.
18   They tested God in their hearts,*
     demanding food for their craving.
19   They railed against God and said,*
     'Can God set a table in the wilderness?
20   'True, he struck the rock, the waters gushed out,
     and the gullies overflowed;*
     but is he able to give bread
     or to provide meat for his people?'
21   When the Lord heard this, he was full of wrath;*
     a fire was kindled against Jacob,
     and his anger mounted against Israel;
22   For they had no faith in God,*
     nor did they put their trust in his saving power.
23   So he commanded the clouds above*
     and opened the doors of heaven.
24   He rained down manna upon them to eat*
     and gave them grain from heaven.
25   So mortals ate the bread of angels;*
     he provided for them food enough.
26   He caused the east wind to blow in the heavens*
     and led out the south wind by his might.
27   He rained down flesh upon them like dust*
     and winged birds like the sand of the sea.
28   He let it fall in the midst of their camp*
     and round about their dwellings.
29   So they ate and were well filled,*
     for he gave them what they craved.

30 But they did not stop their craving,*
  though the food was still in their mouths.

31 So God's anger mounted against them;*
  he slew their strongest men
  and laid low the youth of Israel.

32 In spite of all this, they went on sinning*
  and had no faith in his wonderful works.

33 So he brought their days to an end like a breath*
  and their years in sudden terror.

34 Whenever he slew them, they would seek him,*
  and repent and diligently search for God.

35 They would remember that God was their rock,*
  and the Most High God their redeemer.

36 But they flattered him with their mouths*
  and lied to him with their tongues.

37 Their heart was not steadfast towards him,*
  and they were not faithful to his covenant.

38 But he was so merciful that he forgave their sins
  and did not destroy them;*
  many times he held back his anger
  and did not permit his wrath to be roused.

39 For he remembered that they were but flesh,*
  a breath that goes forth and does not return.

Psalm 78, Part II

40 How often the people disobeyed God in the wilderness*
  and offended him in the desert!

41 Again and again they tempted God*
  and provoked the Holy One of Israel.

42 They did not remember his power*
  in the day when he ransomed them from the enemy;

43 How he wrought his signs in Egypt*
  and his omens in the field of Zoan.

44 He turned their rivers into blood,*
  so that they could not drink of their streams.

45 He sent swarms of flies among them, which ate them up,*
  and frogs, which destroyed them.

46 He gave their crops to the caterpillar,*
  the fruit of their toil to the locust.

47 He killed their vines with hail*
  and their sycamores with frost.

48 He delivered their cattle to hailstones*
  and their livestock to hot thunderbolts.

49 He poured out upon them his blazing anger:*
   fury, indignation and distress,
   a troop of destroying angels.
50 He gave full rein to his anger;
   he did not spare their souls from death;*
   but delivered their lives to the plague.
51 He struck down all the first-born of Egypt,*
   the flower of manhood in the dwellings of Ham.
52 He led out his people like sheep*
   and guided them in the wilderness like a flock.
53 He led them to safety and they were not afraid;*
   but the sea overwhelmed their enemies.
54 He brought them to his holy land,*
   the mountain his right hand had won.
55 He drove out the Canaanites before them
   and apportioned an inheritance to them by lot;*
   he made the tribes of Israel to dwell in their tents.
56 But they tested the Most High God and defied him,*
   and did not keep his commandments.
57 They turned away and were disloyal like their forebears;*
   they were undependable like a warped bow.
58 They grieved him with their hill-altars*
   and provoked his displeasure with their idols.
59 When God heard this, he was angry*
   and utterly rejected Israel.
60 He forsook the shrine at Shiloh,*
   the tabernacle where he had lived among his people.
61 He delivered the ark into captivity,*
   his glory into the adversary's hand.
62 He gave his people to the sword*
   and was angered against his inheritance.
63 The fire consumed their young men;*
   there were no wedding songs for their maidens.
64 Their priests fell by the sword,*
   and their widows made no lamentation.
65 Then the Lord woke as though from sleep,*
   like a warrior refreshed with wine.
66 He struck his enemies from behind*
   and put them to perpetual shame.
67 He rejected the tent of Joseph*
   and did not choose the tribe of Ephraim;
68 He chose instead the tribe of Judah*
   and Mount Zion, which he loved.
69 He built his sanctuary like the heights of heaven,*

like the earth which he founded for ever.
70 He chose David his servant,*
and took him away from the sheepfolds.
71 He brought him from following the ewes,*
to be a shepherd over Jacob his people
and over Israel his inheritance.
72 So he shepherded them with a faithful and true heart*
and guided them with the skilfulness of his hands.

Psalm 79

1 O God, the heathen have come into your inheritance;
they have profaned your holy temple;*
they have made Jerusalem a heap of rubble.
2 They have given the bodies of your servants
as food for the birds of the air,*
and the flesh of your faithful ones
to the beasts of the field.
3 They have shed their blood like water
on every side of Jerusalem,*
and there was no one to bury them.
4 We have become a reproach to our neighbours,*
an object of scorn and derision to those around us.
5 How long will you be angry, O Lord?*
will your fury blaze like fire for ever?
6 Pour out your wrath upon the heathen
who have not known you*
and upon the kingdoms
that have not called upon your name.
7 For they have devoured Jacob*
and made his dwelling a ruin.
8 Remember not our past sins;
let your compassion be swift to meet us;*
for we have been brought very low.
9 Help us, O God our Saviour, for the glory of your name;*
deliver us and forgive us our sins, for your name's sake.
[10 Why should the heathen say, 'Where is their God?'*
Let it be known among the heathen and in our sight
that you avenge the shedding
of your servants' blood.]
11 Let the sorrowful sighing of the prisoners
come before you,*
and by your great might
spare those who are condemned to die.

The Psalter, including Psalm Themes for Prayer

[12   May the revilings with which
　　　they reviled you, O Lord,*
　　　return sevenfold into their bosoms.]

13   We are your people and the sheep of your pasture;*
　　　we will give you thanks for ever
　　　and show forth your praise from age to age.

Psalm 80

1   Hear, O Shepherd of Israel, leading Joseph like a flock;*
　　　shine forth, you that are enthroned upon the cherubim.

2   In the presence of Ephraim, Benjamin and Manasseh,*
　　　stir up your strength and come to help us.

3   Restore us, O God of hosts;*
　　　show the light of your countenance
　　　and we shall be saved.

4   O Lord God of hosts,*
　　　how long will you be angered
　　　despite the prayers of your people?

5   You have fed them with the bread of tears;*
　　　you have given them bowls of tears to drink.

6   You have made us the derision of our neighbours,*
　　　and our enemies laugh us to scorn.

7   Restore us, O God of hosts;*
　　　show the light of your countenance
　　　and we shall be saved.

8   You have brought a vine out of Egypt;*
　　　you cast out the nations and planted it.

9   You prepared the ground for it;*
　　　it took root and filled the land.

10   The mountains were covered by its shadow*
　　　and the towering cedar trees by its boughs.

11   You stretched out its tendrils to the Sea*
　　　and its branches to the River.

12   Why have you broken down its wall,*
　　　so that all who pass by pluck off its grapes?

13   The wild boar of the forest has ravaged it,*
　　　and the beasts of the field have grazed upon it.

14   Turn now, O God of hosts, look down from heaven;
　　　behold and tend this vine;*
　　　preserve what your right hand has planted.

15   They burn it with fire like rubbish;*
　　　at the rebuke of your countenance let them perish.

16   Let your hand be upon the man of your right hand,*

the son of man you have made so strong for yourself.

17 And so will we never turn away from you;*
   give us life, that we may call upon your name.

18 Restore us, O Lord God of hosts;*
   show the light of your countenance
   and we shall be saved.

Psalm 81

1 Sing with joy to God our strength*
   and raise a loud shout to the God of Jacob.

2 Raise a song and sound the timbrel,*
   the merry harp and the lyre.

3 Blow the ram's-horn at the new moon,*
   and at the full moon, the day of our feast.

4 For this is a statute for Israel,*
   a law of the God of Jacob.

5 He laid it as a solemn charge upon Joseph,*
   when he came out of the land of Egypt.

6 I heard an unfamiliar voice saying,*
   'I eased his shoulder from the burden;
   his hands were set free from bearing the load.'

7 You called on me in trouble and I saved you;*
   I answered you from the secret place of thunder
   and tested you at the waters of Meribah.

8 Hear, O my people, and I will admonish you:*
   O Israel, if you would but listen to me!

9 There shall be no strange god among you;*
   you shall not worship a foreign god.

10 I am the Lord your God,
   who brought you out of the land of Egypt and said,*
   'Open your mouth wide and I will fill it.'

11 And yet my people did not hear my voice,*
   and Israel would not obey me.

12 So I gave them over to the stubbornness
   of their hearts,*
   to follow their own devices.

13 O that my people would listen to me!*
   that Israel would walk in my ways!

14 I should soon subdue their enemies*
   and turn my hand against their foes.

15 Those who hate the Lord would cringe before him,*
   and their punishment would last for ever.

16   But Israel would I feed with the finest wheat*
       and satisfy him with honey from the rock.

Psalm 82

1   God takes his stand in the council of heaven;*
       he gives judgement in the midst of the gods:
2   'How long will you judge unjustly,*
       and show favour to the wicked?
3   'Save the weak and the orphan;*
       defend the humble and needy;
4   'Rescue the weak and the poor;*
       deliver them from the power of the wicked.
5   'They do not know, neither do they understand;
       they go about in darkness;*
       all the foundations of the earth are shaken.
6   'Now I say to you, "You are gods,*
       and all of you children of the Most High;
7   ' "Nevertheless, you shall die like mortals,*
       and fall like any prince." '
8   Arise, O God, and rule the earth,*
       for you shall take all nations for your own.

Psalm 83

1   O God, do not be silent;*
       do not keep still nor hold your peace, O God;
2   For your enemies are in tumult,*
       and those who hate you have lifted up their heads.
3   They take secret counsel against your people*
       and plot against those whom you protect.
4   They have said,
       'Come, let us wipe them out from among the nations;*
       let the name of Israel be remembered no more.'
5   They have conspired together;*
       they have made an alliance against you:
6   The tents of Edom and the Ishmaelites,*
       the Moabites and the Hagarenes;
7   Gebal and Ammon and Amalek,*
       the Philistines and those who dwell in Tyre.
8   The Assyrians also have joined them,*
       and have come to help the people of Lot.
[9   Do to them as you did to Midian,*
       to Sisera and to Jabin at the river of Kishon:

10 They were destroyed at Endor;*
   they became like dung upon the ground.
11 Make their leaders like Oreb and Zeeb,*
   and all their commanders like Zebah and Zalmunna,
12 Who said, 'Let us take for ourselves*
   the fields of God as our possession.'
13 O my God, make them like whirling dust*
   and like chaff before the wind;
14 Like fire that burns down a forest,*
   like the flame that sets mountains ablaze.
15 Drive them with your tempest*
   and terrify them with your storm;
16 Cover their faces with shame, O Lord,*
   that they may seek your name.
17 Let them be disgraced and terrified for ever;*
   let them be put to confusion and perish.]
18 Let them know that you, whose name is Yahweh,*
   you alone are the Most High over all the earth.

Psalm 84

1 How dear to me is your dwelling, O Lord of hosts!*
   My soul has a desire and longing
      for the courts of the Lord;
   my heart and my flesh rejoice in the living God.
2 The sparrow has found her a house
   and the swallow a nest
      where she may lay her young;*
   by the side of your altars, O Lord of hosts,
      my King and my God.
3 Happy are they who dwell in your house!*
   they will always be praising you.
4 Happy are the people whose strength is in you!*
   whose hearts are set on the pilgrims' way.
5 Those who go through the desolate valley
   will find it a place of springs,*
   for the early rains have covered it with pools of water.
6 They will climb from height to height,*
   and the God of gods will reveal himself in Zion.
7 Lord God of hosts, hear my prayer;*
   hearken, O God of Jacob.
8 Behold our defender, O God;*
   and look upon the face of your anointed.
9 For one day in your courts

is better than a thousand in my own room,*
and to stand at the threshold of the house of my God
than to dwell in the tents of the wicked.

10   For the Lord God is both sun and shield;*
he will give grace and glory;

11   No good thing will the Lord withhold*
from those who walk with integrity.

12   O Lord of hosts,*
happy are they who put their trust in you!

Psalm 85

1   You have been gracious to your land, O Lord,*
you have restored the good fortune of Jacob.

2   You have forgiven the iniquity of your people*
and blotted out all their sins.

3   You have withdrawn all your fury*
and turned yourself from your wrathful indignation.

4   Restore us then, O God our Saviour;*
let your anger depart from us.

5   Will you be displeased with us for ever?*
will you prolong your anger from age to age?

6   Will you not give us life again,*
that your people may rejoice in you?

7   Show us your mercy, O Lord,*
and grant us your salvation.

8   I will listen to what the Lord God is saying,*
for he is speaking peace to his faithful people
and to those who turn their hearts to him.

9   Truly, his salvation is very near to those who fear him,*
that his glory may dwell in our land.

10   Mercy and truth have met together;*
righteousness and peace have kissed each other.

11   Truth shall spring up from the earth,*
and righteousness shall look down from heaven.

12   The Lord will indeed grant prosperity,*
and our land will yield its increase.

13   Righteousness shall go before him,*
and peace shall be a pathway for his feet.

Psalm 86

1   Bow down your ear, O Lord, and answer me,*
for I am poor and in misery.

A Celtic Primer

2 Keep watch over my life, for I am faithful;*
 save your servant who trusts in you.
3 Be merciful to me, O Lord, for you are my God;*
 I call upon you all the day long.
4 Gladden the soul of your servant,*
 for to you, O Lord, I lift up my soul.
5 For you, O Lord, are good and forgiving,*
 and great is your love towards all who call upon you.
6 Give ear, O Lord, to my prayer,*
 and attend to the voice of my supplications.
7 In the time of my trouble I will call upon you,*
 for you will answer me.
8 Among the gods there is none like you, O Lord,*
 nor anything like your works.
9 All nations you have made
 will come and worship you, O Lord,*
 and glorify your name.
10 For you are great; you do wondrous things;*
 and you alone are God.
11 Teach me your way, O Lord,
 and I will walk in your truth;*
 knit my heart to you that I may fear your name.
12 I will thank you, O Lord my God, with all my heart,*
 and glorify your name for evermore.
13 For great is your love towards me;*
 you have delivered me from the nethermost Pit.
14 The arrogant rise up against me, O God,
 and a violent band seeks my life;*
 they have not set you before their eyes.
15 But you, O Lord, are gracious and full of compassion,*
 slow to anger and full of kindness and truth.
16 Turn to me and have mercy upon me;*
 give your strength to your servant;
 and save the child of your handmaid.
17 Show me a sign of your favour,
 so that those who hate me may see it and be ashamed;*
 because you, O Lord, have helped me and comforted me.

Psalm 87

1 On the holy mountain stands the city he has founded;*
 the Lord loves the gates of Zion
 more than all the dwellings of Jacob.
2 Glorious things are spoken of you,*

O city of our God.
3   I count Egypt and Babylon among those who know me;*
    behold Philistia, Tyre and Ethiopia:
    in Zion were they born.
4   Of Zion it shall be said, 'Everyone was born in her,*
    and the Most High himself shall sustain her.'
5   The Lord will record as he enrols the peoples,*
    'These also were born there.'
6   The singers and the dancers will say,*
    'All my fresh springs are in you.'

Psalm 88

1   O Lord, my God, my Saviour,*
    by day and night I cry to you.
2   Let my prayer enter into your presence;*
    incline your ear to my lamentation.
3   For I am full of trouble;*
    my life is at the brink of the grave.
4   I am counted among those who go down to the Pit;*
    I have become like one who has no strength;
5   Lost among the dead,*
    like the slain who lie in the grave,
6   Whom you remember no more,*
    for they are cut off from your hand.
7   You have laid me in the depths of the Pit,*
    in dark places and in the abyss.
8   Your anger weighs upon me heavily,*
    and all your great waves overwhelm me.
9   You have put my friends far from me;
    you have made me to be abhorred by them;*
    I am in prison and cannot get free.
10 My sight has failed me because of trouble;*
    Lord, I have called upon you daily;
    I have stretched out my hands to you.
11 Do you work wonders for the dead?*
    will those who have died
    stand up and give you thanks?
12 Will your loving-kindness be declared in the grave?*
    your faithfulness in the land of destruction?
13 Will your wonders be known in the dark?*
    or your righteousness in the country
    where all is forgotten?
14 But as for me, O Lord, I cry to you for help;*

in the morning my prayer comes before you.
15 Lord, why have you rejected me?*
why have you hidden your face from me?
16 Ever since my youth,
I have been wretched and at the point of death;*
I have borne your terrors with a troubled mind.
17 Your blazing anger has swept over me;*
your terrors have destroyed me;
18 They surround me all day long like a flood;*
they encompass me on every side.
19 My friend and my neighbour you have put away from me,*
and darkness is my only companion.

PSALMS 89–104

Psalm 89, Part I

1 Your love, O Lord, for ever will I sing;*
from age to age my mouth will proclaim your faithfulness.
2 For I am persuaded that your love is established for ever;*
you have set your faithfulness firmly in the heavens.
3 'I have made a covenant with my chosen one;*
I have sworn an oath to David my servant:
4 ' "I will establish your line for ever,*
and preserve your throne for all generations." '

* * *

5 The heavens bear witness to your wonders, O Lord,*
and to your faithfulness in the assembly of the holy ones;
6 For who in the skies can be compared to the Lord?*
who is like the Lord among the gods?
7 God is much to be feared in the council of the holy ones,*
great and terrible to all those round about him.
8 Who is like you, Lord God of hosts?*
O mighty Lord, your faithfulness is all around you.
9 You rule the raging of the sea*
and still the surging of its waves.
10 You have crushed Rahab of the deep with a deadly wound;*
you have scattered your enemies with your mighty arm.
11 Yours are the heavens; the earth also is yours;*
you laid the foundations of the world
and all that is in it.
12 You have made the north and the south;*
Tabor and Hermon rejoice in your name.

13 You have a mighty arm;*
    strong is your hand and high is your right hand.
14 Righteousness and justice
    are the foundations of your throne;*
    love and truth go before your face.
15 Happy are the people who know the festal shout!*
    they walk, O Lord, in the light of your presence.
16 They rejoice daily in your name;*
    they are jubilant in your righteousness.
17 For you are the glory of their strength,*
    and by your favour our might is exalted.
18 Truly, the Lord is our ruler;*
    the Holy One of Israel is our king.

Psalm 89, Part II

19 You spoke once in a vision
    and said to your faithful people:*
    'I have set the crown upon a warrior
    and have exalted one chosen out of the people.
20 'I have found David my servant;*
    with my holy oil have I anointed him.
21 'My hand will hold him fast*
    and my arm will make him strong.
22 'No enemy shall deceive him,*
    nor the wicked bring him down.
23 'I will crush his foes before him*
    and strike down those who hate him.
24 'My faithfulness and love shall be with him,*
    and he shall be victorious through my name.
25 'I shall make his dominion extend*
    from the Great Sea to the River.
26 'He will say to me, "You are my Father,*
    my God and the rock of my salvation."
27 'I will make him my first-born*
    and higher than the kings of the earth.
28 'I will keep my love for him for ever,*
    and my covenant will stand firm for him.
29 'I will establish his line for ever*
    and his throne as the days of heaven.
30 'If his children forsake my law*
    and do not walk according to my judgements;
31 'If they break my statutes*
    and do not keep my commandments;

A Celtic Primer

32 'I will punish their transgressions with a rod*
and their iniquities with the lash;

33 'But I will not take my love from him,*
nor let my faithfulness prove false.

34 'I will not break my covenant,*
nor change what has gone out of my lips.

35 'Once for all I have sworn by my holiness:*
"I will not lie to David.

36 ' "His line shall endure for ever*
and his throne as the sun before me;

37 ' "It shall stand fast for evermore like the moon,*
the abiding witness in the sky." '

38 But you have cast off and rejected your anointed;*
you have become enraged at him.

39 You have broken your covenant with your servant,*
defiled his crown and hurled it to the ground.

40 You have breached all his walls*
and laid his strongholds in ruins.

41 All who pass by despoil him;*
he has become the scorn of his neighbours.

42 You have exalted the right hand of his foes*
and made all his enemies rejoice.

43 You have turned back the edge of his sword*
and have not sustained him in battle.

44 You have put an end to his splendour*
and cast his throne to the ground.

45 You have cut short the days of his youth*
and have covered him with shame.

46 How long will you hide yourself, O Lord?
will you hide yourself for ever?*
how long will your anger burn like fire?

47 Remember, Lord, how short life is,*
how frail you have made all flesh.

48 Who can live and not see death?*
who can save himself from the power of the grave?

49 Where, Lord, are your loving-kindnesses of old,*
which you promised David in your faithfulness?

50 Remember, Lord, how your servant is mocked,*
how I carry in my bosom the taunts of many peoples,

51 The taunts your enemies have hurled, O Lord,*
which they hurled at the heels of your anointed.

52 Blessèd be the Lord for evermore!*
Amen, I say, Amen.

Psalm 90

1   Lord, you have been our refuge*
    from one generation to another.
2   Before the mountains were brought forth,
    or the land and the earth were born,*
    from age to age you are God.
3   You turn us back to the dust and say,*
    'Go back, O child of earth.'
4   For a thousand years in your sight
    are like yesterday when it is past*
    and like a watch in the night.
5   You sweep us away like a dream;*
    we fade away suddenly like the grass.
6   In the morning it is green and flourishes;*
    in the evening it is dried up and withered.
7   For we consume away in your displeasure;*
    we are afraid because of your wrathful indignation.
8   Our iniquities you have set before you,*
    and our secret sins in the light of your countenance.
9   When you are angry, all our days are gone;*
    we bring our years to an end like a sigh.
10 The span of our life is seventy years,
    perhaps in strength even eighty;*
    yet the sum of them is but labour and sorrow,
    for they pass away quickly and we are gone.
11 Who regards the power of your wrath?*
    who rightly fears your indignation?
12 So teach us to number our days*
    that we may apply our hearts to wisdom.
13 Return, O Lord; how long will you tarry?*
    be gracious to your servants.
14 Satisfy us by your loving-kindness in the morning;*
    so shall we rejoice and be glad all the days of our life.
15 Make us glad by the measure of the days
    that you afflicted us*
    and the years in which we suffered adversity.
16 Show your servants your works*
    and your splendour to their children.
17 May the graciousness of the Lord our God be upon us;*
    prosper the work of our hands;
    prosper our handiwork.

A Celtic Primer

Psalm 91

1 He who dwells in the shelter of the Most High,*
   abides under the shadow of the Almighty.
2 He shall say to the Lord,
   'You are my refuge and my stronghold,*
   my God in whom I put my trust.'
3 He shall deliver you from the snare of the hunter*
   and from the deadly pestilence.
4 He shall cover you with his pinions,
   and you shall find refuge under his wings;*
   his faithfulness shall be a shield and buckler.
5 You shall not be afraid of any terror by night,*
   nor of the arrow that flies by day;
6 Of the plague that stalks in the darkness,*
   nor of the sickness that lays waste at midday.
7 A thousand shall fall at your side
   and ten thousand at your right hand,*
   but it shall not come near you.
8 Your eyes have only to behold*
   to see the reward of the wicked.
9 Because you have made the Lord your refuge,*
   and the Most High your habitation.
10 There shall no evil happen to you,*
   neither shall any plague come near your dwelling.
11 For he shall give his angels charge over you,*
   to keep you in all your ways.
12 They shall bear you in their hands,*
   lest you dash your foot against a stone.
13 You shall tread upon the lion and adder;*
   you shall trample the young lion and the serpent
   under your feet.
14 Because he is bound to me in love,
   therefore will I deliver him;*
   I will protect him, because he knows my name.
15 He shall call upon me and I will answer him;*
   I am with him in trouble,
   I will rescue him and bring him to honour.
16 With long life will I satisfy him,*
   and show him my salvation.

Psalm 92

1 It is a good thing to give thanks to the Lord,*
and to sing praises to your name, O Most High;

2 To tell of your loving-kindness early in the morning*
and of your faithfulness in the night season;

3 On the psaltery and on the lyre*
and to the melody of the harp.

4 For you have made me glad by your acts, O Lord;*
and I shout for joy because of the works of your hands.

5 Lord, how great are your works!*
your thoughts are very deep.

6 The dullard does not know,
nor does the fool understand,*
that though the wicked grow like weeds,
and all the workers of iniquity flourish,

7 They flourish only to be destroyed for ever;*
but you, O Lord, are exalted for evermore.

8 For lo, your enemies, O Lord,
lo, your enemies shall perish,*
and all the workers of iniquity shall be scattered.

9 But my horn you have exalted
like the horns of wild bulls;*
I am anointed with fresh oil.

10 My eyes also gloat over my enemies,*
and my ears rejoice to hear the doom of the wicked
who rise up against me.

11 The righteous shall flourish like a palm tree,*
and shall spread abroad like a cedar of Lebanon.

12 Those who are planted in the house of the Lord*
shall flourish in the courts of our God;

13 They shall still bear fruit in old age;*
they shall be green and succulent;

14 That they may show how upright the Lord is,*
my rock, in whom there is no fault.

Psalm 93

1 The Lord is king; he has put on splendid apparel;*
the Lord has put on his apparel
and girded himself with strength.

2 He has made the whole world so sure*
that it cannot be moved;

3 Ever since the world began,

your throne has been established;*
you are from everlasting.

4   The waters have lifted up, O Lord,
the waters have lifted up their voice;*
the waters have lifted up their pounding waves.

5   Mightier than the sound of many waters,
mightier than the breakers of the sea,*
mightier is the Lord who dwells on high.

6   Your testimonies are very sure,*
and holiness adorns your house, O Lord,
for ever and for evermore.

Psalm 94

1   O Lord God of vengeance,*
O God of vengeance, show yourself.

2   Rise up, O Judge of the world;*
give the arrogant their just deserts.

3   How long shall the wicked, O Lord,*
how long shall the wicked triumph?

4   They bluster in their insolence;*
all evildoers are full of boasting.

5   They crush your people, O Lord,*
and afflict your chosen nation.

6   They murder the widow and the stranger*
and put the orphans to death.

7   Yet they say, 'The Lord does not see,*
the God of Jacob takes no notice.'

8   Consider well, you dullards among the people;*
when will you fools understand?

9   He that planted the ear, does he not hear?*
he that formed the eye, does he not see?

10 He who admonishes the nations, will he not punish?*
he who teaches all the world, has he no knowledge?

11 The Lord knows our human thoughts;*
how like a puff of wind they are.

12 Happy are they whom you instruct, O Lord!*
whom you teach out of your law;

13 To give them rest in evil days,*
until a pit is dug for the wicked.

14 For the Lord will not abandon his people,*
nor will he forsake his own.

15 For judgement will again be just,*
and all the true of heart will follow it.

16 Who rose up for me against the wicked?*
who took my part against the evildoers?
17 If the Lord had not come to my help,*
I should soon have dwelt in the land of silence.
18 As often as I said, 'My foot has slipped',*
your love, O Lord, upheld me.
19 When many cares fill my mind,*
your consolations cheer my soul.
20 Can a corrupt tribunal have any part with you,*
one which frames evil into law?
21 They conspire against the life of the just*
and condemn the innocent to death.
22 But the Lord has become my stronghold,*
and my God the rock of my trust.
23 He will turn their wickedness back upon them
and destroy them in their own malice;*
the Lord our God will destroy them.

Psalm 95

1 Come, let us sing to the Lord;*
let us shout for joy to the rock of our salvation.
2 Let us come before his presence with thanksgiving*
and raise a loud shout to him with psalms.
3 For the Lord is a great God,*
and a great king above all gods.
4 In his hand are the depths of the earth,*
and the heights of the hills are his also.
5 The sea is his, for he made it,*
and his hands have moulded the dry land.
6 Come, let us bow down and bend the knee,*
and kneel before the Lord our Maker.
7 For he is our God,
and we are the people of his pasture
and the sheep of his hand.*
O that today you would hearken to his voice!
8 'Harden not your hearts,
as your forebears did in the wilderness,*
at Meribah, and on that day at Massah,
when they tempted me.
9 'They put me to the test,*
though they had seen my works.
10 'Forty years long I detested that generation and said,*
"This people are wayward in their hearts; they do not know my ways."

A Celtic Primer

11   'So I swore in my wrath,*
      "They shall not enter into my rest." ' '

Psalm 96

1   Sing to the Lord a new song;*
     sing to the Lord, all the whole earth.
2   Sing to the Lord and bless his name;*
     proclaim the good news of his salvation from day to day.
3   Declare his glory among the nations*
     and his wonders among all peoples.
4   For great is the Lord and greatly to be praised;*
     he is more to be feared than all gods.
5   As for all the gods of the nations, they are but idols;*
     but it is the Lord who made the heavens.
6   O the majesty and magnificence of his presence!*
     O the power and the splendour of his sanctuary!
7   Ascribe to the Lord, you families of the peoples;*
     ascribe to the Lord honour and power.
8   Ascribe to the Lord the honour due to his name;*
     bring offerings and come into his courts.
9   Worship the Lord in the beauty of holiness;*
     let the whole earth tremble before him.
10   Tell it out among the nations: 'The Lord is king!*
     he has made the world so firm that it cannot be moved;
     he will judge the peoples with equity.'
11   Let the heavens rejoice and let the earth be glad;
     let the sea thunder and all that is in it;*
     let the field be joyful and all that is therein.
12   Then shall all the trees of the wood shout for joy
     before the Lord when he comes,*
     when he comes to judge the earth.
13   He will judge the world with righteousness*
     and the peoples with his truth.

Psalm 97

1   The Lord is king; let the earth rejoice;*
     let the multitude of the isles be glad.
2   Clouds and darkness are round about him,*
     righteousness and justice
     are the foundations of his throne.
3   A fire goes before him*
     and burns up his enemies on every side.

The Psalter, including Psalm Themes for Prayer   351

4   His lightnings light up the world;*
    the earth sees it and is afraid.
5   The mountains melt like wax
    at the presence of the Lord,*
    at the presence of the Lord of the whole earth.
6   The heavens declare his righteousness,*
    and all the peoples see his glory.
7   Confounded be all who worship carved images
    and delight in false gods!*
    Bow down before him, all you gods.
8   Zion hears and is glad and the cities of Judah rejoice,*
    because of your judgements, O Lord.
9   For you are the Lord: most high over all the earth;*
    you are exalted far above all gods.
10 The Lord loves those who hate evil;*
    he preserves the lives of his saints
    and delivers them from the hand of the wicked.
11 Light has sprung up for the righteous,*
    and joyful gladness for those who are true-hearted.
12 Rejoice in the Lord, you righteous,*
    and give thanks to his holy name.

Psalm 98

1   Sing to the Lord a new song,*
    for he has done marvellous things.
2   With his right hand and his holy arm*
    has he won for himself the victory.
3   The Lord has made known his victory;*
    his righteousness has he openly shown
    in the sight of the nations.
4   He remembers his mercy and faithfulness
    to the house of Israel,*
    and all the ends of the earth have seen
    the victory of our God.
5   Shout with joy to the Lord, all you lands;*
    lift up your voice, rejoice and sing.
6   Sing to the Lord with the harp,*
    with the harp and the voice of song.
7   With trumpets and the sound of the horn*
    shout with joy before the King, the Lord.
8   Let the sea make a noise and all that is in it,*
    the lands and those who dwell therein.
9   Let the rivers clap their hands,*

and let the hills ring out with joy before the Lord,
when he comes to judge the earth.
10   In righteousness shall he judge the world,*
and the peoples with equity.

Psalm 99

1   The Lord is king; let the people tremble;*
he is enthroned upon the cherubim; let the earth shake.
2   The Lord is great in Zion;*
he is high above all peoples.
3   Let them confess his name, which is great and awesome;*
he is the Holy One.
4   'O mighty King, lover of justice,
you have established equity;*
you have executed justice and righteousness in Jacob.'
5   Proclaim the greatness of the Lord our God
and fall down before his footstool;*
he is the Holy One.
6   Moses and Aaron among his priests,
and Samuel among those who call upon his name,*
they called upon the Lord and he answered them.
7   He spoke to them out of the pillar of cloud;*
they kept his testimonies
and the decree that he gave them.
8   'O Lord our God, you answered them indeed;*
you were a God who forgave them,
yet punished them for their evil deeds.'
9   Proclaim the greatness of the Lord our God
and worship him upon his holy hill;*
for the Lord our God is the Holy One.

Psalm 100

1   Be joyful in the Lord, all you lands;*
serve the Lord with gladness
and come before his presence with a song.
2   Know this: The Lord himself is God;*
he himself has made us and we are his;
we are his people and the sheep of his pasture.
3   Enter his gates with thanksgiving;
go into his courts with praise;*
give thanks to him and call upon his name.

4   For the Lord is good; his mercy is everlasting;*
     and his faithfulness endures from age to age.

Psalm 101

1   I will sing of mercy and justice;*
     to you, O Lord, will I sing praises.
2   I will strive to follow a blameless course;
     O when will you come to me?*
     I will walk with sincerity of heart within my house.
3   I will set no worthless thing before my eyes;*
     I hate the doers of evil deeds;
     they shall not remain with me.
4   A crooked heart shall be far from me;*
     I will not know evil.
[5   Those who in secret slander their neighbours
     I will destroy;*
     those who have a haughty look and a proud heart
     I cannot abide.]
6   My eyes are upon the faithful in the land,
     that they may dwell with me,*
     and only those who lead a blameless life
     shall be my servants.
7   Those who act deceitfully shall not dwell in my house,*
     and those who tell lies shall not continue in my sight.
[8   I will soon destroy all the wicked in the land,*
     that I may root out all evildoers
     from the city of the Lord.]

Psalm 102

1   Lord, hear my prayer and let my cry come before you;*
     hide not your face from me in the day of my trouble.
2   Incline your ear to me;*
     when I call, make haste to answer me,
3   For my days drift away like smoke,*
     and my bones are hot as burning coals.
4   My heart is smitten like grass and withered,*
     so that I forget to eat my bread.
5   Because of the voice of my groaning*
     I am but skin and bones.
6   I have become like a vulture in the wilderness,*
     like an owl among the ruins.
7   I lie awake and groan;*

I am like a sparrow, lonely on a house-top.

8   My enemies revile me all day long,*
and those who scoff at me
have taken an oath against me.

9   For I have eaten ashes for bread*
and mingled my drink with weeping.

10   Because of your indignation and wrath*
you have lifted me up and thrown me away.

11   My days pass away like a shadow,*
and I wither like the grass.

12   But you, O Lord, endure for ever,*
and your name from age to age.

13   You will arise and have compassion on Zion,
for it is time to have mercy upon her;*
indeed, the appointed time has come.

14   For your servants love her very rubble,*
and are moved to pity even for her dust.

15   The nations shall fear your name, O Lord,*
and all the kings of the earth your glory.

16   For the Lord will build up Zion,*
and his glory will appear.

17   He will look with favour on the prayer of the homeless;*
he will not despise their plea.

18   Let this be written for a future generation,*
so that a people yet unborn may praise the Lord.

19   For the Lord looked down from his holy place on high;*
from the heavens he beheld the earth;

20   That he might hear the groan of the captive*
and set free those condemned to die;

21   That they may declare in Zion the name of the Lord,*
and his praise in Jerusalem;

22   When the peoples are gathered together,*
and the kingdoms also, to serve the Lord.

23   He has brought down my strength before my time;*
he has shortened the number of my days;

24   And I said, 'O my God,
do not take me away in the midst of my days;*
your years endure throughout all generations.

25   'In the beginning, O Lord,
you laid the foundations of the earth,*
and the heavens are the work of your hands;

26   'They shall perish, but you will endure;
they all shall wear out like a garment;*
as clothing you will change them,

and they shall be changed;

27 'But you are always the same,*
and your years will never end.

28 'The children of your servants shall continue,*
and their offspring shall stand fast in your sight.'

Psalm 103

1 Bless the Lord, O my soul,*
and all that is within me, bless his holy name.

2 Bless the Lord, O my soul,*
and forget not all his benefits.

3 He forgives all your sins*
and heals all your infirmities;

4 He redeems your life from the grave*
and crowns you with mercy and loving-kindness;

5 He satisfies you with good things,*
and your youth is renewed like an eagle's.

6 The Lord executes righteousness*
and judgement for all who are oppressed.

7 He made his ways known to Moses*
and his works to the children of Israel.

8 The Lord is full of compassion and mercy,*
slow to anger and of great kindness.

9 He will not always accuse us,*
nor will he keep his anger for ever.

10 He has not dealt with us according to our sins,*
nor rewarded us according to our wickedness.

11 For as the heavens are high above the earth,*
so is his mercy great upon those who fear him.

12 As far as the east is from the west,*
so far has he removed our sins from us.

13 As a father cares for his children,*
so does the Lord care for those who fear him.

14 For he himself knows whereof we are made;*
he remembers that we are but dust.

15 Our days are like the grass;*
we flourish like a flower of the field;

16 When the wind goes over it, it is gone,*
and its place shall know it no more.

17 But the merciful goodness of the Lord
endures for ever on those who fear him,*
and his righteousness on children's children;

18 On those who keep his covenant*

and remember his commandments and do them.

19 The Lord has set his throne in heaven,*
and his kingship has dominion over all.

20 Bless the Lord, you angels of his,
you mighty ones who do his bidding,*
and hearken to the voice of his word.

21 Bless the Lord, all you his hosts,*
you ministers of his who do his will.

22 Bless the Lord, all you works of his,
in all places of his dominion;*
bless the Lord, O my soul.

Psalm 104

1 Bless the Lord, O my soul;*
O Lord my God, how excellent is your greatness!
you are clothed with majesty and splendour.

2 You wrap yourself with light as with a cloak*
and spread out the heavens like a curtain.

3 You lay the beams of your chambers
in the waters above;*
you make the clouds your chariot;
you ride on the wings of the wind.

4 You make the winds your messengers*
and flames of fire your servants.

5 You have set the earth upon its foundations,*
so that it never shall move at any time.

6 You covered it with the deep as with a mantle;*
the waters stood higher than the mountains.

7 At your rebuke they fled;*
at the voice of your thunder they hastened away.

8 They went up into the hills
and down to the valleys beneath,*
to the places you had appointed for them.

9 You set the limits that they should not pass;*
they shall not again cover the earth.

10 You send the springs into the valleys;*
they flow between the mountains.

11 All the beasts of the field drink their fill from them,*
and the wild asses quench their thirst.

12 Beside them the birds of the air make their nests*
and sing among the branches.

13 You water the mountains from your dwelling on high;*
the earth is fully satisfied by the fruit of your works.

14 You make grass grow for flocks and herds*
    and plants to serve us all;
15 That they may bring forth food from the earth,*
    and wine to gladden our hearts,
16 Oil to make a cheerful countenance,*
    and bread to strengthen the heart.
17 The trees of the Lord are full of sap,*
    the cedars of Lebanon which he planted,
18 In which the birds build their nests,*
    and in whose tops the stork makes his dwelling.
19 The high hills are a refuge for the mountain goats,*
    and the stony cliffs for the rock badgers.
20 You appointed the moon to mark the seasons,*
    and the sun knows the time of its setting.
21 You make darkness that it may be night,*
    in which all the beasts of the forest prowl.
22 The lions roar after their prey*
    and seek their food from God.
23 The sun rises and they slip away*
    and lay themselves down in their dens.
24 The labourer goes forth to work*
    and to toil until the evening.
25 O Lord, how manifold are your works!*
    in wisdom you have made them all;
    the earth is full of your creatures.
26 Yonder is the great and wide sea
    with its living things too many to number,*
    creatures both small and great.
27 There move the ships,
    and there is that Leviathan,*
    which you have made for the sport of it.
28 All of them look to you*
    to give them their food in due season.
29 You give it to them, they gather it;*
    you open your hand and they are filled with good things.
30 You hide your face and they are terrified;*
    you take away their breath
    and they die and return to their dust.
31 You send forth your Spirit and they are created;*
    and so you renew the face of the earth.
32 May the glory of the Lord endure for ever;*
    may the Lord rejoice in all his works.
33 He looks at the earth and it trembles;*
    he touches the mountains and they smoke.

34 I will sing to the Lord as long as I live;*
    I will praise my God while I have my being.

35 May these words of mine please him;*
    I will rejoice in the Lord.

36 Let sinners be consumed out of the earth,*
    and the wicked be no more.

37 Bless the Lord, O my soul.*
    Alleluia!

PSALMS 105–118

Psalm 105

1 Give thanks to the Lord and call upon his name;*
    make known his deeds among the peoples.

2 Sing to him, sing praises to him,*
    and speak of all his marvellous works.

3 Glory in his holy name;*
    let the hearts of those who seek the Lord rejoice.

4 Search for the Lord and his strength;*
    continually seek his face.

5 Remember the marvels he has done,*
    his wonders and the judgements of his mouth,

6 O offspring of Abraham his servant,*
    O children of Jacob his chosen.

7 He is the Lord our God;*
    his judgements prevail in all the world.

8 He has always been mindful of his covenant,*
    the promise he made for a thousand generations:

9 The covenant he made with Abraham,*
    the oath that he swore to Isaac,

10 Which he established as a statute for Jacob,*
    an everlasting covenant for Israel,

11 Saying, 'To you will I give the land of Canaan*
    to be your allotted inheritance.'

12 When they were few in number,*
    of little account and sojourners in the land,

13 Wandering from nation to nation*
    and from one kingdom to another,

14 He let no one oppress them*
    and rebuked kings for their sake,

15 Saying, 'Do not touch my anointed*
    and do my prophets no harm.'

16 Then he called for a famine in the land*
    and destroyed the supply of bread.
17 He sent a man before them,*
    Joseph, who was sold as a slave.
18 They bruised his feet in fetters;*
    his neck they put in an iron collar.
19 Until his prediction came to pass,*
    the word of the Lord tested him.
20 The king sent and released him;*
    the ruler of the peoples set him free.
21 He set him as master over his household,*
    as a ruler over all his possessions,
22 To instruct his princes according to his will*
    and to teach his elders wisdom.

                    *   *   *

23 Israel came into Egypt,*
    and Jacob became a sojourner in the land of Ham.
24 The Lord made his people exceedingly fruitful;*
    he made them stronger than their enemies;
25 Whose heart he turned, so that they hated his people,*
    and dealt unjustly with his servants.
26 He sent Moses his servant,*
    and Aaron whom he had chosen.
27 They worked his signs among them,*
    and portents in the land of Ham.
28 He sent darkness and it grew dark;*
    but the Egyptians rebelled against his words.
29 He turned their waters into blood*
    and caused their fish to die.
30 Their land was overrun by frogs,*
    in the very chambers of their kings.
31 He spoke and there came swarms of insects*
    and gnats within all their borders.
32 He gave them hailstones instead of rain,*
    and flames of fire throughout their land.
33 He blasted their vines and their fig trees*
    and shattered every tree in their country.
34 He spoke and the locust came,*
    and young locusts without number,
35 Which ate up all the green plants in their land*
    and devoured the fruit of their soil.
36 He struck down the first-born of their land,*
    the first-fruits of all their strength.
37 He led out his people with silver and gold;*

in all their tribes there was not one that stumbled.
38   Egypt was glad of their going,*
     because they were afraid of them.
39   He spread out a cloud for a covering*
     and a fire to give light in the night season.
40   They asked and quails appeared,*
     and he satisfied them with bread from heaven.
41   He opened the rock and water flowed,*
     so the river ran in the dry places.
42   For God remembered his holy word*
     and Abraham his servant.
43   So he led forth his people with gladness,*
     his chosen with shouts of joy.
44   He gave his people the lands of the nations,*
     and they took the fruit of others' toil,
45   That they might keep his statutes*
     and observe his laws.
     Alleluia!

Psalm 106

1   Alleluia!
     Give thanks to the Lord, for he is good,*
     for his mercy endures for ever.
2   Who can declare the mighty acts of the Lord*
     or show forth all his praise?
3   Happy are those who act with justice*
     and always do what is right!
4   Remember me, O Lord,
     with the favour you have for your people,*
     and visit me with your saving help;
5   That I may see the prosperity of your elect
     and be glad with the gladness of your people,*
     that I may glory with your inheritance.
6   We have sinned as our forebears did;*
     we have done wrong and dealt wickedly.
7   In Egypt they did not consider your marvellous works,
     nor remember the abundance of your love;*
     they defied the Most High at the Red Sea.
8   But he saved them for his name's sake,*
     to make his power known.
9   He rebuked the Red Sea and it dried up,*
     and he led them through the deep as through a desert.
10   He saved them from the hand of those who hated them*

and redeemed them from the hand of the enemy.
11   The waters covered their oppressors;*
     not one of them was left.
12   Then they believed his words*
     and sang him songs of praise.
13   But they soon forgot his deeds*
     and did not wait for his counsel.
14   A craving seized them in the wilderness,*
     and they put God to the test in the desert.
15   He gave them what they asked,*
     but sent leanness into their soul.
16   They envied Moses in the camp,*
     and Aaron, the holy one of the Lord.
17   The earth opened and swallowed Dathan*
     and covered the company of Abiram.
18   Fire blazed up against their company,*
     and flames devoured the wicked.
19   Israel made a bull-calf at Horeb*
     and worshipped a molten image;
20   And so they exchanged their Glory*
     for the image of an ox that feeds on grass.
21   They forgot God their saviour,*
     who had done great things in Egypt,
22   Wonderful deeds in the land of Ham,*
     and fearful things at the Red Sea.
23   So he would have destroyed them,
     had not Moses his chosen
     stood before him in the breach,*
     to turn away his wrath from consuming them.

       *   *   *

24   Our forebears refused the pleasant land*
     and would not believe God's promise.
25   They grumbled in their tents*
     and would not listen to the voice of the Lord.
26   So he lifted his hand against them,*
     to overthrow them in the wilderness,
27   To cast out their seed among the nations,*
     and to scatter them throughout the lands.
28   They joined themselves to Baal-Peor*
     and ate sacrifices offered to the dead.
29   They provoked him to anger with their actions,*
     and a plague broke out among them.
30   Then Phinehas stood up and interceded,*
     and the plague came to an end.

A Celtic Primer

31 This was reckoned to him as righteousness*
   throughout all generations for ever.
32 Again they provoked his anger at the waters of Meribah,*
   so that he punished Moses because of them;
33 For they so embittered his spirit*
   that he spoke rash words with his lips.
34 They did not destroy the peoples*
   as the Lord had commanded them.
35 They intermingled with the heathen*
   and learned their pagan ways,
36 So that they worshipped their idols,*
   which became a snare to them.
37 They sacrificed their sons*
   and their daughters to evil spirits.
38 They shed innocent blood,
   the blood of their sons and daughters,*
   which they offered to the idols of Canaan,
   and the land was defiled with blood.
39 Thus they were polluted by their actions*
   and went whoring in their evil deeds;
40 Therefore the wrath of the Lord
   was kindled against his people*
   and he abhorred his inheritance.
41 He gave them over to the hand of the heathen,*
   and those who hated them ruled over them.
42 Their enemies oppressed them,*
   and they were humbled under their hand.
43 Many a time did he deliver them,
   but they rebelled through their own devices,*
   and were brought down in their iniquity.
44 Nevertheless, he saw their distress,*
   when he heard their lamentation.
45 He remembered his covenant with them*
   and relented in accordance with his great mercy.
46 He caused them to be pitied*
   by those who held them captive.
47 Save us, O Lord our God,
   and gather us from among the nations,*
   that we may give thanks to your holy name
   and glory in your praise.
48 Blessèd be the Lord, the God of Israel,
   from everlasting and to everlasting;*
   and let all the people say, 'Amen!'
   Alleluia!

Psalm 107

1   Give thanks to the Lord, for he is good,*
     and his mercy endures for ever.
2   Let all those whom the Lord has redeemed proclaim*
     that he redeemed them from the hand of the foe.
3   He gathered them out of the lands;*
     from the east and from the west,
     from the north and from the south.
4   Some wandered in desert wastes;*
     they found no way to a city where they might dwell.
5   They were hungry and thirsty;*
     their spirits languished within them.
6   Then they cried to the Lord in their trouble,*
     and he delivered them from their distress.
7   He put their feet on a straight path*
     to go to a city where they might dwell.
8   Let them give thanks to the Lord for his mercy*
     and the wonders he does for his children.
9   For he satisfies the thirsty*
     and fills the hungry with good things.
10   Some sat in darkness and deep gloom,*
     bound fast in misery and iron;
11   Because they rebelled against the words of God*
     and despised the counsel of the Most High.
12   So he humbled their spirits with hard labour;*
     they stumbled and there was none to help.
13   Then they cried to the Lord in their trouble,*
     and he delivered them from their distress.
14   He led them out of darkness and deep gloom*
     and broke their bonds asunder.
15   Let them give thanks to the Lord for his mercy*
     and the wonders he does for his children.
16   For he shatters the doors of bronze*
     and breaks in two the iron bars.
17   Some were fools and took to rebellious ways;*
     they were afflicted because of their sins.
18   They abhorred all manner of food*
     and drew near to death's door.
19   Then they cried to the Lord in their trouble,*
     and he delivered them from their distress.
20   He sent forth his word and healed them*
     and saved them from the grave.
21   Let them give thanks to the Lord for his mercy*

A Celtic Primer

and the wonders he does for his children.
22 Let them offer a sacrifice of thanksgiving*
and tell of his acts with shouts of joy.
23 Some went down to the sea in ships*
and plied their trade in deep waters;
24 They beheld the works of the Lord*
and his wonders in the deep.
25 Then he spoke and a stormy wind arose,*
which tossed high the waves of the sea.
26 They mounted up to the heavens
and fell back to the depths;*
their hearts melted because of their peril.
27 They reeled and staggered like drunkards*
and were at their wits' end.
28 Then they cried to the Lord in their trouble,*
and he delivered them from their distress.
29 He stilled the storm to a whisper*
and quieted the waves of the sea.
30 Then were they glad because of the calm,*
and he brought them
to the harbour they were bound for.
31 Let them give thanks to the Lord for his mercy*
and the wonders he does for his children.
32 Let them exalt him in the congregation of the people*
and praise him in the council of the elders.

*   *   *

33 The Lord changed rivers into deserts,*
and water-springs into thirsty ground,
34 A fruitful land into salt flats,*
because of the wickedness of those who dwell there.
35 He changed deserts into pools of water*
and dry land into water-springs.
36 He settled the hungry there,*
and they founded a city to dwell in.
37 They sowed fields and planted vineyards,*
and brought in a fruitful harvest.
38 He blessed them, so that they increased greatly;*
he did not let their herds decrease.
39 Yet when they were diminished and brought low,*
through stress of adversity and sorrow,
40 He lifted up the poor out of misery*
and multiplied their families like flocks of sheep.
41 He pours contempt on princes*
and makes them wander in trackless wastes.

42   The upright will see this and rejoice,*
      but all wickedness will shut its mouth.

43   Whoever is wise will ponder these things,*
      and consider well the mercies of the Lord.

Psalm 108

1   My heart is firmly fixed, O God, my heart is fixed;*
      I will sing and make melody.

2   Wake up, my spirit; awake, lute and harp;*
      I myself will waken the dawn.

3   I will confess you among the peoples, O Lord;*
      I will sing praises to you among the nations.

4   For your loving-kindness is greater than the heavens,*
      and your faithfulness reaches to the clouds.

5   Exalt yourself above the heavens, O God,*
      and your glory over all the earth.

6   So that those who are dear to you may be delivered,*
      save with your right hand and answer me.

7   God spoke from his holy place and said,*
      'I will exult and parcel out Shechem;
      I will divide the valley of Succoth.

8   'Gilead is mine and Manasseh is mine;*
      Ephraim is my helmet and Judah my sceptre.

9   'Moab is my wash-basin,
      on Edom I throw down my sandal to claim it,*
      and over Philistia will I shout in triumph.'

10   Who will lead me into the strong city?*
      who will bring me into Edom?

11   Have you not cast us off, O God?*
      you no longer go out, O God, with our armies.

12   Grant us your help against the enemy,*
      for vain is any human help.

13   With God we will do valiant deeds,*
      and he shall tread our enemies under foot.

Psalm 109

1   Hold not your tongue, O God of my praise;*
      for the mouth of the wicked,
      the mouth of the deceitful, is opened against me.

2   They speak to me with a lying tongue;*
      they encompass me with hateful words
      and fight against me without a cause.

3   Despite my love, they accuse me;*
      but as for me, I pray for them.
4   They repay evil for good,*
      and hatred for my love.
[5   Set the wicked against him,*
      and let an accuser stand at his right hand.
6   When he is judged, let him be found guilty,*
      and let his appeal be in vain.
7   Let his days be few,*
      and let another take his office.
8   Let his children be fatherless,*
      and his wife become a widow.
9   Let his children be waifs and beggars;*
      let them be driven from the ruins of their homes.
10   Let the creditor seize everything he has;*
      let strangers plunder his gains.
11   Let there be no one to show him kindness,*
      and none to pity his fatherless children.
12   Let his descendants be destroyed,*
      and his name be blotted out in the next generation.
13   Let the wickedness of his forebears
      be remembered before the Lord,*
      and his mother's sin not be blotted out;
14   Let their sin be always before the Lord;*
      but let him root out their names from the earth;
15   Because he did not remember to show mercy,*
      but persecuted the poor and needy
      and sought to kill the brokenhearted.
16   He loved cursing: let it come upon him;*
      he took no delight in blessing: let it depart from him.
17   He put on cursing like a garment:*
      let it soak into his body like water
      and into his bones like oil;
18   Let it be to him like the cloak
      which he wraps around himself,*
      and like the belt that he wears continually.
19   Let this be the recompense from the Lord to my accusers,*
      and to those who speak evil against me.]
20   But you, O Lord my God,
      O deal with me according to your name;*
      for your tender mercy's sake, deliver me.
21   For I am poor and needy,*
      and my heart is wounded within me.
22   I have faded away like a shadow when it lengthens;*

I am shaken off like a locust.

23   My knees are weak through fasting,*
and my flesh is wasted and gaunt.

24   I have become a reproach to them;*
they see and shake their heads.

25   Help me, O Lord my God;*
save me for your mercy's sake.

26   Let them know that this is your hand,*
that you, O Lord, have done it.

27   They may curse, but you will bless;*
let those who rise up against me be put to shame,
and your servant will rejoice.

28   Let my accusers be clothed with disgrace*
and wrap themselves in their shame as in a cloak.

29   I will give great thanks to the Lord with my mouth;*
in the midst of the multitude will I praise him;

30   Because he stands at the right hand of the needy,*
to save his life from those who would condemn him.

Psalm 110

1   The Lord said to my lord, 'Sit at my right hand,*
until I make your enemies your footstool.'

2   The Lord will send the sceptre of your power
out of Zion,*
saying, 'Rule over your enemies round about you.

3   'Princely state has been yours
from the day of your birth,*
in the beauty of holiness have I begotten you,
like dew from the womb of the morning.'

4   The Lord has sworn and he will not recant:*
'You are a priest for ever after the order of Melchizedek.'

5   The Lord who is at your right hand
will smite kings in the day of his wrath;*
he will rule over the nations.

6   He will heap high the corpses;*
he will smash heads over the wide earth.

7   He will drink from the brook beside the road;*
therefore he will lift high his head.

Psalm 111

1   Alleluia!
I will give thanks to the Lord with my whole heart,*

in the assembly of the upright, in the congregation.
2   Great are the deeds of the Lord!*
    they are studied by all who delight in them.
3   His work is full of majesty and splendour,*
    and his righteousness endures for ever.
4   He makes his marvellous works to be remembered;*
    the Lord is gracious and full of compassion.
5   He gives food to those who fear him;*
    he is ever mindful of his covenant.
6   He has shown his people the power of his works*
    in giving them the lands of the nations.
7   The works of his hands are faithfulness and justice;*
    all his commandments are sure.
8   They stand fast for ever and ever,*
    because they are done in truth and equity.
9   He sent redemption to his people;
    he commanded his covenant for ever;*
    holy and awesome is his name.
10 The fear of the Lord is the beginning of wisdom;*
    those who act accordingly have a good understanding;
    his praise endures for ever.

Psalm 112

1   Alleluia!
    Happy are they who fear the Lord*
    and have great delight in his commandments!
2   Their descendants will be mighty in the land;*
    the generation of the upright will be blessed.
3   Wealth and riches will be in their house,*
    and their righteousness will last for ever.
4   Light shines in the darkness for the upright;*
    the righteous are merciful and full of compassion.
5   It is good for them to be generous in lending*
    and to manage their affairs with justice.
6   For they will never be shaken;*
    the righteous will be kept in everlasting remembrance.
7   They will not be afraid of any evil rumours;*
    their heart is right;
    they put their trust in the Lord.
8   Their heart is established and will not shrink,*
    until they see their desire upon their enemies.
9   They have given freely to the poor,*
    and their righteousness stands fast for ever;

they will hold up their head with honour.
10   The wicked will see it and be angry;
     they will gnash their teeth and pine away;*
     the desires of the wicked will perish.

Psalm 113

1   Alleluia!
     Give praise, you servants of the Lord;*
     praise the name of the Lord.
2   Let the name of the Lord be blessed,*
     from this time forth for evermore.
3   From the rising of the sun to its going down*
     let the name of the Lord be praised.
4   The Lord is high above all nations,*
     and his glory above the heavens.
5   Who is like the Lord our God,
     who sits enthroned on high,*
     but stoops to behold the heavens and the earth?
6   He takes up the weak out of the dust*
     and lifts up the poor from the ashes.
7   He sets them with the princes,*
     with the princes of his people.
8   He makes the woman of a childless house*
     to be a joyful mother of children.

Psalm 114

1   Alleluia!
     When Israel came out of Egypt,*
     the house of Jacob from a people of strange speech,
2   Judah became God's sanctuary*
     and Israel his dominion.
3   The sea beheld it and fled;*
     Jordan turned and went back.
4   The mountains skipped like rams,*
     and the little hills like young sheep.
5   What ailed you, O sea, that you fled?*
     O Jordan, that you turned back?
6   You mountains, that you skipped like rams?*
     you little hills like young sheep?
7   Tremble, O earth, at the presence of the Lord,*
     at the presence of the God of Jacob,
8   Who turned the hard rock into a pool of water*
     and flint-stone into a flowing spring.

Psalm 115

1   Not to us, O Lord, not to us,
    but to your name give glory;*
    because of your love and because of your faithfulness.
2   Why should the heathen say,*
    'Where then is their God?'
3   Our God is in heaven;*
    whatever he wills to do he does.
4   Their idols are silver and gold,*
    the work of human hands.
5   They have mouths, but they cannot speak;*
    eyes have they, but they cannot see;
6   They have ears, but they cannot hear;*
    noses, but they cannot smell;
7   They have hands, but they cannot feel;
    feet, but they cannot walk;*
    they make no sound with their throat.
8   Those who make them are like them,*
    and so are all who put their trust in them.
9   O Israel, trust in the Lord;*
    he is their help and their shield.
10 O house of Aaron, trust in the Lord;*
    he is their help and their shield.
11 You who fear the Lord, trust in the Lord;*
    he is their help and their shield.
12 The Lord has been mindful of us and he will bless us;*
    he will bless the house of Israel;
    he will bless the house of Aaron;
13 He will bless those who fear the Lord,*
    both small and great together.
14 May the Lord increase you more and more,*
    you and your children after you.
15 May you be blessed by the Lord,*
    the maker of heaven and earth.
16 The heaven of heavens is the Lord's,*
    but he entrusted the earth to its peoples.
17 The dead do not praise the Lord,*
    nor all those who go down into silence;
18 But we will bless the Lord,*
    from this time forth for evermore.
    Alleluia!

Psalm 116

1 I love the Lord,
   because he has heard the voice of my supplication,*
   because he has inclined his ear to me
   whenever I called upon him.

2 The cords of death entangled me;
   the grip of the grave took hold of me;*
   I came to grief and sorrow.

3 Then I called upon the name of the Lord:*
   'O Lord, I pray you, save my life.'

4 Gracious is the Lord and righteous;*
   our God is full of compassion.

5 The Lord watches over the innocent;*
   I was brought very low and he helped me.

6 Turn again to your rest, O my soul,*
   for the Lord has treated you well.

7 For you have rescued my life from death,*
   my eyes from tears and my feet from stumbling.

8 I will walk in the presence of the Lord*
   in the land of the living.

9 I believed, even when I said,
   'I have been brought very low.'*
   In my distress I said, 'No one can be trusted.'

10 How shall I repay the Lord*
   for all the good things he has done for me?

11 I will lift up the cup of salvation*
   and call upon the name of the Lord.

12 I will fulfil my vows to the Lord*
   in the presence of all his people.

13 Precious in the sight of the Lord*
   is the death of his servants.

14 O Lord, I am your servant;*
   I am your servant and the child of your handmaid;
   you have freed me from my bonds.

15 I will offer you the sacrifice of thanksgiving*
   and call upon the name of the Lord.

16 I will fulfil my vows to the Lord*
   in the presence of all his people.

17 In the courts of the Lord's house,*
   in the midst of you, O Jerusalem.
   Alleluia!

A Celtic Primer

Psalm 117

1   Praise the Lord, all you nations;*
    laud him, all you peoples.

2   For his loving-kindness towards us is great,*
    and the faithfulness of the Lord endures for ever.
    Alleluia!

Psalm 118

1   Give thanks to the Lord, for he is good;*
    his mercy endures for ever.

2   Let Israel now proclaim,*
    'His mercy endures for ever.'

3   Let the house of Aaron now proclaim,*
    'His mercy endures for ever.'

4   Let those who fear the Lord now proclaim,*
    'His mercy endures for ever.'

5   I called to the Lord in my distress;*
    the Lord answered by setting me free.

6   The Lord is at my side, therefore I will not fear;*
    what can anyone do to me?

7   The Lord is at my side to help me;*
    I will triumph over those who hate me.

8   It is better to rely on the Lord*
    than to put any trust in flesh.

9   It is better to rely on the Lord*
    than to put any trust in rulers.

10   All the ungodly encompass me;*
    in the name of the Lord I will repel them.

11   They hem me in, they hem me in on every side;*
    in the name of the Lord I will repel them.

12   They swarm about me like bees;
    they blaze like a fire of thorns;*
    in the name of the Lord I will repel them.

13   I was pressed so hard that I almost fell,*
    but the Lord came to my help.

14   The Lord is my strength and my song,*
    and he has become my salvation.

15   There is a sound of exultation and victory*
    in the tents of the righteous:

16   'The right hand of the Lord has triumphed!*
    the right hand of the Lord is exalted!
    the right hand of the Lord has triumphed!'

17 I shall not die, but live,*
    and declare the works of the Lord.
18 The Lord has punished me sorely,*
    but he did not hand me over to death.
19 Open for me the gates of righteousness;*
    I will enter them; I will offer thanks to the Lord.
20 'This is the gate of the Lord;*
    whoever is righteous may enter.'
21 I will give thanks to you, for you answered me*
    and have become my salvation.
22 The same stone which the builders rejected*
    has become the chief corner-stone.
23 This is the Lord's doing,*
    and it is marvellous in our eyes.
24 On this day the Lord has acted;*
    we will rejoice and be glad in it.
25 Hosanna, Lord, hosanna!*
    Lord, send us now success.
26 Blessèd is he who comes in the name of the Lord;*
    we bless you from the house of the Lord.
27 God is the Lord; he has shined upon us;*
    form a procession with branches
    up to the horns of the altar.
28 'You are my God and I will thank you;*
    you are my God and I will exalt you.'
29 Give thanks to the Lord, for he is good;*
    his mercy endures for ever.

Psalms 119–131

Psalm 119

1 Happy are they whose way is blameless,*
    who walk in the law of the Lord!
2 Happy are they who observe his decrees*
    and seek him with all their hearts!
3 Who never do any wrong,*
    but always walk in his ways.
4 You laid down your commandments,*
    that we should fully keep them.
5 O that my ways were made so direct*
    that I might keep your statutes!
6 Then I should not be put to shame,*

A Celtic Primer

when I regard all your commandments.
7   I will thank you with an unfeigned heart,*
     when I have learned your righteous judgements.
8   I will keep your statutes;*
     do not utterly forsake me.

        *   *   *

9   How shall the young cleanse their way?*
     By keeping to your words.
10   With my whole heart I seek you;*
     let me not stray from your commandments.
11   I treasure your promise in my heart,*
     that I may not sin against you.
12   Blessèd are you, O Lord;*
     instruct me in your statutes.
13   With my lips will I recite*
     all the judgements of your mouth.
14   I have taken greater delight in the way of your decrees*
     than in all manner of riches.
15   I will meditate on your commandments*
     and give attention to your ways.
16   My delight is in your statutes;*
     I will not forget your word.

        *   *   *

17   Deal bountifully with your servant,*
     that I may live and keep your word.
18   Open my eyes, that I may see*
     the wonders of your law.
19   I am a stranger here on earth;*
     do not hide your commandments from me.
20   My soul is consumed at all times*
     with longing for your judgements.
21   You have rebuked the insolent;*
     cursed are they who stray from your commandments!
22   Turn from me shame and rebuke,*
     for I have kept your decrees.
23   Even though rulers sit and plot against me,*
     I will meditate on your statutes.
24   For your decrees are my delight,*
     and they are my counsellors.

        *   *   *

25   My soul cleaves to the dust;*
     give me life according to your word.
26   I have confessed my ways and you answered me;*
     instruct me in your statutes.

27 Make me understand the way of your commandments,*
   that I may meditate on your marvellous works.
28 My soul melts away for sorrow;*
   strengthen me according to your word.
29 Take from me the way of lying;*
   let me find grace through your law.
30 I have chosen the way of faithfulness;*
   I have set your judgements before me.
31 I hold fast to your decrees;*
   O Lord, let me not be put to shame.
32 I will run the way of your commandments,*
   for you have set my heart at liberty.

                *   *   *

33 Teach me, O Lord, the way of your statutes,*
   and I shall keep it to the end.
34 Give me understanding and I shall keep your law;*
   I shall keep it with all my heart.
35 Make me go in the path of your commandments,*
   for that is my desire.
36 Incline my heart to your decrees*
   and not to unjust gain.
37 Turn my eyes from watching what is worthless;*
   give me life in your ways.
38 Fulfil your promise to your servant,*
   which you make to those who fear you.
39 Turn away the reproach which I dread,*
   because your judgements are good.
40 Behold, I long for your commandments;*
   in your righteousness preserve my life.

                *   *   *

41 Let your loving-kindness come to me, O Lord,*
   and your salvation, according to your promise.
42 Then shall I have a word for those who taunt me,*
   because I trust in your words.
43 Do not take the word of truth out of my mouth,*
   for my hope is in your judgements.
44 I shall continue to keep your law;*
   I shall keep it for ever and ever.
45 I will walk at liberty,*
   because I study your commandments.
46 I will tell of your decrees before kings*
   and will not be ashamed.
47 I delight in your commandments,*
   which I have always loved.

A Celtic Primer

48   I will lift up my hands to your commandments,*
and I will meditate on your statutes.

           *   *   *

49   Remember your word to your servant,*
because you have given me hope.

50   This is my comfort in my trouble,*
that your promise gives me life.

51   The proud have derided me cruelly,*
but I have not turned from your law.

52   When I remember your judgements of old,*
O Lord, I take great comfort.

53   I am filled with a burning rage,*
because of the wicked who forsake your law.

54   Your statutes have been like songs to me*
wherever I have lived as a stranger.

55   I remember your name in the night, O Lord,*
and dwell upon your law.

56   This is how it has been with me,*
because I have kept your commandments.

           *   *   *

57   You only are my portion, O Lord;*
I have promised to keep your words.

58   I entreat you with all my heart,*
be merciful to me according to your promise.

59   I have considered my ways*
and turned my feet towards your decrees.

60   I hasten and do not tarry*
to keep your commandments.

61   Though the cords of the wicked entangle me,*
I do not forget your law.

62   At midnight I will rise to give you thanks,*
because of your righteous judgements.

63   I am a companion of all who fear you*
and of those who keep your commandments.

64   The earth, O Lord, is full of your love;*
instruct me in your statutes.

           *   *   *

65   O Lord, you have dealt graciously with your servant,*
according to your word.

66   Teach me discernment and knowledge,*
for I have believed in your commandments.

67   Before I was afflicted I went astray,*
but now I keep your word.

68   You are good and you bring forth good;*

instruct me in your statutes.
69   The proud have smeared me with lies,*
      but I will keep your commandments
      with my whole heart.
70   Their heart is gross and fat,*
      but my delight is in your law.
71   It is good for me that I have been afflicted,*
      that I might learn your statutes.
72   The law of your mouth is dearer to me*
      than thousands in gold and silver.

                *   *   *

73   Your hands have made me and fashioned me;*
      give me understanding,
      that I may learn your commandments.
74   Those who fear you will be glad when they see me,*
      because I trust in your word.
75   I know, O Lord, that your judgements are right*
      and that in faithfulness you have afflicted me.
76   Let your loving-kindness be my comfort*
      as you have promised to your servant.
77   Let your compassion come to me, that I may live,*
      for your law is my delight.
78   Let the arrogant be put to shame,
      for they wrong me with lies;*
      but I will meditate on your commandments.
79   Let those who fear you turn to me,*
      and also those who know your decrees.
80   Let my heart be sound in your statutes,*
      that I may not be put to shame.

                *   *   *

81   My soul has longed for your salvation;*
      I have put my hope in your word.
82   My eyes have failed from watching for your promise,*
      and I say, 'When will you comfort me?'
83   I have become like a leather flask in the smoke,*
      but I have not forgotten your statutes.
84   How much longer must I wait?*
      when will you give judgement
      against those who persecute me?
85   The proud have dug pits for me;*
      they do not keep your law.
86   All your commandments are true;*
      help me, for they persecute me with lies.
87   They had almost made an end of me on earth,*

but I have not forsaken your commandments.
88 In your loving-kindness, revive me,*
that I may keep the decrees of your mouth.

      *   *   *

89 O Lord, your word is everlasting;*
it stands firm in the heavens.
90 Your faithfulness remains
from one generation to another;*
you established the earth and it abides.
91 By your decree these continue to this day,*
for all things are your servants.
92 If my delight had not been in your law,*
I should have perished in my affliction.
93 I will never forget your commandments,*
because by them you give me life.
94 I am yours; O that you would save me!*
for I study your commandments.
95 Though the wicked lie in wait for me to destroy me,*
I will apply my mind to your decrees.
96 I see that all things come to an end,*
but your commandment has no bounds.

      *   *   *

97 O how I love your law!*
all the day long it is in my mind.
98 Your commandment has made me wiser
than my enemies,*
and it is always with me.
99 I have more understanding than all my teachers,*
for your decrees are my study.
100 I am wiser than the elders,*
because I observe your commandments.
101 I restrain my feet from every evil way,*
that I may keep your word.
102 I do not shrink from your judgements,*
because you yourself have taught me.
103 How sweet are your words to my taste!*
they are sweeter than honey to my mouth.
104 Through your commandments I gain understanding;*
therefore I hate every lying way.

      *   *   *

105 Your word is a lantern to my feet*
and a light upon my path.
106 I have sworn and am determined*
to keep your righteous judgements.

107 I am deeply troubled;*
    preserve my life, O Lord, according to your word.
108 Accept, O Lord, the willing tribute of my lips,*
    and teach me your judgements.
109 My life is always in my hand,*
    yet I do not forget your law.
110 The wicked have set a trap for me,*
    but I have not strayed from your commandments.
111 Your decrees are my inheritance for ever;*
    truly, they are the joy of my heart.
112 I have applied my heart to fulfil your statutes*
    for ever and to the end.

            *   *   *

113 I hate those who have a divided heart,*
    but your law do I love.
114 You are my refuge and shield;*
    my hope is in your word.
115 Away from me, you wicked!*
    I will keep the commandments of my God.
116 Sustain me according to your promise, that I may live,*
    and let me not be disappointed in my hope.
117 Hold me up and I shall be safe,*
    and my delight shall be ever in your statutes.
118 You spurn all who stray from your statutes;*
    their deceitfulness is in vain.
119 In your sight all the wicked of the earth are but dross;*
    therefore I love your decrees.
120 My flesh trembles with dread of you;*
    I am afraid of your judgements.

            *   *   *

121 I have done what is just and right;*
    do not deliver me to my oppressors.
122 Be surety for your servant's good;*
    let not the proud oppress me.
123 My eyes have failed from watching for your salvation*
    and for your righteous promise.
124 Deal with your servant
    according to your loving-kindness*
    and teach me your statutes.
125 I am your servant; grant me understanding,*
    that I may know your decrees.
126 It is time for you to act, O Lord,*
    for they have broken your law.
127 Truly, I love your commandments*

more than gold and precious stones.
128 I hold all your commandments to be right for me;*
all paths of falsehood I abhor.

       *   *   *

129 Your decrees are wonderful;*
therefore I obey them with all my heart.
130 When your word goes forth it gives light;*
it gives understanding to the simple.
131 I open my mouth and pant;*
I long for your commandments.
132 Turn to me in mercy,*
as you always do to those who love your name.
133 Steady my footsteps in your word;*
let no iniquity have dominion over me.
134 Rescue me from those who oppress me,*
and I will keep your commandments.
135 Let your countenance shine upon your servant*
and teach me your statutes.
136 My eyes shed streams of tears,*
because people do not keep your law.

       *   *   *

137 You are righteous, O Lord,*
and upright are your judgements.
138 You have issued your decrees*
with justice and in perfect faithfulness.
139 My indignation has consumed me,*
because my enemies forget your words.
140 Your word has been tested to the uttermost,*
and your servant holds it dear.
141 I am small and of little account,*
yet I do not forget your commandments.
142 Your justice is an everlasting justice*
and your law is the truth.
143 Trouble and distress have come upon me,*
yet your commandments are my delight.
144 The righteousness of your decrees is everlasting;*
grant me understanding, that I may live.

       *   *   *

145 I call with my whole heart;*
answer me, O Lord, that I may keep your statutes.
146 I call to you; O that you would save me!*
I will keep your decrees.
147 Early in the morning I cry out to you,*
for in your word is my trust.

148   My eyes are open in the night watches,*
     that I may meditate upon your promise.
149   Hear my voice, O Lord,
     according to your loving-kindness;*
     according to your judgements, give me life.
150   They draw near who in malice persecute me;*
     they are very far from your law.
151   You, O Lord, are near at hand,*
     and all your commandments are true.
152   Long have I known from your decrees*
     that you have established them for ever.

          *   *   *

153   Behold my affliction and deliver me,*
     for I do not forget your law.
154   Plead my cause and redeem me;*
     according to your promise, give me life.
155   Deliverance is far from the wicked,*
     for they do not study your statutes.
156   Great is your compassion, O Lord;*
     preserve my life, according to your judgements.
157   There are many who persecute and oppress me,*
     yet I have not swerved from your decrees.
158   I look with loathing at the faithless,*
     for they have not kept your word.
159   See how I love your commandments!*
     O Lord, in your mercy, preserve me.
160   The heart of your word is truth;*
     all your righteous judgements endure for evermore.

          *   *   *

161   Rulers have persecuted me without a cause,*
     but my heart stands in awe of your word.
162   I am as glad because of your promise*
     as one who finds great spoils.
163   As for lies, I hate and abhor them,*
     but your law is my love.
164   Seven times a day do I praise you,*
     because of your righteous judgements.
165   Great peace have they who love your law;*
     for them there is no stumbling block.
166   I have hoped for your salvation, O Lord,*
     and I have fulfilled your commandments.
167   I have kept your decrees*
     and I have loved them deeply.

                                      A Celtic Primer

168 I have kept your commandments and decrees,*
　　for all my ways are before you.

　　　　*　　　*　　　*

169 Let my cry come before you, O Lord;*
　　give me understanding, according to your word.
170 Let my supplication come before you;*
　　deliver me, according to your promise.
171 My lips shall pour forth your praise,*
　　when you teach me your statutes.
172 My tongue shall sing of your promise,*
　　for all your commandments are righteous.
173 Let your hand be ready to help me,*
　　for I have chosen your commandments.
174 I long for your salvation, O Lord,*
　　and your law is my delight.
175 Let me live and I will praise you,*
　　and let your judgements help me.
176 I have gone astray like a sheep that is lost;*
　　search for your servant,
　　for I do not forget your commandments.

Psalm 120

1　When I was in trouble I called to the Lord,*
　　I called to the Lord and he answered me.
2　Deliver me, O Lord, from lying lips*
　　and from the deceitful tongue.
3　What shall be done to you and what more besides,*
　　O you deceitful tongue?
4　The sharpened arrows of a warrior,*
　　along with hot glowing coals.
5　How hateful it is that I must lodge in Meshech*
　　and dwell among the tents of Kedar!
6　Too long have I had to live*
　　among the enemies of peace.
7　I am on the side of peace,*
　　but when I speak of it, they are for war.

Psalm 121

1　I lift up my eyes to the hills;*
　　from where is my help to come?
2　My help comes from the Lord,*
　　the maker of heaven and earth.

The Psalter, including Psalm Themes for Prayer

3   He will not let your foot be moved*
    and he who watches over you will not fall asleep.
4   Behold, he who keeps watch over Israel*
    shall neither slumber nor sleep;
5   The Lord himself watches over you;*
    the Lord is your shade at your right hand,
6   So that the sun shall not strike you by day,*
    nor the moon by night.
7   The Lord shall preserve you from all evil;*
    it is he who shall keep you safe.
8   The Lord shall watch over your going out
    and your coming in,*
    from this time forth for evermore.

Psalm 122

1   I was glad when they said to me,*
    'Let us go to the house of the Lord.'
2   Now our feet are standing*
    within your gates, O Jerusalem.
3   Jerusalem is built as a city*
    that is at unity with itself.
4   To which the tribes go up, the tribes of the Lord,*
    the assembly of Israel, to praise the name of the Lord.
5   For there are the thrones of judgement,*
    the thrones of the house of David.
6   Pray for the peace of Jerusalem:*
    'May they prosper who love you.
7   'Peace be within your walls*
    and quietness within your towers.
8   'For my family and companions' sake,*
    I pray for your prosperity.
9   'Because of the house of the Lord our God,*
    I will seek to do you good.'

Psalm 123

1   To you I lift up my eyes,*
    to you enthroned in the heavens.
2   As the eyes of servants look to the hand of their masters,*
    and the eyes of a maid to the hand of her mistress,
3   So our eyes look to the Lord our God,*
    until he show us his mercy.
4   Have mercy upon us, O Lord, have mercy,*

for we have had more than enough of contempt,

5   Too much of the scorn of the indolent rich,*
     and of the derision of the proud.

Psalm 124

1   If the Lord had not been on our side,*
     let Israel now say;
2   If the Lord had not been on our side,*
     when enemies rose up against us;
3   Then would they have swallowed us up alive*
     in their fierce anger towards us;
4   Then would the waters have overwhelmed us*
     and the torrent gone over us;
5   Then would the raging waters*
     have gone right over us.
6   Blessèd be the Lord!*
     he has not given us over to be a prey for their teeth.
7   We have escaped like a bird
     from the snare of the fowler;*
     the snare is broken and we have escaped.
8   Our help is in the name of the Lord,*
     the maker of heaven and earth.

Psalm 125

1   Those who trust in the Lord are like Mount Zion,*
     which cannot be moved, but stands fast for ever.
2   The hills stand about Jerusalem;*
     so does the Lord stand round about his people,
     from this time forth for evermore.
3   The sceptre of the wicked shall not hold sway
     over the land allotted to the just,*
     so that the just shall not put their hands to evil.
4   Show your goodness, O Lord, to those who are good*
     and to those who are true of heart.
5   As for those who turn aside to crooked ways,
     the Lord will lead them away with the evildoers;*
     but peace be upon Israel.

Psalm 126

1   When the Lord restored the fortunes of Zion,*
     then were we like those who dream.

The Psalter, including Psalm Themes for Prayer   385

2 Then was our mouth filled with laughter,*
   and our tongue with shouts of joy.
3 Then they said among the nations,*
   'The Lord has done great things for them.'
4 The Lord has done great things for us,*
   and we are glad indeed.
5 Restore our fortunes, O Lord,*
   like the watercourses of the Negev.
6 Those who sowed with tears*
   will reap with songs of joy.
7 Those who go out weeping, carrying the seed,*
   will come again with joy, shouldering their sheaves.

Psalm 127

1 Unless the Lord builds the house,*
   their labour is in vain who build it.
2 Unless the Lord watches over the city,*
   in vain the guard keeps vigil.
3 It is in vain that you rise so early
   and go to bed so late;*
   vain, too, to eat the bread of toil,
   for he gives to his belovèd sleep.
4 Children are a heritage from the Lord,*
   and the fruit of the womb is a gift.
5 Like arrows in the hand of a warrior*
   are the children of one's youth.
6 Happy are they who have their quiver full of them!*
   they shall not be put to shame
   when they contend with their enemies in the gate.

Psalm 128

1 Happy are they all who fear the Lord,*
   and who follow in his ways!
2 You shall eat the fruit of your labour;*
   happiness and prosperity shall be yours.
3 Your wife shall be like a fruitful vine
   within your house,*
   your children like olive shoots round about your table.
4 Whoever fears the Lord*
   shall thus indeed be blessed.
5 The Lord bless you from Zion,*
   and may you see the prosperity of Jerusalem

A Celtic Primer

all the days of your life.
6   May you live to see your children's children;*
    may peace be upon Israel.

Psalm 129

1   'Greatly have they oppressed me since my youth',*
    let Israel now say;
2   'Greatly have they oppressed me since my youth,*
    but they have not prevailed against me.'
3   The ploughers ploughed upon my back*
    and made their furrows long.
4   The Lord, the Righteous One,*
    has cut the cords of the wicked.
5   Let them be put to shame and thrown back,*
    all those who are enemies of Zion.
6   Let them be like grass upon the housetops,*
    which withers before it can be plucked;
7   Which does not fill the hand of the reaper,*
    nor the bosom of him who binds the sheaves;
8   So that those who go by say not so much as,
    'The Lord prosper you.*
    We wish you well in the name of the Lord.'

Psalm 130

1   Out of the depths have I called to you, O Lord;
    Lord, hear my voice;*
    let your ears consider well the voice of my supplication.
2   If you, Lord, were to note what is done amiss,*
    O Lord, who could stand?
3   For there is forgiveness with you;*
    therefore you shall be feared.
4   I wait for the Lord; my soul waits for him;*
    in his word is my hope.
5   My soul waits for the Lord,
    more than the night-watch for the morning,*
    more than the night-watch for the morning.
6   O Israel, wait for the Lord,*
    for with the Lord there is mercy;
7   With him there is plenteous redemption,*
    and he shall redeem Israel from all their sins.

Psalm 131

1   O Lord, I am not proud;*
    I have no haughty looks.
2   I do not occupy myself with great matters,*
    or with things that are too hard for me.
3   But I still my soul and make it quiet,
    like a child upon its mother's breast;*
    my soul is quieted within me.
4   O Israel, wait upon the Lord,*
    from this time forth for evermore.

PSALMS 132–150

Psalm 132

1   Lord, remember David*
    and all the hardships he endured;
2   How he swore an oath to the Lord*
    and vowed a vow to the Mighty One of Jacob:
3   'I will not come under the roof of my house,*
    nor climb up into my bed;
4   'I will not allow my eyes to sleep,*
    nor let my eyelids slumber;
5   'Until I find a place for the Lord,*
    a dwelling for the Mighty One of Jacob.'
6   'The Ark! We heard it was in Ephratha;*
    we found it in the fields of Jearim.
7   'Let us go to God's dwelling place;*
    let us fall upon our knees before his footstool.'
8   Arise, O Lord, into your resting-place,*
    you and the ark of your strength.
9   Let your priests be clothed with righteousness;*
    let your faithful people sing with joy.
10 For your servant David's sake,*
    do not turn away the face of your anointed.
11 The Lord has sworn an oath to David;*
    in truth, he will not break it:
12 'A son, the fruit of your body*
    will I set upon your throne.
13 'If your children keep my covenant
    and my testimonies that I shall teach them,*
    their children will sit upon your throne for evermore.'

14   For the Lord has chosen Zion,*
      he has desired her for his habitation:
15   'This shall be my resting-place for ever;*
      here will I dwell, for I delight in her.
16   'I will surely bless her provisions,*
      and satisfy her poor with bread.
17   'I will clothe her priests with salvation,*
      and her faithful people will rejoice and sing.
18   'There will I make the horn of David flourish;*
      I have prepared a lamp for my anointed.
19   'As for his enemies, I will clothe them with shame;*
      but as for him, his crown will shine.'

Psalm 133

1   O how good and pleasant it is,*
      when a family lives together in unity!
2   It is like fine oil upon the head*
      that runs down upon the beard,
3   Upon the beard of Aaron,*
      and runs down upon the collar of his robe.
4   It is like the dew of Hermon*
      that falls upon the hills of Zion.
5   For there the Lord has ordained the blessing:*
      life for evermore.

Psalm 134

1   Behold now, bless the Lord,
      all you servants of the Lord,*
      you that stand by night in the house of the Lord.
2   Lift up your hands in the holy place
      and bless the Lord;*
      the Lord who made heaven and earth
      bless you out of Zion.

Psalm 135

1   Alleluia! Praise the name of the Lord;*
      give praise, you servants of the Lord,
2   You who stand in the house of the Lord,*
      in the courts of the house of our God.
3   Praise the Lord, for the Lord is good;*
      sing praises to his name, for it is lovely.

4   For the Lord has chosen Jacob for himself*
    and Israel for his own possession.
5   For I know that the Lord is great,*
    and that our Lord is above all gods.
6   The Lord does whatever pleases him,
    in heaven and on earth,*
    in the seas and all the deeps.
7   He brings up rain clouds from the ends of the earth;*
    he sends out lightning with the rain,
    and brings the winds out of his storehouse.
8   It was he who struck down the first-born of Egypt,*
    the first-born both of human and beast.
9   He sent signs and wonders
    into the midst of you, O Egypt,*
    against Pharaoh and all his servants.
10 He overthrew many nations*
    and put mighty kings to death:
11 Sihon, king of the Amorites,
    and Og, the king of Bashan,*
    and all the kingdoms of Canaan.
12 He gave their land to be an inheritance,*
    an inheritance for Israel his people.
13 O Lord, your name is everlasting;*
    your renown, O Lord, endures from age to age.
14 For the Lord gives his people justice*
    and shows compassion to his servants.
15 The idols of the heathen are silver and gold,*
    the work of human hands.
16 They have mouths, but they cannot speak;*
    eyes have they, but they cannot see.
17 They have ears, but they cannot hear;*
    neither is there any breath in their mouth.
18 Those who make them are like them,*
    and so are all who put their trust in them.
19 Bless the Lord, O house of Israel;*
    O house of Aaron, bless the Lord.
20 Bless the Lord, O house of Levi;*
    you who fear the Lord, bless the Lord.
21 Blessèd be the Lord out of Zion,*
    who dwells in Jerusalem. Alleluia!

Psalm 136

1   Give thanks to the Lord, for he is good,*
    for his mercy endures for ever.

2   Give thanks to the God of gods,*
    for his mercy endures for ever.

3   Give thanks to the Lord of lords,*
    for his mercy endures for ever.

4   Who only does great wonders,*
    for his mercy endures for ever;

5   Who by his wisdom made the heavens,*
    for his mercy endures for ever;

6   Who spread out the earth upon the waters,*
    for his mercy endures for ever;

7   Who created great lights,*
    for his mercy endures for ever;

8   The sun to rule the day,*
    for his mercy endures for ever;

9   The moon and the stars to govern the night,*
    for his mercy endures for ever.

10   Who struck down the first-born of Egypt,*
    for his mercy endures for ever;

11   And brought out Israel from among them,*
    for his mercy endures for ever;

12   With a mighty hand and a stretched-out arm,*
    for his mercy endures for ever;

13   Who divided the Red Sea in two,*
    for his mercy endures for ever;

14   And made Israel to pass through the midst of it,*
    for his mercy endures for ever;

15   But swept Pharaoh and his army into the Red Sea,*
    for his mercy endures for ever;

16   Who led his people through the wilderness,*
    for his mercy endures for ever.

17   Who struck down great kings,*
    for his mercy endures for ever;

18   And slew mighty kings,*
    for his mercy endures for ever;

19   Sihon, king of the Amorites,*
    for his mercy endures for ever;

20   And Og, the king of Bashan,*
    for his mercy endures for ever;

21   And gave away their lands for an inheritance,*
    for his mercy endures for ever;

22   An inheritance for Israel his servant,*
       for his mercy endures for ever.

23   Who remembered us in our low estate,*
       for his mercy endures for ever;

24   And delivered us from our enemies,*
       for his mercy endures for ever;

25   Who gives food to all creatures,*
       for his mercy endures for ever;

26   Give thanks to the God of heaven,*
       for his mercy endures for ever.

Psalm 137

1   By the waters of Babylon we sat down and wept,*
       when we remembered you, O Zion.

2   As for our harps, we hung them up*
       on the trees in the midst of that land.

3   For those who led us away captive asked us for a song,
       and our oppressors called for mirth:*
       'Sing us one of the songs of Zion.'

4   How shall we sing the Lord's song*
       upon an alien soil?

5   If I forget you, O Jerusalem,*
       let my right hand forget its skill.

6   Let my tongue cleave to the roof of my mouth
       if I do not remember you,*
       if I do not set Jerusalem above my highest joy.

[7   Remember the day of Jerusalem, O Lord,
       against the people of Edom,*
       who said, 'Down with it! down with it!
       even to the ground!'

8   O Daughter of Babylon, doomed to destruction,*
       happy the one who pays you back
       for what you have done to us!

9   Happy shall he be who takes your little ones,*
       and dashes them against the rock!]

Psalm 138

1   I will give thanks to you, O Lord, with my whole heart;*
       before the gods I will sing your praise.

2   I will bow down towards your holy temple
       and praise your name,*
       because of your love and faithfulness;

3   For you have glorified your name*
and your word above all things.

4   When I called, you answered me;*
you increased my strength within me.

5   All the kings of the earth will praise you, O Lord,*
when they have heard the words of your mouth.

6   They will sing of the ways of the Lord,*
that great is the glory of the Lord.

7   Though the Lord be high, he cares for the lowly;*
he perceives the haughty from afar.

8   Though I walk in the midst of trouble,
you keep me safe;*
you stretch forth your hand
against the fury of my enemies;
your right hand shall save me.

9   The Lord will make good his purpose for me;*
O Lord, your love endures for ever;
do not abandon the works of your hands.

Psalm 139

1   Lord, you have searched me out and known me;*
you know my sitting down and my rising up;
you discern my thoughts from afar.

2   You trace my journeys and my resting-places*
and are acquainted with all my ways.

3   Indeed, there is not a word on my lips,*
but you, O Lord, know it altogether.

4   You press upon me behind and before*
and lay your hand upon me.

5   Such knowledge is too wonderful for me;*
it is so high that I cannot attain to it.

6   Where can I go then from your Spirit?*
where can I flee from your presence?

7   If I climb up to heaven, you are there;*
if I make the grave my bed, you are there also.

8   If I take the wings of the morning*
and dwell in the uttermost parts of the sea,

9   Even there your hand will lead me*
and your right hand hold me fast.

10   If I say, 'Surely the darkness will cover me,*
and the light around me turn to night',

11   Darkness is not dark to you;
the night is as bright as the day;*

darkness and light to you are both alike.

12 For you yourself created my inmost parts;*
 you knit me together in my mother's womb.

13 I will thank you because I am marvellously made;*
 your works are wonderful and I know it well.

14 My body was not hidden from you,*
 while I was being made in secret
 and woven in the depths of the earth.

15 Your eyes beheld my limbs, yet unfinished in the womb;
 all of them were written in your book;*
 they were fashioned day by day,
 when as yet there was none of them.

16 How deep I find your thoughts, O God!*
 how great is the sum of them!

17 If I were to count them,
 they would be more in number than the sand;*
 to count them all,
 my life span would need to be like yours.

[18 O that you would slay the wicked, O God!*
 You that thirst for blood, depart from me.

19 They speak despitefully against you;*
 your enemies take your name in vain.

20 Do I not hate those, O Lord, who hate you?*
 and do I not loathe those who rise up against you?

21 I hate them with a perfect hatred;*
 they have become my own enemies.]

22 Search me out, O God, and know my heart;*
 try me and know my restless thoughts.

23 Look well whether there be any wickedness in me*
 and lead me in the way that is everlasting.

Psalm 140

1 Deliver me, O Lord, from evildoers;*
 protect me from the violent,

2 Who devise evil in their hearts*
 and stir up strife all day long.

3 They have sharpened their tongues like a serpent;*
 adder's poison is under their lips.

4 Keep me, O Lord, from the hands of the wicked;*
 protect me from the violent,
 who are determined to trip me up.

5 The proud have hidden a snare for me
 and stretched out a net of cords;*

394

they have set traps for me along the path.

6 I have said to the Lord, 'You are my God;*
   listen, O Lord, to my supplication.

7 'O Lord God, the strength of my salvation,*
   you have covered my head in the day of battle.

8 'Do not grant the desires of the wicked, O Lord,*
   nor let their evil plans prosper.

[9 'Let not those who surround me lift up their heads;*
   let the evil of their lips overwhelm them.

10 'Let hot burning coals fall upon them;*
   let them be cast into the mire, never to rise up again.'

11 A slanderer shall not be established on the earth,*
   and evil shall hunt down the lawless.]

12 I know that the Lord will maintain the cause of the poor*
   and render justice to the needy.

13 Surely, the righteous will give thanks to your name,*
   and the upright shall continue in your sight.

Psalm 141

1 O Lord, I call to you; come to me quickly;*
   hear my voice when I cry to you.

2 Let my prayer be set forth in your sight as incense,*
   the lifting up of my hands as the evening sacrifice.

3 Set a watch before my mouth, O Lord,
   and guard the door of my lips;*
   let not my heart incline to any evil thing.

4 Let me not be occupied in wickedness with evildoers,*
   nor eat of their choice foods.

5 Let the righteous smite me in friendly rebuke;
   let not the oil of the unrighteous anoint my head;*
   for my prayer is continually against their wicked deeds.

6 Let their rulers be overthrown in stony places,*
   that they may know my words are true.

7 As when a plough turns over the earth in furrows,*
   let their bones be scattered at the mouth of the grave.

8 But my eyes are turned to you, Lord God;*
   in you I take refuge; do not strip me of my life.

9 Protect me from the snare which they have laid for me*
   and from the traps of the evildoers.

10 Let the wicked fall into their own nets,*
   while I myself escape.

Psalm 142

1 I cry to the Lord with my voice;*
  to the Lord I make loud supplication.
2 I pour out my complaint before him*
  and tell him all my trouble.
3 When my spirit languishes within me, you know my path;*
  in the way wherein I walk they have hidden a trap for me.
4 I look to my right hand and find no one who knows me;*
  I have no place to flee to and no one cares for me.
5 I cry out to you, O Lord;*
  I say, 'You are my refuge,
  my portion in the land of the living.'
6 Listen to my cry for help,
  for I have been brought very low;*
  save me from those who pursue me,
  for they are too strong for me.
7 Bring me out of prison,
  that I may give thanks to your name;*
  when you have dealt bountifully with me,
  the righteous will gather around me.

Psalm 143

1 Lord, hear my prayer,
  and in your faithfulness heed my supplications;*
  answer me in your righteousness.
2 Enter not into judgement with your servant,*
  for in your sight shall no one living be justified.
3 For my enemy has sought my life
  and has crushed me to the ground;*
  making me live in dark places
  like those who are long dead.
4 My spirit faints within me;*
  my heart within me is desolate.
5 I remember the time past;
  I muse upon all your deeds;*
  I consider the works of your hands.
6 I spread out my hands to you;*
  my soul gasps to you like a thirsty land.
7 O Lord, make haste to answer me; my spirit fails me;*
  do not hide your face from me
  or I shall be like those who go down to the Pit.
8 Let me hear of your loving-kindness in the morning,

A Celtic Primer

for I put my trust in you;*
show me the road that I must walk,
for I lift up my soul to you.

9   Deliver me from my enemies, O Lord,*
for I flee to you for refuge.

10 Teach me to do what pleases you, for you are my God;*
let your good Spirit lead me on level ground.

11 Revive me, O Lord, for your name's sake;*
for your righteousness' sake, bring me out of trouble.

[12 Of your goodness, destroy my enemies
and bring all my foes to naught,*
for truly I am your servant.]

Psalm 144

1 Blessèd be the Lord my rock!*
who trains my hands to fight and my fingers to battle;

2 My help and my fortress,
my stronghold and my deliverer,*
my shield in whom I trust,
who subdues the peoples under me.

3 O Lord, what are we that you should care for us?*
mere mortals that you should think of us?

4 We are like a puff of wind;*
our days are like a passing shadow.

5 Bow your heavens, O Lord, and come down;*
touch the mountains and they shall smoke.

6 Hurl the lightning and scatter them;*
shoot out your arrows and rout them.

7 Stretch out your hand from on high;*
rescue me and deliver me from the great waters,
from the hand of foreign peoples,

8 Whose mouths speak deceitfully*
and whose right hand is raised in falsehood.

9 O God, I will sing to you a new song;*
I will play to you on a ten-stringed lyre.

10 You give victory to kings*
and have rescued David your servant.

11 Rescue me from the hurtful sword*
and deliver me from the hand of foreign peoples,

12 Whose mouths speak deceitfully*
and whose right hand is raised in falsehood.

13 May our sons be like plants
well nurtured from their youth,*

and our daughters like sculptured corners of a palace.

14   May our barns be filled to overflowing*
     with all manner of crops;

15   May the flocks in our pastures
     increase by thousands and tens of thousands;*
     may our cattle be fat and sleek.

16   May there be no breaching of the walls,
     no going into exile,*
     no wailing in the public squares.

17   Happy are the people of whom this is so!*
     happy are the people whose God is the Lord!

Psalm 145

1   I will exalt you, O God my King,*
     and bless your name for ever and ever.

2   Every day will I bless you*
     and praise your name for ever and ever.

3   Great is the Lord and greatly to be praised;*
     there is no end to his greatness.

4   One generation shall praise your works to another*
     and shall declare your power.

5   I will ponder the glorious splendour of your majesty*
     and all your marvellous works.

6   They shall speak of the might of your wondrous acts,*
     and I will tell of your greatness.

7   They shall publish the remembrance
     of your great goodness;*
     they shall sing of your righteous deeds.

8   The Lord is gracious and full of compassion,*
     slow to anger and of great kindness.

9   The Lord is loving to everyone*
     and his compassion is over all his works.

10   All your works praise you, O Lord,*
     and your faithful servants bless you.

11   They make known the glory of your kingdom*
     and speak of your power;

12   That the peoples may know of your power*
     and the glorious splendour of your kingdom.

13   Your kingdom is an everlasting kingdom;*
     your dominion endures throughout all ages.

14   The Lord is faithful in all his words*
     and merciful in all his deeds.

15 The Lord upholds all those who fall;*
   he lifts up those who are bowed down.

16 The eyes of all wait upon you, O Lord,*
   and you give them their food in due season.

17 You open wide your hand*
   and satisfy the needs of every living creature.

18 The Lord is righteous in all his ways*
   and loving in all his works.

19 The Lord is near to those who call upon him,*
   to all who call upon him faithfully.

20 He fulfils the desire of those who fear him,*
   he hears their cry and helps them.

21 The Lord preserves all those who love him,*
   but he destroys all the wicked.

22 My mouth shall speak the praise of the Lord;*
   let all flesh bless his holy name for ever and ever.

Psalm 146

1 Alleluia!
  Praise the Lord, O my soul!*
  I will praise the Lord as long as I live;
  I will sing praises to my God while I have my being.

2 Put not your trust in rulers,
  nor in any child of earth,*
  for there is no help in them.

3 When they breathe their last, they return to earth,*
  and in that day their thoughts perish.

4 Happy are they who have the God of Jacob
  for their help!*
  whose hope is in the Lord their God;

5 Who made heaven and earth, the seas,
  and all that is in them;*
  who keeps his promise for ever;

6 Who gives justice to those who are oppressed,*
  and food to those who hunger.

7 The Lord sets the prisoners free;
  the Lord opens the eyes of the blind;*
  the Lord lifts up those who are bowed down;

8 The Lord loves the righteous;
  the Lord cares for the stranger;*
  he sustains the orphan and widow,
  but frustrates the way of the wicked.

9   The Lord shall reign for ever,*
    your God, O Zion, throughout all generations.
    Alleluia!

Psalm 147, Part I

1   Alleluia!
    How good it is to sing praises to our God!*
    how pleasant it is to honour him with praise!
2   The Lord rebuilds Jerusalem;*
    he gathers the exiles of Israel.
3   He heals the brokenhearted*
    and binds up their wounds.
4   He counts the number of the stars*
    and calls them all by their names.
5   Great is our Lord and mighty in power;*
    there is no limit to his wisdom.
6   The Lord lifts up the lowly,*
    but casts the wicked to the ground.
7   Sing to the Lord with thanksgiving;*
    make music to our God upon the harp.
8   He covers the heavens with clouds*
    and prepares rain for the earth;
9   He makes grass to grow upon the mountains*
    and green plants to serve us all.
10 He provides food for flocks and herds*
    and for the young ravens when they cry.
11 He is not impressed by the might of a horse,*
    he has no pleasure in human strength;
12 But the Lord has pleasure in those who fear him,*
    in those who await his gracious favour.

Psalm 147, Part II

13 Worship the Lord, O Jerusalem;*
    praise your God, O Zion;
14 For he has strengthened the bars of your gates;*
    he has blessed your children within you.
15 He has established peace on your borders;*
    he satisfies you with the finest wheat.
16 He sends out his command to the earth,*
    and his word runs very swiftly.
17 He gives snow like wool;*
    he scatters hoarfrost like ashes.

A Celtic Primer

18 He scatters his hail like bread crumbs;*
    who can stand against his cold?
19 He sends forth his word and melts them;*
    he blows with his wind and the waters flow.
20 He declares his word to Jacob,*
    his statutes and his judgements to Israel.
21 He has not done so to any other nation;*
    to them he has not revealed his judgements.
    Alleluia!

Psalm 148

1   Alleluia!
    Praise the Lord from the heavens;*
    praise him in the heights.
2   Praise him, all you angels of his;*
    praise him, all his host.
3   Praise him, sun and moon;*
    praise him, all you shining stars.
4   Praise him, heaven of heavens,*
    and you waters above the heavens.
5   Let them praise the name of the Lord;*
    for he commanded and they were created.
6   He made them stand fast for ever and ever;*
    he gave them a law which shall not pass away.
7   Praise the Lord from the earth,*
    you sea-monsters and all deeps;
8   Fire and hail, snow and fog,*
    tempestuous wind, doing his will;
9   Mountains and all hills,*
    fruit trees and all cedars;
10 Wild beasts and all cattle,*
    creeping things and winged birds;
11 Kings of the earth and all peoples,*
    princes and all rulers of the world;
12 Young men and maidens,*
    old and young together.
13 Let them praise the name of the Lord,*
    for his name only is exalted,
    his splendour is over earth and heaven.
14 He has raised up strength for his people
    and praise for all his loyal servants,*
    the children of Israel, a people who are near him.
    Alleluia!

Psalm 149

1 Alleluia!
Sing to the Lord a new song;*
sing his praise in the congregation of the faithful.

2 Let Israel rejoice in his maker;*
let the children of Zion be joyful in their king.

3 Let them praise his name in the dance;*
let them sing praise to him with timbrel and harp.

4 For the Lord takes pleasure in his people*
and adorns the poor with victory.

5 Let the faithful rejoice in triumph;*
let them be joyful on their beds.

6 Let the praises of God be in their throat*
and a two-edged sword in their hand;

7 To wreak vengeance on the nations*
and punishment on the peoples;

8 To bind their kings in chains*
and their nobles with links of iron;

9 To inflict on them the judgement decreed;*
this is glory for all his faithful people.
Alleluia!

Psalm 150

1 Alleluia!
Praise God in his holy temple;*
praise him in the firmament of his power.

2 Praise him for his mighty acts;*
praise him for his excellent greatness.

3 Praise him with the blast of the ram's-horn;*
praise him with lyre and harp.

4 Praise him with timbrel and dance;*
praise him with strings and pipe.

5 Praise him with resounding cymbals;*
praise him with loud-clanging cymbals.

6 Let everything that has breath*
praise the Lord.
Alleluia!

REFERENCES, SOURCES
AND NOTES

1. Robin Flower, *The Irish Tradition*, Clarendon Press, Oxford, 1947.
2. Robin Flower, *Poems and Translations*, London, 1931.
3. Charles Plummer, *Irish Litanies*, Henry Bradshaw Society, London, Harrison & Sons, 1925.
4. George Sigerson, *Bards of the Gael and Gall*, Talbot, Dublin, 1925.
5. *Thesaurus Paleohibernicus*, ed. Whitley Stokes and John Strachan, Cambridge University Press, 1901–1903.
6. *Maidin Uinseann – The Celtic Monk – Rules and Writings of Early Irish Monks*, Cistercian Publications, Kalamazoo, Michigan, Massachusetts, 1996.
7. Oliver Davies and Thomas O'Loughlin, *Celtic Spirituality*, Paulist Press, New York, 1999.
8. Brendan O'Malley, *A Welsh Pilgrim's Manual*, Gomer Press, Llandysul, Ceredigion, 1989, 1995.
9. J. Carney, *The Poems of Blathmac*, Irish Texts Society, Dublin, 1964.
10. J. Carney, *Early Irish Poetry*, Cork, 1965.
11. Kuno Meyer, *Ancient Irish Poetry*, Constable, 1913.
12. Helen Waddell (trans.), *Mediaeval Latin Lyrics*, Holt, New York, 1929.
13. Alexander Carmichael (ed.), *Carmina Gadelica*, 5 Volumes, Oliver & Boyd, Edinburgh, 1900–54.
14. Whitley Stokes (ed. and trans.), *Lives of the Saints from the 'Book of Lismore'*, Clarendon Press, Oxford 1890.
15. Thomas Owen Clancy and Gilbert Markus, *Iona, the Earliest Poetry of a Celtic Monastery*, Edinburgh, 1995.
16. O. Davies and F. Bowie, *Celtic Christian Spirituality*, SPCK, 1995.
17. Alfred P. Graves, *A Celtic Psaltery*, SPCK, 1917.
18. John Carey, *King of Mysteries – Early Irish Religious Writings*, Four Courts Press, Dublin, 1998, 2000.
19. G. Murphy, *Early Irish Lyrics*, Oxford, 1956.
20. K. Meyer, *Selections from Ancient Irish Poetry*, London, 1911.
21. Ifor Williams, *The Beginnings of Welsh Poetry*, University of Wales Press, 1972.
22. Meirion Pennar, *The Black Book of Carmarthen*, Llanerch Enterprises, 1989.
23. Eleanor Hull, *The Poem-Book of the Gael*, Chatto & Windus, 1913.
24. H. A. Hodges, *Homage to Ann Griffiths*, Church in Wales Publications, 1976.
25. Donald Allchin, Densil D. Morgan and Patrick Thomas, *Sensuous Glory – The Poetic Vision of D. Gwenallt Jones*, Canterbury Press, Norwich, 2000.
26. Dafydd Johnston (trans.), *Iolo Goch: Poems*, Gomer Press, Llandysul, Ceredigion, 1993.
27. Gwyn Thomas (trans.), *Dafydd ap Gwilym*, University of Wales Press, Cardiff, 2001.

28. Thomas Parry (ed.), *The Oxford Book of Welsh Verse*, Oxford, 1962.
29. Dame Fellicitas Corrigan, *Helen Waddell: A Biography*, London 1986.
30. From 'Keep the Feast, Plygain', published by the Board of Mission of the Church in Wales, Cardiff.
31. Collects for the Office are taken from *Proclaiming All Your Wonders: Prayers From a Pilgrim People*, Dominican Publications, Dublin, 1991. Used with permission.
32. Adapted by the author.
33. Antiphony of Bangor VIII Century, 'The Lighting of the Vesper Light or Paschal Candle'; translated by Dr Oliver Davies.
34. The Gloria is the modern translation, International Committee on English in the Liturgy, Inc. (ICEL) 1983. The Gloria is a song of praise usually sung at a morning celebration of the Eucharist. If the Lighting of the Vesper Light hymn is used at an evening Eucharist, the Gloria may be omitted.
35. Tírechán's Creed (from *The Patrician Texts from the Book of Armach AD 670* (Dublin), Ludwig Bieler) and Patrick's Confession translated by Dr Thomas O'Loughlin.
36. Deprecatio Sancti Martini Pro Populo Incipit (Bidding Prayer of St Martin). The association of these in the *Stowe Missal* with the name of St Martin, Bishop of Tours 271–401, indicates that, though of Eastern origin, they reached Ireland through a Gallican channel. I am grateful to the Revd J. W. Hunwicke for this translation.
37. The Litany of the Trinity – adapted from the Litany of the same title by Mugron, the coarb of Columba in Ireland and Scotland, i.e., Abbot of the Federated Columban Monasteries in the two counties of which the chief were respectively Iona in Scotland and Durrow in Ireland. Mugron held the abbacy from 964 to 980 (Plummer, *Irish Litanies*, 1925).
38. The Stowe Preface – a translation of the preface from the *Stowe Missal* by Dr Thomas O'Loughlin; adapted by Brendan O'Malley. The *Stowe Missal* was owned by the Marquis of Buckinghamshire, of Stowe House. It is the oldest book from the early Irish Church still extant. It is of monastic origin linked with Tallaght and dated to the eighth/early ninth centuries. It is now in the Royal Irish Academy in Dublin.
39. *Stowe Missal* Eucharistic Prayer – an adapted translation of the canon of St Gelasius (AD 494) which was not further revised until AD 600. (In the *Stowe Missal* it is labelled, 'the Canon of the lord Pope Gelasius'.) I have removed the reference 'N our Pope' and added local Celtic saints alongside the universal college of bishops. I have done this as an ecumenical gesture without in any way denying the Petrine Primacy.
40. The Gallican Liturgy is the generic title of a large number of rites in the eighth century, which has much in common with Eastern liturgies and was used throughout France. There was a constant to-and-fro between the British and Gallican churches during the first six centuries, and an intimate connection between Wales and Brittany can be traced up to the eleventh century. The Bobbio Missal, a seventh or eighth century text of Celtic origin, contains Gallican elements. The Gallican Eucharistic Prayer used here, albeit in adapted form, would have been known and probably used by the Church of the Celts.
41. Hippolytus: The Apostolic Tradition of the third century. This is the first version of a definitive Eucharistic Prayer in the early church circa AD 215. This may not be an invariable form although it may have been a model for all later Eucharistic Prayers.
42. 'Cognuerunt Dominum', translated by Dr Thomas O'Loughlin.
43. The Psalms are taken from *The Standard Book of Common Prayer of the Episcopal Church of the USA*, on which no copyright is claimed.